The Cultic Origins of Christianity

The Cultic Origins
of Christianity

The Dynamics of Religious Development

W. W. Meissner, S.J., M.D.

A Michael Glazier Book
THE LITURGICAL PRESS
Collegeville, Minnesota

A Michael Glazier book published by The Liturgical Press

Cover design by David Manahan, O.S.B. Illustration courtesy of Scala/Art Resource, New York. Duccio (c. 1260–1318), *Christ Appearing to His Disciples*, Siena, Italy.

1   2   3   4   5   6   7   8   9

Library of Congress Cataloging-in-Publication Data

Meissner, W. W. (William W.), 1931–
    The cultic origins of Christianity : the dynamics of religious development / W. W. Meissner.
        p.   cm.
    "A Michael Glazier book."
    Includes bibliographical references and index.
    ISBN 0-8146-5076-7 (alk. paper)
    1. Church history—Primitive and early church, ca. 30–600.   I. Title.

BR148.M45   2000
270.1—dc21
                                                                99-054673

Contents

SECTION II

Pre-Christian Context

SECTION III

Early Christianity

Preface

One of the elusive phenomena in the study of religious development is the conjunction of factors that give rise to new religious movements. The subject has been actively explored by anthropologists and sociologists of religion, but it has drawn minimal attention from psychologists, especially psychoanalysts.

Needless to say the conjunction of circumstances and influences that would lead to the emergence of a new religious movement are complex and not always easily identifiable. There are unquestionably external factors to be taken into account, whether they be economic, political, social, or cultural. The interplay of such factors goes a long way toward illuminating the terms and conditions of religious evolution, but when all is said and done there remains a missing component that these extrinsic influences do not take into consideration. The missing link has to do with those aspects of the individual believer's beliefs and motives for belief that come into play and give the integration of external circumstances and the emergent belief system such appeal and evocative emotional power. What, we might ask, is it that makes the religious participant respond to an emergent religious articulation, to find in it a source of emotional resolution and satisfaction, and motivates him to endorse, affiliate with and commit himself to that belief system in ways that are personally transforming and powerfully convincing?

To ask this question opens the way to exploring the inner workings of the minds and hearts of the human beings who become the adherents to the new religion and participate in the group dynamics that compose the inner life of the religious group. This approach would, then, draw into consideration the intrapsychic dimensions of the religious experiences that contribute to and complement the other forces that propel the nascent religious movement into existence. Behind the turmoil of externally derived and even public events, there lies the less observable interplay of subjective events and powerful psychic forces generating and sustaining the phenomenon of individual participation and commitment that are vital to the survival and perdurance of the religious group.

It is this complex interweaving of inner and external influences that I am calling the "cultic process." I will argue that the dynamic forces underlying the cultic process are operative in religious groups of all kinds. The argument will carry us back through the annals of the history of religion to discern workings of the cultic process in the origins and historical evolution of Judeo-Christian beliefs and in the emergence of orthodox and heterodox religious groups involved in the historical evolution of religious groupings that contributed to the establishment of the Christian church.

To the extent that the cultic process can be identified in those contexts, I will argue further that the driving forces underlying the cultic process in intrapsychic terms derive from interplay of psychic mechanisms that constitute a more general process that I have described as "the paranoid process." I have articulated these mechanisms specifically introjection, projection, and paranoid construction, which I will elaborate in due course, but the core of my argument rests on the degree with which these psychic elements can be focused in relation to processes that are more familiar on the level of social organization and integration. In this sense, the group phenomena that are evident in the formation of the religious group do not take place in isolation from intrapsychic dynamics and processes; my effort in this discussion is to try to bring those processes into meaningful conjunction with mechanisms operative on the group level in terms of social processes.

The cogency of my thesis rests on the persuasiveness of the translation of mechanisms and processes defined originally in the context of intrapsychic dynamics into processes taking place in the more complex and problematic contexts of group processes and sociohistorical influences. The argument in the text will pursue the following progression:

(1) Exposition of the basic ideas of the paranoid process which entails the primary psychological configuration on which the fun-

damentals of my argument rest. The paranoid process takes its
origin from the clinical setting, in the dynamics of patients afflicted with paranoid psychopathology. Presentation of this set
of ideas will utilize the classical case example of Judge Schreber,
whose paranoid disease became the subject of Freud's now famous discussion of paranoid dynamics. Chapter 1. I should urge
the caution that the Schreber case is not presented as the basis
for the analysis of the paranoid process; the evidential base for
that analysis is clinical and the evidence has been presented
elsewhere in considerable detail (Meissner 1978, 1986/1994).
The Schreber case is used simply to exemplify the mechanisms
and processes in question, since the case is familiar to psychiatric and analystic audiences and has a degree of prominence
because of Freud's interpretation of it.

(2) Exposition of the cultic process as the central idea on which the
strength of the argument rests. The cultic process is an expression of the dynamics of the paranoid process cast in the perspective of group forces and dynamics and specifically of the
articulation of these processes in the formation and maintenance
of religious groups and movements. Chapter 2.

(3) Exploration of the operation of the cultic process in the pre-
Christian Palestinian background within which Christianity
came into being through the mission and preaching of Jesus of
Nazareth. Effects of the cultic process are identified in Palestinian sectarian movements and in the rise of Christianity as a Jewish heterodox religious movement. Chapters 3, 4, 5, and 6.

(4) Extension of the analysis of divisive and consolidating influences of the cultic process in the subsequent development of the
early Christian churches, particularly in the gradual separation
between the Hellenistically oriented churches like Antioch,
Corinth, Rome and the Johannine community and the more conservative Jewish Christian orientation of the original Jerusalem
church. Chapters 7, 8, and 9.

(5) Exploration of the origins and development of Gnostic thought
systems and the rise of Gnostic churches out of the same heterodox Judaic background as Christianity. The influence of Gnostic
viewpoints in Christianity gave way to a gradual redefinition of
the boundaries of the Christian church and a progressive delineation of Gnostic systems as heretical and not consistent with
union with the Christian church and system of beliefs increasingly consolidated under the leadership of the church of Rome.
Chapters 10, 11, and 12.

(6) Analysis of these historical and sociological developments as expressions of the operation of the cultic process, deriving its driving force and power from the underlying dynamics of the paranoid process and the psychoanalytically based implementation of constitutive drives and defenses, especially those involved in the integration of narcissistic and aggressive components. The relevance of these dimensions for the integration and sustaining of personality structure and identity for both individual believers and for the religious group as a whole are delineated. Chapters 13 and 14.

The overall argument, I would hope, provides another perspective within which the relevance of psychological and specifically psychoanalytic processes intersect with and influence religious motivation and experience and thus offers another facet to the endlessly fascinating interface between psychoanalysis and religion.

Needless to say, there are complex and endlessly problematic questions that continually dog the steps of any argument attempting to bridge the chasm between individual intrapsychic dynamics and the understanding of group processes. My argument rests on certain presumptions about the influence of intrapsychic dynamic processes on the group phenomena I will be dealing with in this study. It would be presumptuous to think that one could resolve such troublesome issues, and I can make no such claim. But the questions cannot be ignored—whether one's approach to them brings consensus or debate, they must at least be faced and one's position clearly stated. I have tried to do so, and have included these discussions in a methodological prelude anticipating the ensuing exploration and discussion. Readers who take such issues seriously can find my approach stated there; readers who would find such arguments distracting, irrelevant, or obsessive, could readily skip the prelude and move on to the conceptual and historical exploration.

I make no pretense of comprehensiveness in the exploration of the history of religious movements—the material is far-reaching and overwhelmingly complex. My approach is selective and partial—the material has been chosen to illuminate and illustrate the development of my argument. The focus is restricted to Western religious experience and to Judaic and Christian religious traditions. I will argue that the mechanisms of the cultic and paranoid processes operate in these sect formations and developments with as much impact as any.

My gratitude and appreciation are due to several colleagues who have contributed their expertise in criticizing earlier drafts of this manuscript and offering helpful suggestions to bolster the argument and upgrade the scholarly quality of this effort. My thanks are due to Rev. Daniel Harrington, S.J., of the Weston School of Theology, and Professors Anthony Saldarini and Pheme Perkins of the Boston College Theology Department.

I express my gratitude also to Dr. Bryce Boyer, editor of *The Psychoanalytic Study of Society*, and to his thoughtful and enterprising co-editors and reviewers, who have read, criticized, and constructively evaluated several essays that were previously published in the *Study*. Their comments and suggestions have added significantly to the development of my argument. I would also like to thank Dr. Boyer for his kind permission to utilize material from those previously published papers in the present book. These papers are:

(1984) The cult phenomenon: psychoanalytic perspective. *The Psychoanalytic Study of Society*, 10:91–111—part of chapters 1 and 2.

(1987) The cult phenomenon and the paranoid process. *The Psychoanalytic Study of Society*, 12:69–95—parts of chapters 1, 2 and 14.

(1988) The origins of Christianity. *The Psychoanalytic Study of Society*, 13:29–62—parts of chapters 6 and 7.

(1989) Cultic elements in early Christianity: Antioch and Jerusalem. *The Psychoanalytic Study of Society*, 14:89–117—chapter 7.

(1991) Cultic elements in early Christianity: Rome, Corinth, and the Johannine community. *The Psychoanalytic Study of Society*, 16:265–85—parts of chapters 8 and 9.

My gratitude is also due for the editorial suggestions and guidance provided by editorial reviewers of the *Study*.

W. W. Meissner, S.J., M.D.

Training and Supervising Analyst
Boston Psychoanalytic Institute

University Professor of Psychoanalysis
Boston College

Prelude:
A Note on Methodology

Questions

An interdisciplinary study of this nature, involving the convergence of data and theories from several areas and approaches to understanding the phenomena under investigation, unavoidably raises serious methodological issues that may not yield completely to thoughtful analysis, but at least deserve serious consideration. Moreover, an author owes it to his readers, particularly his scholarly readers for whom methodological issues may take on greater valence, to be as clear as possible about how he thinks about these problems and to what degree he is able to illumine them. I have reserved a fuller discussion of some of these questions for this separate section, since, however inherently interesting, their appeal is bound to be narrow and there is no need to inflict these reflections on readers who have less interest or concern about them.

The problems I will take up here concern the concept of paranoia, specifically the question of the extension of the meaning of "paranoid" from the restrictively clinical and pathological realm to broader non-pathological considerations, the transition from the level of individual and intrapsychic processes to social and cultural applications, specifically the issue of extrapolation from the significance and implication of individual analysis to group and social processes involving larger numbers of people, and finally some issues related to the problem of applying psychological and social analyses to religious phenomena. In addition, another term that requires comment is "cultic," specifically in reference to my use of it in reference to the cultic process.

The Nature of Paranoia

The origins of the concept of paranoia lie buried in late nineteenth and early twentieth descriptive psychiatry. As a diagnostic term it came to fruition in the work of Kraepelin, the great diagnostician and classifier of severe mental diseases. In 1904, in the seventh edition of his famous textbook of psychiatry, Kraepelin emphasized the delusional symptomatology. He wrote: "There is undoubtedly a group of cases in which delusions are the most prominent, if not the only, symptoms of the disease. In these cases a chronic, stable system of delusions gradually develops without any disorder of the train of thought, of will, or of action." It was not long, however, before this pure form of paranoia began to meet serious challenges arising from the fact that delusional formations seemed to occur in a variety of psychotic and toxic conditions. Even Kraepelin found it necessary to group such nonconforming cases under another heading, separating them from the true paranoias of his original description. The effect was to increasingly segregate paranoia from the other forms of dementia praecox (the schizophrenias as we know them today) and establish it as a differentiated diagnostic category.

This diagnostic clarification brought with it further uncertainties and controversies about the nature of this disorder. Some thought the problem was primarily affective; others emphasized the intellectual component. The seriousness of the disorder was generally acknowledged and accepted. Bleuler, for example, regarded it as a form of psychosis in which a complex of ideas associated with powerful emotions dominated the patient's thinking so that any thought was largely determined by affective influences rather than any facts or logic. The persistence of this "autistic" tendency gave rise to errors such that whenever anything in the individual's experience aroused these associations, the errors were extended into delusions that became persistent and more fully elaborated. The rest of the patient's thinking was relatively little affected, so that progressive mental deterioration, which had been the hallmark of dementia praecox, or other psychotic symptoms seemed lacking.

Within this context with its emphasis on disordered thinking and psychotic potential, the term "paranoia" causes bells to ring in the mind of any clinician and carries with it all the diagnostic baggage of severe mental illness and delusional distortion. This is still largely the case—

the word "paranoia" seemingly automatically elicits associations to pathology and disordered mental processes. But the intervening years have seen a broadening and diffusion of the connotations of the term, largely abetted by Freud's analysis of the Schreber case. Not only has the occurrence of paranoid characteristics a much wider distribution among other diagnostic categories, both psychotic and nonpsychotic, but the appreciation of the degree to which paranoid or quasi-paranoid traits can be identified in nonclinical and presumably normal populations has changed much of our thinking about paranoia and its significance. While efforts continue among descriptively committed psychiatrists and psychologists to refine the diagnostic categories, there has also been a shift from narrowly descriptive preoccupations in the tradition of Kraepelin to a greater concern for understanding developmental and defensive aspects of paranoid mechanisms. It is the conceptual drift in this direction that led me to develop the analysis of the paranoid process (Meissner 1978b) and to the development of concepts pertaining to nonpathological expressions of paranoid traits (Pinderhughes 1970, 1971, 1982) and to the analysis of such processes in social and political contexts (Volkan 1988). The development of this direction in thinking about paranoid processes remains an active focus of current clinical interest (Oldham and Bone 1994).

Paranoia—from Pathology to Process

I would like to emphasize at this juncture the shift from a diagnostic preoccupation to that of interpretive understanding. This involves a shift from an orientation toward paranoia as pathology to a consideration of paranoia as process. Our contemporary understanding of paranoia is increasingly conditioned by awareness of the variety of manifestations of paranoid mechanisms, not only in forms of psychopathology, but in relatively normal ranges of personality as well. Within this broader perspective, the operation of paranoid mechanisms can be identified in a broad range of pathological, near pathological, and relatively normal contexts.

The first step would be to acknowledge and put aside the pathology of paranoia. Besides the classic kraepelinian paranoia, the pathological paranoid states include paranoid schizophrenia, paraphrenia, involutional paranoid state, and the paranoid personality. With the exception of the paranoid personality these are forms of psychotic deterioration. Even in the nonpsychotic and characterological form of frank paranoid disturbance, the paranoid personality, however, the characteristic paranoid mechanisms are identifiable. Patients suffering from paranoid personality are characteristically hypersensitive, argumentative, suspicious, and constantly maintain a guarded and defensive attitude toward other people. They are constantly afraid of being taken advantage of, constantly expecting attacks and injury from people around them. They may be quite tense, hostile, and anxious, but often enough are quiet and unassuming; in any case, they tend to maintain a rigid guardedness and control of their environment and relationships. They avoid close involvements with other people and are prone to jealous and angry outbursts. The paranoid personality, then, is one in which the paranoid process has become highly structuralized and embedded in the organization of the personality so that it comes to dominate the inner workings of the psychic apparatus without necessarily impeding the structural and functional organization of the personality. This particular form of paranoid pathology makes it abundantly clear that the paranoid mechanisms can operate in fairly intense ways without leading to psychotic disorganization.

There are also pathological states related to the paranoid process which are so frequent and so endemic in the general population that one hesitates to call them pathological. Nonetheless they display the operation of paranoid mechanisms as dramatically and clearly as in the forms of frank paranoid pathology. Here I would include forms of envy and jealousy and particularly the phenomenon of prejudice. In addition, paranoid mechanisms can be seen operating characteristically in the authoritarian personality (Meissner 1978b).

Taking the argument even a step further, the manifestations of paranoid mechanisms can be found operative in a broad range of phenomena which not only must be characterized as normal, but also are to be regarded as positive and sustaining forces in the life experience of normal individuals. They not only serve as sustaining and integrating forces in the organization and functioning of individual personalities, but come to serve important functions in the integration and sustaining of social and cultural processes as well. Here we must include a variety of belief systems which operate in a broad range of important human contexts: we must concern ourselves with political ideologies, with social and cultural ideologies, with religious belief systems of various kinds, and even with a variety of value systems.

In all of these contexts, the operation of paranoid mechanisms can be identified so that they may be regarded as variant manifestations of the paranoid process. Consequently, the shift in perspective from a view of paranoia as pathology to a view of paranoia as process carries us out of the clinical realm into a broad range of social, political, religious, and cultural phenomena which serve to shape and sustain the life of mankind in general. Moreover, the shift in perspective implies that the paranoid process has relevance not only for the understanding of certain forms of pathological deviation, but is also an important contributing force to the shaping of normal personality development and functioning. Further exploration of this perspective requires that we bring into focus precisely what it is that constitutes the paranoid process.

The Concept of Process

The concept of process carries several connotations worthy of consideration. The notion of process carries implications of dynamic change and progression through time. The concept of process is thus linked with structural progression, particularly in terms of the emergence, shaping, and sustaining of structural continuity through time. Thus, the process perspective cannot simply be reduced to static structural terms, since over and above the structural derivatives themselves the notion of process deals with the continuity and dynamic progression between structures. Moreover, the process does not take place in a vacuum, but rather is subject to multiple extrinsic influences, which come to bear on it and influence its patterning, and with which it must fit in, through a mixture of what Piaget called assimilative and accommodative operations. Consequently, the notion of process has implicit in it a developmental reference and an adaptational and directive component. The developmental perspective in this regard concerns more the inherently internal progression and organization of elements, intrinsic to the operation of the process as it were, while the latter adaptive aspect carries more explicit reference to the direction, intention, external modification and fitting in of the process with its environment. In the latter sense, the adaptive connotation of the notion of process comes close analogously to the notion of biological purpose in physical organisms.

The notion of process also remains relatively nonspecific in its denotation. As we have suggested, the operation of the paranoid process plays itself out at multiple levels of psychological and social integration. We can describe the operation of the mechanisms characterizing the paranoid process in individual personalities. The description is applicable to the deviant forms of pathological expression found in a variety of forms of psychopathology, most particularly in paranoid pathology. However, the same mechanisms can be found operating in the genesis of normal personality structure and functioning. The same process is operative in both contexts, so that neither realm of application can claim to be the exclusive realm of operation of the paranoid process. By the same token, the analogous mechanisms can be found operating in the psychological substructure of more complex social and cultural phenomena. Here again the process reference remains nonspecific, so that when we designate the operation of these same mechanisms, we are not by that reason, dealing with some different form of process, but rather a variant manifestation of the same process, now however expressing the products of its operation in farther-reaching and more complex realms of human involvement. Consequently, it can be seen that a shift to the perspective of process in regard to the study of paranoia moves from a rather specific and confined area of consideration, namely, the focusing and definition of a form of pathology, to a much broader and far-reaching perspective which places the understanding of paranoid in a far-reaching context embracing developmental, adaptive, defensive, functional, social, and cultural perspectives.

Extension of the Paranoid Process

The Schreber material[1] brings the components of the paranoid process into sharp relief. My primary reason for appealing to this classic case is that in their pathological expressions the paranoid mechanisms reveal themselves in sharp and unequivocal delineation. This has considerable advantage for purposes of description and clarification of the mechanisms. The distinction, however, between the paranoid process and paranoid psychopathology is central to my argument—they are not synonymous. The shift in emphasis from pathology to process implies that the paranoid process has a much broader range of application and implication than paranoid psychopathology. While the mechanisms of the paranoid process are found in all forms of paranoid psychopathology, these same mechanisms can also be identified, as I have suggested, in a broad range of nonpathological and even normal contexts. The paranoid process also plays a considerable part in a variety of nonparanoid pathological states—I refer to a series of fairly common, admittedly pathological, conditions such as envy, jealousy, prejudice, depression, and even certain forms of personality organization (Meissner 1978b, 1986c). While these emotionally ladened affective states bear some of the marks of pathogenicity, they are also generally accepted as the common lot of humankind and consequently more often than not never come to professional attention. When they do, however, the elements of the paranoid process are not difficult to identify.

If we extend our exploration beyond the pathological into areas of socially acceptable and relatively normal human experience, we find similar mechanisms at work. Such areas would include belief systems, particularly in the form of political ideologies and religious belief systems, value systems forming contexts of shared meaning and human cultural participation, and even certain aspects of scientific thinking

[1] See chapter 1.

(Monti 1981). Subsequent study has made it clear that the paranoid process is a quite general, even universal, process active in many aspects of human experience and personality functioning. It plays an important role in psychological development and in the formation and consolidation of personality structure. This is equally true whether that evolving personality structure is healthy and productive, leading to establishment of a mature and positive sense of personal identity, or whether the process takes a pathological turn and eventuates in personality structures that are essentially pathogenic and defective.

There are certain clear links between the pathology of paranoia and more normal nonpathological expressions of the paranoid process. The process itself and the mechanisms involved can be discerned with the greatest clarity and descriptive differentiation in frank paranoid pathology—as in the Schreber case. Particularly in the extreme forms of paranoia, the pathology serves as a sort of *experimentum naturae* permitting a clear vision of the nature of these processes and their interrelationships. It is as though the effects of the pathology were to separate the various elements of the paranoid process and display them in clear and unequivocal delineation, providing us the opportunity for careful and detailed study.

Further, even in its nonpathological applications, the paranoid process retains an inherent potentiality, even in well-integrated personalities, to shift under appropriate eliciting conditions in the direction of paranoid pathology. In other words, all human beings carry within them, by reason of the inherent organization of the paranoid process, the potentiality for the emergence of psychopathology as a result of pathological diversion of elements inherent in the normal paranoid process. The paranoid process carries within it a potentiality for pathological expression that can be activated or elicited by the proper constellation of stimulating or stressful conditions.

Keeping the distinction between pathological and nonpathological expressions of the paranoid process clearly in mind, we can make certain critical clarifications. Recognition of such a paranoid potential as inherent in human psychological makeup would not justify the conclusion that the cultic process or any similar group process involving paranoid mechanisms was in itself inherently pathological, or that the individual personalities involved in the group process were all of the same personality structure (i.e., paranoid personalities). The main forms of this pathological expression seem to be either paranoid or depressive manifestations of varying degrees, and can be elicited by certain life stresses, alterations in the contexts of social and environmental support, or by changes in the physiological functioning of the body itself (as in aging or other physiologically induced changes in mental capacity or functioning) and a host of other factors having to do with the sustaining and the reinforcement of the capacity for psychic integration and inner psychic cohesiveness. The fact that similar mechanisms can be identified in group and social contexts does not mean that the outcome is pathological in any sense. In fact, I would argue even further, that society provides certain forms of group structure and process that offer a vehicle for the absorption and more or less constructive channeling of this same paranoid potential in ways that are socially and culturally constructive. The problem remains, however, that these same processes, because of their inherent paranoid potential, can be rechanneled in more pathological and destructive directions, given the right eliciting conditions. If such paranoid processes can serve the adaptive interests of society, they can also be diverted into serving more destructive and maladaptive purposes. This is the central thesis on which the argument concerning the paranoid process and its embellishment in the cultic process is founded.

I would conclude, then, as a corollary to this argument, that frank paranoid psychopathology is merely the tip of an iceberg, encompassing the vast body of humankind. In fact, the impact of the paranoid process can be traced in social contexts, first of all in family systems (Meissner 1978a), and then in social systems more generally. Thus, the term "paranoid" points in two directions, on the one hand to the origin of the conceptualization and the understanding of the paranoid process in paranoid psychopathology, and on the other hand to an inherent capacity for the activation of paranoid potentialities in the broad spectrum of humankind, even in populations whose mental normality and emotional stability can be assumed. To take a familiar example, the extent to which malignant prejudice can be found in otherwise normal and well-adapted populations, and the extent to which, given the proper eliciting conditions, prejudicial attitudes can be generated in otherwise reasonable and psychologically mature groups of people has been frequently documented. Such observations would argue to the existence of an inherent potentiality for such paranoid trends, even in normal populations (Meissner 1978b, 1994). It is this potentiality that I am formulating in terms of the paranoid process, a potentiality that comes into play, I contend, in the formation and development of religious groups as well.

Relation of Socio-cultural Analysis to Psychoanalysis— Social Structures and Processes

The above argument involves a basic hypothesis that social processes organize appropriate contexts within which the paranoid process comes into play, to preserve certain specific adaptive functions and provide a context within which individuals may find a sense of appropriate belonging and useful social and cultural participation. Achievement of these goals is intimately linked to sustaining a sense of identity in the individual: substantially the same dynamic issues were addressed by Erikson (1959, 1963) in his analysis of the developmental emergence and resolution of psychosocial crises. The intrapsychic organization of the self and the social participation and embeddedness of the self are intimately intertwined. My argument here extends the eriksonian schema to include the manner in which society provides structures and contexts within which the basic mechanisms of the paranoid process—internalizations in terms of which personal identity as a group member is consolidated, and externalizations determining group boundaries and differentiation from other groups—can be turned to adaptive and useful purposes. These mechanisms can be read as further specifications of the intrapsychic processes in Erikson's epigenetic progression of crisis resolutions.

An important methodological question arises from applying a process arising within the context of individual psychodynamics to group phenomena. In what sense can the group be said to embody the paranoid process that has its primary locus of application in the individual mind? Does the "paranoid process" have the same reference and connotations when applied to groups as when applied to the individual psyche? Does the argument rest merely on analogy between these levels of explanation? Do we not have to face the difficulties of different, if related, frames of reference? It may clarify matters to address these questions in the following points.

(1) The proper and immediate context of the paranoid process is the individual psyche (Meissner 1978b, 1994b). In the description and analysis of the relevant intrapsychic dynamics, it plays its immediate and most appropriate role. In groups, its role is analogous to the effect of such mechanisms in the individual psyche. Its group effects, I would suggest, reflect the aggregate operation of these mechanisms in enough members of the group to promote analogous group effects. However, there is no paranoid process operating in the group other than the intrapsychic processes effective in individual members. But, when complex extrinsic factors—social, cultural, historical, economic, political, and so on—impinge in similar ways on large numbers of group members, paranoid potentialities are mobilized within respective members that find expression in group processes bearing striking similarities to paranoid dynamics. These include ingroup vs. outgroup differentiation, prejudicial attitudes affecting both ingroup and outgroup, intensification of boundary delineations, denigration of and hostility to

outgroup values and activities along with increased valuation and en-hancement of corresponding ingroup qualities, and so on.[2]

(2) However, as such, the paranoid process is not an isolated phe-nomenon—as though it arose and functioned exclusive of interaction with other extrapsychic social and cultural processes. Not only does the paranoid process originate in virtue of interpersonal and interac-tional influences coming to bear on it throughout the developmental years—stemming from familial interactions, social influences, cultural influences, core processes of internalization that necessarily derive from relational contexts involving other significant human beings, and so on[3]—but, in its more mature and adult expressions, it remains highly reactive to, reflective of, and to an extent determined by contin-uing influences from these extrapsychic sources.

(3) An essential note of the paranoid process (Meissner 1978b) is that the potential for paranoid pathology exists in every human being. In many its expressions are minimal and for the most part remain in-distinguishable from normal behaviors. In many others, its expressions take the form of often subtle and run-of-the-mill prejudices, beliefs, at-titudes, and convictions that usually find some form of societal appro-bation and integration—prejudicial religious beliefs and attitudes, racial and sexual prejudices, political divisions, social stratifications, value systems—as well as minor degrees of pathological expression, e.g., envy, jealousy, authoritarian attitudes, obsessions with power, and so on. Because of the matrix of social absorption and even endorse-ment, these properties are regarded as within the limits of normality. In others, the paranoid potential reaches a threshold of frank psycho-pathology that may prove in varying degrees problematic and disrup-tive both personally and socially, and in the most extremely deviant cases may even reach the level of psychosis.

Underlying this spectrum of paranoid pathological-nonpathological assertions, there lies the core continuum of paranoid potential con-tained in the paranoid process. To the extent that developmental, inter-personal, familial, social and cultural elements contribute to the shaping of the potentiality of the paranoid process in each individual, we can argue that there is a body of paranoid potential and resulting degrees of paranoid expression within the social groupings them-selves—so that particular groups can be classified and analyzed in terms of this potential. Corresponding to the degree of actualization of paranoid potential in the members of the group, the group itself can

---

[2] These characteristics are discussed in greater detail in chapters 13 and 14.

[3] See the more extended discussion of developmental aspects of the paranoid process in chapter 1.

take on paranoid characteristics—in the hatred of enemies, even the at times delusional paranoid extremes to which national and religious groups can go in seeking the destruction of their enemies (Meissner 1978b; Volkan 1988). I would argue that the group paranoia—if we may call it that—serves a certain economic function, namely that it effects a compromise by which the individual paranoid potential is shunted into and conjoined with similar paranoid tendencies in other group members and is effectively channeled in aspects of group dynamic processes that both contribute to group formation and maintenance on one hand, and provide a communal buffer that prevents the individual paranoia from becoming undermining and destructive to the individual. Social processes of this sort thus serve a vital function by converting pathological potential into group structuring and confirming effects. My argument here is, as far as I can see, congruent with that advanced by Volkan (1988) regarding the need for enemies and its effects in cultural adaptation and social cohesion.

(4) Thus the primary intrapsychic frame of reference for the paranoid process differs from that of the group—the similarities cannot be stretched beyond analogy. But if the paranoid expressions of the group differ from those of the individual both in quality and character, they are also causally related. The national group paranoia leading to hatred of an enemy and war rides on a substratum of individual paranoias in the members of the nation, sufficient in number and strength to lend conviction to the paranoid impulse of the group and mobilize the support of the members to the paranoid crusade. The group paranoia, then, arises out of the paranoid matrix provided by the paranoid potential of individuals, and cannot be sustained without the persistence of paranoid expression in the members. Otherwise, it falters and falls short of the paranoid threshold.

The implications of this intertwining of social and paranoid processes are multiple. It suggests that the organization of social processes and institutions can have a positive psychological impact, in that it draws the operation of paranoid mechanisms into more adaptive and self-sustaining contexts. At the same time, these same processes, operating typically across a broad spectrum of less pathological human contexts, can be viewed as playing an role, under deviant conditions, in the genesis of possible paranoid psychopathology. A point not to be ignored is that the same mechanisms are brought into play whether the process operates with positive and constructive outcomes, or not.

Social Prejudice

The differentiation between social groupings and the attribution of negative stereotypes to the outgroup and the corresponding attribution of positive stereotypes to the ingroup is an expression of social prejudice. In discussing such paranoid manifestations, the question is not one of the reality of such distinctions as opposed to, let us say, some form of fanciful distortion. The realities often do not correspond to perceptions and a good case can usually be made for subjective distortion or, at the least, interpretation. The question I would prefer to focus on here is rather about the ways and extent to which paranoid mechanisms come into play. In many situations of social prejudice, the underlying issues have to do with competition between subgroups. While the threat inherent in the competition might be seen at one level, let us say, as economic, e.g., as competition for available jobs, the same threat may also be posed at an intrapsychic level as a threat to narcissism. Paranoid mechanisms, then, would be mobilized to defend against this potential narcissistic threat. From clinical experience, we are quite familiar with the propensity for threatened or injured narcissism to result in thinking in terms of extreme alternatives, to blur realistic distinctions, to conceptualize in terms of stereotypical categories, and to seize upon any identifiable differences as the basis for drawing the line between that to which one affiliates oneself and that to which one is opposed—to draw the line, that is, between those who belong and those who do not, between those who are members of the ingroup and those who must be regarded as enemies.

The formation of such extreme and radical groupings provides a context within which the paranoid resources of members can be mobilized to sustain both a significant sense of self and personal identity, and a context within which purposeful striving and belonging can be realized. The provision of such a matrix provides an important source of sustenance and support for an emergent sense of identity otherwise in danger of being undermined and overwhelmed. As Volkan (1988) comments:

> A sense of self is the impression one has of how his emotional, intellectual, and physical components respond together to the world about him and to pressures arising within himself. . . . The obstacles encountered along the way contribute to the developing concept of the enemy, partly through their coalescence with issues pertaining to the sense of self. Finally, as adults equipped with their own value system and the values belonging to their culture, they know whom they like and dislike and who is safe and who is not (p. 4).

The danger, of course, is the same danger that is always inherent in the mobilization of such paranoid resources. It runs the risk of verifying its own projections, and eliciting a mutually responsive paranoid rejoinder from the larger community within which it functions or from the outgroup that provides the exclusionary target. To the extent that paranoia elicits and generates a reciprocal paranoid response, the process becomes mutually destructive and pathological. This scenario has been sufficiently dramatically enacted on various conflict-ridden stages of our modern world to require little further comment.

On both sides of the dividing line between the subjective group and the outside world, there grows up a mythology erected on the history of significant episodes in which such essentially paranoid distortions were apparently realized and verified. What is noteworthy here, as in so many other areas in which the paranoid process plays itself out, is not only that the paranoid mechanisms have a propensity for eliciting their own verification, but that the paranoid construction tends to generate a mythology based on a small number of verifiable incidents, which it uses as the basis for a general ideology expressing both the victimization of one's own group and the malicious and untrustworthy evil of the other. In such contexts we can clearly see the mythopoeic potentiality of the paranoid process, as an aspect of the paranoid construction, coming into clear elaboration.

Application to the Religious Sphere

Another important set of methodological questions arise from the application of forms of sociological and psychological analysis to religious phenomena. There are valid issues concerning the degree and manner in which such scientifically oriented frames of reference can legitimately be used to explore the structure and meaning of religious experience—whether in individual or group terms. The issues are similar on both levels, but there are dissimilarities that make room for separate consideration.

The use of sociological interpretations in the understanding of religious phenomena gives rise to conceptual difficulties. The objection arises that the sociological-psychological approach tends to explain religion away rather than deepen our understanding—religion becomes a byproduct of group processes or a projection of individual wishful fantasies. The objection is not without merit since sociological approaches have often enough proven or have been interpreted as reductionistic.[4] The Marxist critique (Kautsky 1925), for example, traced the origins of Christianity to the class struggle in ancient societies; the Chicago school (Case 1923) found the roots of the ideas and practices of

---

[4] My use of the terms "reductionistic" and "reductive" deserve comment. I use "reductionistic" to describe a situation in which lower-order concepts are used to

first-century Christianity in the social needs of the time. More recent Marxist understanding has contributed a more nuanced concept of the dialectic between social and belief structures and patterns, and the early functionalist naiveté of early Chicagoans has given way to a more relevant application of functionalist perspectives including a greater sensitivity to the interplay of participant and observer viewpoints, of manifest and latent content and function, of transcultural and transhistorical variants, and of the complex dialectic of cognitive and structural cultural elements. These developments have made it clear that sociological analysis, or for that matter psychological analysis, does not imply reductionistic conclusions, but that such analyses remain essentially reductive insofar as they illuminate the cultural, social, economic and historical factors shaping and influencing religious movements.

The conclusion regarding the application of psychological analyses to religious phenomena is much the same. My interest and the focus of the discussion in the present work is specifically on the role of psychoanalysis in the understanding of religious phenomena. I have discussed this problem in previous publications (Meissner 1984, 1992) and would refer the interested reader to those works. Psychoanalytic interest in religious manifestations, following Freud's lead, has largely been restricted to efforts to reduce religious experiences to unconscious dynamic factors or to interpret religious symbols and rites in psychoanalytic terms. The gist of such studies has tended to be reductionistic

---

explain a set of higher-order phenomena in such a way that the lower-order explanation is regarded as complete and exclusive and the higher-order phenomena are regarded as having no independent explanatory validity on their own terms. Thus, explanation of affective states by an appeal to basically physiological processes and accepting this explanation as total and excluding any intelligibility of affective experience beyond the explanatory account would be reductionistic. Similarly, explanation of chemical processes by appeal to physical mechanisms without taking into account that chemical analyses or complex reactions might involve anything proper to chemical analysis beyond the explanatory power of physical models would also be reductionistic. The same explanations, however, might be reductive. I use the term "reductive" to indicate that lower-order explanations might have validity in further extending understanding of higher-order phenomena, but they do not replace higher-order understanding, but serve a complementary function adding another dimension to higher-order interpretations. Thus, the physiological aspect of affective states is an important component of the understanding of these phenomena, but they do not substitute for or replace other interpretive approaches based on experiential and/or psychological bases. In the present discussion, I regard sociological and psychological analyses and the interpretive accounts they contribute to understanding religious phenomena as reductive, and not necessarily reductionistic.

rather than reductive in tone and intent. The present study attempts to extend psychoanalytic understanding to a different dimension of religious experience and meaning. The focus of interest is on the dynamic forces and processes contributing to the emergence, development, and subsequent evolution of religious groups and belief systems rather than on the individual intrapsychic aspects of religious experience.

The first step in my explanatory hypothesis is to establish the validity of the cultic process as an identifiable phenomenon in religious group development; the second step is to establish the basis for the cultic process in the individual mechanisms of the paranoid process. The reader will have to judge the success of that enterprise for himself. It remains to be seen whether the paranoid process, as one formulation of psychoanalytic principles and mechanisms, can adequately sustain the explanatory weight of this understanding. My intention in developing this line of thought is in no sense reductionistic, but it is reductive insofar as it recasts the emergence and historical development of religious movements in a framework that allows a clearer focus to emerge on the intrapsychic components and the manner of their contribution to these social and cultural developments. None of the sociological or psychological conceptualizations involved in these considerations are intended nor do they necessarily lend themselves to a reductionistic interpretation that would exclude a more theologically or faith-impregnated understanding of the same phenomena.

Another corollary of this argument, one that is more directed to what is not being said than to what is, is concerned with the discrimination of the pathological and the nonpathological in religious movements—whether of the cultic variety or of more developed structure. The question is frequently asked about how one might decide on what religious movements are pathological and how does one discriminate them from nonpathological religious expressions. This concern probably reflects the persistence of the automatic association of "paranoid" with its pathological implications rather than with its role as a form of psychic process as noted above. Even so, historically the problem was one that perplexed Freud and led him to fix on pathological aspects of religious experience, particularly the infantile and neurotic components, and draw his classic analogy to obsessional states and behaviors. From one point of view, the question is irrelevant—the upshot of the analysis in terms of the cultic process is that pathological and nonpathological elements are discernible in all religious groups, large and small, structured and unstructured, in cults and sects as well as in larger denominations and fully formed and institutionalized churches. The mixtures of the pathological and the nonpathological in the sectarian movements described in this study bear ample testimony to that conclusion.

One could refine the question to mean, if all religious movements have their pathological as well as nonpathological elements, to what extent can we discriminate between those groups manifesting predominantly or excessively pathological traits as opposed to those that show a lesser degree of pathogenicity? This question is less prejudicial and offers an opportunity to apply a more refined analysis to particular religious groups to determine what aspects of group beliefs, ritual behaviors, and credal commitments smack of the pathological and what do not. If the paranoid process operates as my hypothesis indicates, we would expect a mixture of relatively paranoid expressions in any religious community—some of which are in some degree adaptive and others more maladaptive. Even in the more established churches, aspects of the belief system can reflect pathological determinants—belief in the devil and hell in Christian churches may be a case in point, particularly in regard to the excessive preoccupations with guilt, worthlessness, and sinfulness that can pervade the believer's consciousness as byproducts of such belief orientations. These expressions can reflect depressive dynamics that would seem to be clinically pathological in some degree, more certain in specific instances than in others.

If one were to take the question seriously, where would one look to make some estimate of relative pathogenicity or adaptiveness? My best guess is the cult investigator might advisedly examine those parameters of group functioning that most directly have the potential of expressing underlying pathological influences. Aspects of sect characteristics that might carry this potential include the degree of separateness from the world, whether by isolation or insulation; the degree of coherence of sect values and the degree of correspondence or deviance of sect values from the surrounding culture—recognizing that pathology may lie in either excessive coherence and demands for adherence, or in the lack of coherence, and that either set of values, those of the cult or of the society, may express pathological components; and the nature of group commitments and loyalties, particularly the degree of adherence to a cult leader whose style of leadership and guiding ideology may reflect degrees of pathological deviation. This list is not meant to be exhaustive, but serves only to suggest that there are identifiable parameters of group life and commitment that may lend themselves to the evaluation of potential pathogenicity. Obviously, all religious groups have elements of positive adaptation and negative distortion, but we can presume—as with equality—some are more equal than others.

This consideration does, however, raise an important point—that the validity of religious beliefs is not determined by their inherent pathogenicity. This logical error was made by Freud, when he argued that the neurotic aspects of religious belief and praxis undermined the credibility and validity of religious commitments. The validity of religious beliefs, their truth value in a sense, rests on the basis of faith and the acceptance of a revelation—not on the degree to which particular beliefs may reflect pathological influences or determinants (Meissner 1992). Thus pathogenicity and religious truth-value are orthogonal dimensions. There is no contradiction between a valid credal system and psychopathology—the dynamics of religious belief does not base its faith commitments on the basis of what is psychologically mature or not. In other words, what seems pathological to the psychiatric or psychoanalytic view may seem religiously valid and true to the religious or theological perspective. Part of the richness and complexity of the psychoanalytic study of religious phenomena lies precisely in this mixture of elements—a situation that prevails in the psychoanalytic study of all human enterprises, whether religious, political, cultural, artistic, or historical. The pathological and the nonpathological find their way, in varying degrees and complex interminglings, in all human endeavors.

This consideration leads me to one last preliminary comment. This consideration confronted me when I began to get feedback from scholars studying new religious movements who bridled at my use of the term "cultic process." It had not occurred to me that the term was prejudicial—I had intended it as merely descriptive at most. Their concern, expressed by a number of scholars involved in this field, was that despite my obvious intention the terminology remained open to prejudicial cooptation by those who were invested in attacking and condemning cult movements of all kinds. The risk of potential harm, they felt, exceeded any gain from use of the terminology. The objection gave me considerable pause and forced me to rethink some of my own suppositions. My response at this juncture is not to abandon the concept nor the term, but to assure myself and others that the term "cultic" does not refer exclusively to cults, however that designation is to be conceived. Its reference extends to all religious groups, old, new, large, small, orthodox, heterodox, etc. Moreover, my frame of reference in the present work is not contemporary but ancient. I will attempt to explore the implications of these concepts in the framework of the early centuries of the development of Christianity, beginning with pre-Christian religious groupings and following the evolution of religious structures through the ensuing first centuries of the Christian dispensation.

This creates something of a methodological problem. Although the material I am focusing on is historical and quite ancient, the technical resources at my command, both borrowed from more contemporary studies in the sociology and psychology of religion, particularly psychoanalysis, arise out of the study of contemporary religious movements. Those studies are caught up in the tensions and controversies

that have arisen over the evaluation and understanding of cult movements in our own day and which reflect the reverberations of the paranoid process operative between cult advocates and cult opponents. My
problem is whether I can put some of the conceptual apparatus of contemporary thinking to work in evaluating ancient religious phenomena without carrying along the excess baggage that would be involved
in any evaluation of cult phenomena in the modern context. I argue
that I can and have. But this has required that my use of terms be judi-
cious and cautious, ensuring that my evaluations even in the displacement of two millennia are evenhanded and nonprejudicial. I hope that
I have sufficiently succeeded in that endeavor to satisfy potential critics
without sacrificing the complexity and nuancedness of my discussion.
Again, I will have to leave it to the reader to judge.

Introduction

.

1

The Paranoid Process

Introduction

This study seeks to formulate an understanding of patterns of motivation and psychological integration involved in the origin and evolution of religious movements. The conceptual centerpiece of the argument will be the cultic process;[1] the cultic process is essentially a group process by which the group establishes and defines itself over against other competing and oppositional groups. As such, it does not speak to the level of intrapsychic dynamic processes that give force, conviction, and motivational power to the formation of religious groups and belief systems. These forces require a specifically psychological perspective to lend its explanatory power to the religious group dynamic. In this chapter I will discuss my understanding of the psychological process serving this function for the cultic process—the paranoid process.

Since the understanding of the paranoid process originates from clinical experience (Meissner 1978b), I would like to be clear as to what we are talking about in applying these concepts to social and cultural contexts. In this first chapter, therefore, I will summarize the basic ideas involved in the "paranoid process," so that this perspective can serve as a frame of reference for our subsequent considerations of the cultic process. The argument proceeds from the pathological to the presumably normal, and from the individual to the group. I would like to

---

[1] The concept of the cultic process is developed in greater detail in chapter 2.

begin the argument with a clinical case—one that has become noteworthy because of Freud's (1911) discussion of it and one that allows us to
delineate the components of the paranoid process *in vivo*—I refer to the
case of Daniel Paul Schreber. My interest is less in Schreber's pathology
than in delineating the mechanisms of the paranoid process and the
cultic process it lays bare.[2]

Schreber Case

Daniel Paul Schreber was a distinguished jurist who stood as a
candidate for the *Reichstag* in the autumn of 1884, but soon after his
election began to experience hypochondriacal delusions requiring
hospitalization. He was discharged in the following year and then appointed to the Leipzig *Landgericht*. He functioned reasonably effectively
in this office until 1893, at which point he was elevated to the more
prestigious Court of Appeals. In October of the same year, he was appointed presiding judge of the court, but in the following month again
decompensated and had to be readmitted to the hospital. Altogether,
Schreber spent thirteen of the next twenty-seven years in mental asy-
lums. His *Memoirs of My Nervous Illness* (Schreber 1903) is a remarkable
document, written between 1900–1902, recounting the development of
his illness and describing graphically his elaborate delusional system.
The *Memoirs* did not come to Freud's attention until 1910, but then provided him with ripe material for his germinating ideas about paranoia.

Schreber's delusions were bizarre and elaborate. His physician at
the Leipzig Clinic had been Flechsig, the famous neuropsychiatrist.
Schreber had originally admired and esteemed Flechsig, but later on
felt, as a part of his persecutory delusions, that Flechsig was perform-
ing "soul murder" on him—Schreber never explained what he meant
by the term.[3] Freud interpreted this powerful persecutor as a substitute
for an important figure in the patient's emotional life prior to his illness: a once loved and honored object became a hated and feared persecutor. In terms of his libidinal hypothesis, Freud speculated that the

---

[2] I emphasize again that the Schreber case is in no sense providing the evidential
base on which my argument rests. That evidence is collected and discussed in
Meissner (1978b). I am using this discussion of the Schreber case simply as a convenient device for explaining and dramatizing the concepts involved in the understanding of the paranoid process. The case serves merely an expository function,
not evidential.

[3] See the discussion of soul murder in Schreber in Niederland (1974), Schatzman
(1974), and Shengold (1989).

reason for the paranoid delusion was the wish/fear of sexual abuse by Flechsig and that the precipitating cause of the illness was an outburst of homosexual libido. Later in the course of his illness, Schreber developed the delusion that he was being transformed into a woman by the power of God—that his genitalia were changing into those of a woman, and that he was developing breasts.

The place of the divinity in these delusions was very special, and incidentally makes Schreber's delusional system an interesting case study for relating paranoid mechanisms to religious belief systems. In Schreber's view, God consisted purely of nerves; he was convinced that God was changing his body by influencing Schreber's own nerves. The nerves of God had a creative capacity, possessing all of the properties of human nerves to a greatly intensified degree. In addition, they could transform themselves into any kind of object in the created world through rays emanating from the Deity. In terms of this theocosmology, after the work of creation, God had withdrawn to an immense distance and left the world to its own meager devices. God's activities were restricted to drawing to himself the souls of the dead. Schreber felt that he was selected by God for a special mission and that, consequently, God worked his power on Schreber's nerves to give them the character of female "nerves of voluptuousness," transforming his body gradually into a female body. Schreber was able to reconcile himself to this sexual transformation by accepting the higher purposes of God. God demanded femaleness from him as part of his special mission in the world, to be God's special agent and to save and redeem God's creation. He was the chosen messenger of God, selected to carry out the special mission of saving the world by means of this subordination to the divine will and the transformation of his body into that of a woman. Only in this way was the world to be saved from imminent and complete destruction. Schreber was to become the wife of God and by divine impregnation would give birth to a new race of men, and thus become the redeemer of the world. Consequently, Schreber developed an elaborate theocosmology articulating his ideas of God's special relation to the world and his own special relation to God.

Schreber's concept of God was also of interest. Briefly, Schreber identified his God with the sun, but following a Zoroastrian pattern, divided this God into an upper God called Ormuzd and a lower God called Ahriman. In this ancient Manichean tradition, Ormuzd was the good divinity who created and guided the world; Ahriman was the Evil Spirit who entered into universal conflict with the Good Spirit for the control of the world and men's souls. Schreber's God combined these attributes of good and evil, reflecting according to Freud's hypothesis Schreber's ambivalence toward both the physician Flechsig and, behind Flechsig as the primary transferential figure, Schreber's father (Freud 1911; Meissner 1976; Niederland 1974; Westphal 1990).

Schreber's relation to God included a mixture of blasphemous criticism and mutinous insubordination, on one hand, and reverent devotion, on the other. He felt that God was incapable of learning anything by experience and, since he only knew how to deal with corpses, did not understand living men. Freud speculated that God stood for Schreber's distinguished father; the sun thus became the symbol of the father, and the conflict with God could be construed as representing the infantile conflict with the father whom the patient also loved and to whom he was forced to submit. It was the oedipal threat of the father, namely, the threat of castration, that provided the basic material for Schreber's wishful fantasy of transformation into a woman. Part of Schreber's delusional system was his belief in the imminent destruction of the world, interpreted by Freud in terms of the withdrawal of cathexis from the environment, so that the expected end of the world became a projection of the patient's inner catastrophe. The libido thus liberated according to Freud's theoretical schema was attached to the ego in the form of self-aggrandizement and megalomania.

The Projective System

The major emphasis in Freud's consideration of Schreber's pathology fell on the projective system. Later studies have exquisitely documented the relation between specific elements in Schreber's projective delusions and detailed aspects of what he must have experienced as a child—particularly the persecution at the hands of his father (Niederland 1974; Schatzman 1974). The father was a physician and well-known writer and lecturer, who specialized in orthopedics and developed a system for the discipline and physical culture of children called "therapeutic gymnastics." This involved an elaborate series of compulsive and rigid techniques and mechanical restraints calculated to break the child's will. Severe corporal punishments were advised for the slightest infringement of these many rules, since the unruly and disruptive aspects of the child's crude nature had to be weakened and brought under control through the greatest strictness—even from the earliest years. Dr. Schreber applied these methods rigorously to his own children, so that the infant Schreber was subjected to relentless mental and physical torment under the guise of education.

The elder Schreber was pathologically obsessed with control, especially of masturbatory and aggressive manifestations, but his compulsive sadism was rationalized as a fanatical missionary crusade for improved physical culture and moral formation. These exercises in child discipline, described in some detail by Niederland (1974), can be regarded as compulsive-sadistic-projective rituals in self-control. In this sense, Schreber's projective system preserves and extrapolates his pathological relationship to his father. The price of relation with the father, therefore, was subjugation and submission, just as the price of becoming the special agent and instrument of God's divine purposes for redemption of the world was transformation into a woman. Schreber's projective system was founded on recognition and acceptance by, and special relationship to, the projected father-figure of God.

The projective system can thus be seen as an attempt to redeem and salvage Schreber's damaged narcissism. Within the delusional system he retained a grandiose and narcissistically embellished position as the agency of divine purpose. His self-esteem and his impaired sense of inner value and worth were in this fashion generously restored. Transformation into a woman, on one level, served to redeem the narcissistic loss experienced through his failure to generate healthy children; his wife's many miscarriages were narcissistic injuries for him. On another level, the transformation into a woman consolidated his underlying identification with his mother.

In terms of the paranoid process (Meissner, 1978b, 1986c), the projective system has a derivative relation to the patterning of introjects[4] around which the sense of self is organized. The roots of the projective system must be sought in the patterning of introjects, even as the structure of the projective system is a response to the undermined and deprived narcissism embedded in the introjective economy. In Schreber's case, his early developmental experiences left him with a crippled sense of himself as valueless, humiliated, evil, unlovable, and ultimately worthy only of sadistic subjugation and cruel restraint (victim introject). Around this nuclear formation was erected a context of object relatedness defined by the emerging sense of self based on the central introjects.

The introjective economy rests on crucial introjections from both parents. The dominant element in the traditional view of the Schreber case is the introjection of the aggressive and punitive father figure (aggressor introject). Even as he suffered as the vulnerable victim of his father's punitive attacks, Schreber identified with the implicit power of his father's aggression, and this identification with the aggressor, formed around this paternal introject, became the basis for the persecutory projection. But other elements are also present. Although we have very little direct knowledge of Schreber's mother, we can infer that she must have been a woman whose character contained strong depressive

---

[4] These mechanisms are considered in greater detail below.

and masochistic elements. Sustaining a relationship with her severely sadistic and authoritarian husband would have suggested strongly masochistic elements in her own character structure.

In a powerful and convincing manner, Schreber identified himself with the castrated figure of the mother-victim. His delusional system realized the ultimate in victimized subjugation to the power of the father-God. Schreber's position as victim was engendered by his sado-masochistic and homosexual relation with his father in conjunction with his identification with his victim-mother. Close study of paranoid pathology indicates that the combined elements of identification with the aggressor and identification with the victim are persistent and central elements in the introjective economy of paranoid patients. In one aspect at least, the paranoid process can be seen as a reinforcement of the victim introject as a means of defending against the aggressive and victimizing introject by projection (Meissner, 1976). Permutations in the dynamics of these introjects provide the basis for some of the complex manifestations of the paranoid process. Consequently, the projective system serves an important function in the preservation of a sense of self. The pathogenic introjects do not allow establishment or organization of an authentic sense of self meaningfully related to real objects. To sustain the pathological sense of self based on these introjects, the subject must organize a projective system allowing for substitute relatedness of the pathological self and providing it with a sense of meaningful belongingness within the system of projective relations.

Schreber's projective system was elaborated into a highly complex theocosmological mythic ideology connecting his inner sense of psychic need and defensive dynamics with the cosmic implications of a special relation with God and divine purposes spanning time and history. The dynamics of this delusional system have been analyzed elsewhere (Freud 1911; Niederland 1974; Meissner 1976; Westphal 1990), but my focus here is on the belief system itself as an example of the paranoid construction which encompasses and rationalizes the projective system. The paranoid construction provides the point of transition from a paranoid delusional system to theological belief systems. We would regard Schreber's system as delusional and pathological, but the belief systems of pre-Christian Palestinian religious sects, or of the Jesus movement and early Christianity, or even the Gnostic cosmologies, as legitimate and nonpathological convictions. Yet I would argue that they involve the same basic psychic mechanisms of the paranoid process. Why is one pathological and others not?

Why, then, do we regard Schreber's delusional system as pathological? First, it is an idiosyncratic system entirely personal in derivation and connected with no current or consensual religious tradition or organized religious group. It has, therefore, no group culture connected with it; it incorporates elements of an ancient tradition with respect to the divine names and their essential duality, but it has no real connection with that or any other religious tradition. The conviction of the imminent end of the world is common to many cultic, especially millennarian, beliefs, and was even part of the early Christian kerygma regarding the imminence of the *parousia* in which the triumphant Christ would return in glory (Meissner 1995). Other details carry the stamp of unreality and delusional wish fulfillment—especially the "nerves" and the sexual transformation so graphically expressing the sexual dynamics along with powerful themes of narcissistic grandiosity and self-enhancement (narcissistic introjects). Elevation to the status of God's wife and redeemer of the world would do very nicely in satisfying unresolved grandiose narcissistic desires of a quite primitive and pathological order.

Paranoid Process

Frank paranoid psychopathology is merely the tip of an iceberg, encompassing the vast body of humankind. In fact, the impact of the paranoid process can be traced in social contexts, first of all in family systems (Meissner 1978a), and then in social systems more generally. Thus, the term "paranoid" points in two directions, on the one hand to the origin of the conceptualization and the understanding of the paranoid process in paranoid psychopathology, and on the other hand to an inherent capacity for the activation of paranoid potentialities in the broad spectrum of humankind, even in populations whose mental normality and emotional stability can be assumed. To take a familiar example, the extent to which malignant prejudice can be found in otherwise normal and well-adapted populations, and the extent to which, given the proper eliciting conditions, prejudicial attitudes can be generated in otherwise reasonable and psychologically mature groups of people has been frequently documented. Such observations would argue to the existence of an inherent potentiality for such paranoid trends, even in normal populations (Meissner 1978b, 1994). It is this potentiality that I am formulating in terms of the paranoid process, a potentiality that comes into play in the formation and development of religious groups as well.

Mechanisms of the Paranoid Process

The "paranoid process" has both developmental and defensive components that delineate the individual's inner psychic world and experience of an emerging sense of self, and correlatively, in shaping the individual's interaction with the significant objects in his experiential world. Consequently, the paranoid process contributes in important ways to the process of individuation and the development of inner cohesiveness and self-awareness (Meissner, 1978b).

The three core dimensions of the paranoid process I would like to discuss are introjection, projection, and the paranoid construction.

Introjection

Introjection is the central mechanism of the paranoid process, insofar as it provides the intrapsychic basis from which projections arise as correlative secondary derivatives. The notion of introjection arose out of Freud's (1917) original formulation of narcissistic identification, proposed originally in his analysis of melancholy and later applied as the essential internalizing mechanism in the formation of the superego (1923). The mechanism of introjection, in that context, was based on loss of an object and preservation of the object intrapsychically through internalization.

Within the range of forms of internalization, introjection must be distinguished from more primitive and global incorporations on the one hand, and from higher-level, more differentiated, secondary process identifications that provide the basis for positive and constructive integration of healthy and adaptive personality functioning (Meissner, 1970, 1971, 1972, 1981). Between the level of (usually psychotic) incorporation, in which all differentiation between self and object is obliterated, and more differentiated identifications, that maintain the differentiation between self and object and allow for acknowledging the separateness and individuality of the object, introjections form an intermediate level of internalization by which the object is internalized, that is, becomes part of the subject's inner world, but at the same time retains some connection to the object realm. In melancholia, internalizing the lost object results in taking on attributes of that object, just as in the internalizations in the formation of the superego lead to adopting attitudes, ethical standards and even values of the (parental) objects. These internalized objects may never become completely integrated as part of the subjective inner world, but always retain the potentiality for objectification, for creating an experienced distance between the internalized object derivative (introject) and the subjective sense of self. Expressed in representational terms, it retains a capacity to be re-externalized or transformed from the realm of self-representations to that of object-representations. This inherent quality of continuing object connection of introjects forms the basis of its potentiality for projection. Projection, when and if it occurs, derives from the introjective organization, and only from that basis.

Formation of introjects results from defense mechanisms reflecting the individual's inability to accept and tolerate the separateness of the objects of dependence; he or she resorts to internalization as a means of avoiding the threat posed by separation, loss, or abandonment. In this sense, then, the introject comes to have a set of characteristic and inter-related qualities: it is defensively organized and maintained, vulner-able to drive influences in varying degrees, has an inherent regressive potential, and finally is susceptible to re-externalization by projection.

Developmentally, the introjective configuration comes about by the internalization of elements derived primarily from the personality organization of the parents, specifically the parents' own introjective configurations, so that the organization of any individual's introjects reflects elements combined from both parents in characteristic pattern-ings. Most often in family settings where pathological elements are at work, the patterns serving as the basis for the pathological organiza-tion of the patient's introjects can be seen plainly in the parental rela-tionship. The relationship between these patterns of parental interaction and the organization of the internalized derivatives in the patient's introjective alignment is often quite direct, since the child readily inter-nalizes aspects of both parents as he experiences them. These introjec-tive patterns in Schreber were highly influenced by his relations with both parents—the sadistic, punitive, and rigidly authoritarian aspects of his father's personality, and the pliant, passive, vulnerable and vic-timized aspects of his mother.

Reflection on the process of introjection as related to the paranoid process considerably broadens the meaning of the term from the nar-row focus of Freud's original formulations. Introjection comes to refer generally to that process of internalization by which aspects of objects or object relationships are taken in to form part of the subject's inner world, thus giving rise to the inner organization of some of the core ele-ments of the sense of self. When all goes well, forming of the introjec-tive configuration is expressed developmentally in an increasingly individuated and integrated sense of self. The process is, of course, subject to all the vicissitudes of development itself. I shall return to this subject shortly, but the point to be emphasized here is that there is a progressive differentiation in the organization of the introjects and their economy. At the earliest developmental levels, the introjective configuration is relatively primitive, undifferentiated, and global. At progressive stages of development, it becomes more delineated, more specifically differentiated, and increasingly structuralized.

While the developmental aspects of introjection are of major signifi-cance, the mechanism functions basically in defensive terms—that is, broadly speaking, the mechanism of introjection is called into operation by the defensive need to salvage and preserve the residues of narcissism jeopardized by losses and separations in the developmental progression. Schreber's sense of himself as victimized, vulnerable, and humiliated resulted from subjection to his father's disciplinary torments; narcissism could only be salvaged by internalizations based on the powerful and sadistic father and the passive, weak and vulnerable mother. These narcissistic and defensive dynamics give a characteristic stamp to the introjective organization, embodying drive derivatives and defensive configurations (Meissner, 1978b).

The characteristic alignment of the introjects can be expressed in terms of polar configurations based on both aggression and narcissism. The aggressive polarities take the form of the hostile and destructive aspects of aggression (aggressor-introject) versus a sense of helpless weakness and vulnerable victimization (victim-introject). In a similar fashion, the narcissistic components express themselves in a sense of superiority (superior introject) versus inferiority (inferior introject). Around one or other or some combination of these introjective components, the individual structures his sense of self. In terms of the victim-introject, the person sees himself as weak, ineffectual, inadequate, helpless, vulnerable and victimized. In terms of the aggressor-introject, he would see himself as strong, powerful, domineering, controlling, sadistic, hostile and destructive. In terms of the superior introject, in narcissistic terms, he would see himself as superior, special, privileged, perfect, entitled, and even grandiose or omnipotent. In terms of the inferior introject, the opposite pole to the narcissistic superior introject, he would see himself as inferior, worthless, valueless, shameful and humiliated. For Schreber, his early developmental experiences at the hands of his father left him with a crippled sense of himself as valueless, humiliated, unlovable, filled with evil impulses and desires, and worthy only of sadistic subjugation and cruel restraint. Introjection of the sadistic and aggressive aspects of his father offered the basis for his persecutory projection—the image of the persecuting father was displaced first to the physician Flechsig, and then to God. In both cases, his own sense of himself as victim, vulnerable, suffering, and humiliated was reinforced by his introjection of the image of his castrated mother-victim. In his delusional system, he realized the ultimate in victimized subjugation to the power of the father-God by transformation into a woman.

To the extent that the introjective process organizes and expresses a specific configuration of drive derivatives and serves specific defensive functions, this drive-and-defense organization leaves the self relatively susceptible to regressive drive influences, allowing the introjects to serve as points of origin for further defensive operations, specifically projection. It is the inherent relationship of the introjective organization to drive derivatives—whether libidinal, aggressive, or narcissistic—its susceptibility to regressive pulls, and its propensity to projection that allows us to delineate and identify it clinically (Meissner, 1971).

I will argue, in connecting the paranoid process to the cultic process, that, although introjects are primarily based developmentally on the child's experience of parental objects, social, economic, and cultural conditions can impinge on these intrapsychic configurations to reinforce, intensify, and modify the character and shape that these intrapsychic structures might take, as well as determining in large measure what form of expression they may seek. Persecution, deprivation, or oppression in the sociopolitical realm, for example, may interact with the individual's sense of victimization to intensify and radicalize his inner sense of humiliation, worthlessness, and impotence, and provoke countermeasures intended to redress the psychic balance even as they lead to revolution or social disruption. This dynamic can be traced in the origins of many cult movements.

Projection

The mechanism of projection derives from the introjective organization and draws its content from it. As we saw in the Schreber case, the persecutory objects—Dr. Flechsig and God—were modeled on Schreber's internalization of the sense of sadistic power and destructiveness acquired through introjection of his powerful and castrating father ("identification with the aggressor"). The externalization involved in projection involves modification of object images or representations and has a critical function in relation to object relationships. The correlative interaction of projection and introjection plays itself out throughout the whole of the developmental course. Projection is a central dimension of the process by which objects are differentiated and the quality of object relationships continually shaped and reworked.

Insofar as projections externalize elements of the introjective configuration, they bear the characteristic stamp of introjective components, and can be expected to reflect the organization of drives and defenses built into the introjects. While projection tends to occur primarily with other people, it may operate in any context in which human qualities can be attributed to the external world, as in primitive animistic or magically superstitious interactions with the environment, but also in more mundane contexts of interaction with pets or other forms of animal interaction (e.g., animal phobias), or even in determining the quality of interaction between the individual and the social environment—attributing personal qualities to social organizations, institutions, business organizations, government, and so forth.

Even from this sketchy description, it can be seen that projection is highly complex with many gradations and variations. The interplay of introjective and projective mechanisms weaves a pattern of relatedness to the world of objects and provides the fabric out of which the individual fashions his own self-image. His capacity to relate to and identify with the objects in his environment also develops out of this interplay, and determines the quality of his object relations. Projection and introjection must be seen in a developmental and differentiating perspective, which does not merely reduce them to defense mechanisms. They also serve important developmental functions, particularly in the early course of development. As development progresses, intrapsychic differentiation and the differentiation between subject and object reach a point at which further developmental progress depends on the emergence of other, more highly integrated and less drive-dependent types of processes. The persistence of projection and introjection beyond this point suggests that they are being employed more in the service of defensive needs than in facilitating interactions between subject and object.

It is difficult to say when their developmental relevance ceases. The persistence of introjective and projective mechanisms in development extends at least through the resolution of the oedipal situation, insofar as introjection and projection continue to play a vital role in the formation of the superego and the ego ideal. They may play a role in the reworking of previous developmental crises during adolescence, but beyond that their function is primarily defensive. Introjective responses to loss, while they provide the matrix for adaptive change and personal growth in the course of the life cycle, are primarily defensive responses (Rochlin 1965). It may be most accurate to say that the balance between the developmental and defensive aspects of introjection and projection shifts in the course of the life cycle and that these mechanisms therefore undergo a change in function, adjusting the balance of instinctual pressures between the inner and the outer worlds. The process is always in some degree defensive and in some degree developmental, in that its effects involve the emergence or consolidation of structure.

It is important to realize that introjection and projection are correlative. The understanding of projection requires an understanding of the introjective mechanisms underlying them. To understand what comes from the inner world we must try to understand what comprises the inner world and how it got there. In group process, projections play a critical role in establishing and maintaining group boundaries—attribution to outside groups of qualities oppositional to those characterizing the ingroup are a common mechanism based on projection. Outsiders are dishonest, deceitful, and dangerous, not us—even when these undesirable characteristics are as generously distributed within the ingroup as outside it.

The projective system, whatever the degree of its elaboration and complexity, does not stand on its own. The projective components, as we have indicated, derive from the subject's inner world and are reinforced by the motivational components—the drive and defensive configurations—that characterize that realm of inner experience. But the projective elaboration cannot be sustained simply by means of drives and their derivatives. This is particularly true in the case of more pathological projective distortions, which unavoidably run afoul of other dimensions of the subject's experience of reality. Without some secondary considerations, one would have to anticipate that such projective distortions would be equivalently self-limiting and self-correcting. Projections thus require a stabilizing framework.

Paranoid Construction

Clinical experience tells us that in more severe forms of paranoid psychopathology, the projective system acquires a degree of delusional fixity and conviction making it all but impermeable to therapeutic intervention and correction. The projective system in such cases is usually reinforced by the "paranoid construction" (Meissner, 1978b). The paranoid construction is a form of cognitive reorganization of one's experience in a broader conceptual framework including and integrating the elements of the projective system. In paranoid states, this cognitive organization takes the form of an elaborate system of beliefs, attitudes, convictions, and formulations serving to justify and sustain the projective components, as in the elaborate theocosmological construction of Judge Schreber. The projective elements in his delusional system could not have been sustained without a conceptual framework to provide support and meaning for them. His delusional system had to include a concept of God and a series of beliefs concerning the relation of God to the world and the special place appointed for Schreber himself in this divine plan.

The paranoid construction thus plays a critical role in the operation of the paranoid process, specifically in sustaining and reinforcing the projective elements. The projective elements themselves are articulated within a stabilizing framework in the service of the inner necessity for sustaining, to whatever degree possible, a sense of cohesiveness and integration within the experienced sense of self. Insofar as the introjective organization provides the core elements around which the sense of self is constructed, maintaining and reinforcing the introjective organization becomes vital for the economy of self-organization and integration. Thus, the entire apparatus—paranoid construction, projections, and introjective formations—has the overriding purpose of preserving and sustaining a coherent and integrated sense of self. This is the inner driving force and motivation behind the paranoid process. Moreover, this motivation not only operates in pathological expressions of the paranoid process but also plays a vital role in the relatively normal and adaptive development of human personality and in maintaining a mature and integrated sense of identity.

The paranoid construction can, therefore, be envisioned as providing a context within which the organization of the self finds a sense of belonging, participation, sharing, meaningful involvement, and relevance. We do not have far to go in our own experience to understand the importance of this dynamic in human life and experience. If the paranoid process operates in certain ways to separate and divide us from a sense of communion and belonging with our fellow men, that same process creates pressures that drive us in the direction of establishing another context, another matrix, within which these needs can be adequately satisfied. This inherent dynamic lies behind the shaping of social groupings and provides the inner dynamism for social processes. Particularly the formation and coherence of religious movements depends on an articulated belief system or creed that lends credibility and motivational conviction to the believers; to the extent that individual believers embrace the consensual belief system, they achieve a sense of sharing, belonging, participation and communion with their fellowmen, a powerful motivational dynamic in the formation of religious groups.

Developmental Aspects

I have noted in passing the role of the paranoid process in development, but its significance merits further discussion. The paranoid process plays a key role in the differentiation of both self and objects. Through the interplay of introjection and projection, the intrapsychic components of the emerging sense of self are gradually established. These processes contribute both to the organization of object-representations and to their gradual internalization as core elements of the self-system (Meissner 1981, 1986a). These modifications of object-representations are in the beginning primitive, undifferentiated, and global, and only gradually does the degree of differentiation between these elements allow the critical developmental step of the differentiation between self and object and between the internal and the external.

We can translate this process into terms of Mahler's (1975) separation-individuation process. This view would have to be qualified by more recent findings in early psychological development (Stern 1985; Dowling and Rothstein 1989), but our concern here is with the function of introjective-projective processes. In Mahler's terms, the infant begins life in a state of autistic immersion within the mother-child unit. Within this normal autistic unity there is no differentiation, and no distinction in the child's experience between internal and external stimuli. Within this omnipotent autistic orbit, the infant's waking experience centers around the continuing efforts to achieve physiological homeostasis. This view has to be balanced with the pre-adaptive responsiveness of the infant to object stimulation, but the viewpoints may not be irreconcilable since stimulus responsiveness does not imply the quality of the infant's experience—differentiated or not. The mother's ministrations may not be subjectively distinguishable from the infant's own tension-reducing processes—including urination, defecation, coughing, spitting, and so forth. Little by little, however, in Mahler's schema, the infant begins to differentiate between the pleasurable and the less pleasurable or painful qualities of his experience. Gradually, a dim awareness of the mother as a need-satisfying object begins to take shape, but he and the mother form an omnipotent system, contained within a common boundary.

This marks the transition to a more symbiotic phase characterized by a delusional omnipotent fusion with the representation of the mother in which primitively differentiated physiological affect states, governed by pleasure and unpleasure, begin to emerge. Attachment to the mother and response to her ministrations are governed by the pressure of these physiological needs. The perception dawns ever so dimly that need satisfaction derives from a need-satisfying object—even though that object is still retained within the orbit of the omnipotent symbiotic unity. Only to the extent that separation begins to take place does the infant begin to experience the receiving of milk that is not his own narcissistic (omnipotent) creation. These developments involve a critical shift of cathexis from a predominantly proprioceptive-enteroceptive focus toward the sensory perceptive and peripheral aspects of the infant's body. At this juncture, projective mechanisms come into play, not merely contributing to the construction of a more or less separate need-satisfying object, but beginning to serve specific defensive functions of deflecting more destructive and unneutralized aggressive impulses beyond the gradually emerging body-self boundaries.

As this developmental process works itself out, the organization of object-representations reflects inputs from external reality, particularly and most significantly from the primary objects of the infant's experience. Object-representations become increasingly differentiated as the child's cognitive capacities become more developed and articulated. The capacity for development of sensory and perceptual images, the gradual emergence of more complex forms of memory organization—shifting from more immediate and stimulus-bound forms of memory processing to the gradual emergence of more sophisticated and persistent forms of recognitional and finally evocative memory—the emergence of object constancies, and a variety of important influences from various forms of developmental learning, all contribute in meaningful and important ways to the gradual building-up, differentiation, and organization of object-representations (Meissner 1974).

As the object-representation is increasingly elaborated, elements of it are correlatively internalized and introjected as parts of the infant's globally emerging and relatively undifferentiated sense of self. Even in the earliest phases of the symbiotic matrix, these internalizations are taking place so that critical elements of the inchoate core of the infant's self are being shaped (Meissner 1986; Stern 1985). At this point, we can only guess at the significance of the balance of pleasurable versus unpleasurable components and the significance of the contribution of maternal attitudes to these nascent stirrings within the child. Winnicott (1965) stressed the importance of "good-enough mothering" and "holding" environment in the laying down of these primitive, yet crucial, early internalizations.

As these processes continue their interplay, the organization of elements of the self becomes more decisive and is more clearly and definitively separated from representations of the object in the separation and individuation process. In the view I am proposing here, projection and introjection are the mechanisms which subserve separation-individuation. At each step of the process, there is a critical reworking of internalized elements that gradually allows the child to establish a more autonomous sense of self and to separate himself from the dependency on the parental object. In this sense, the individuation would seem to be related to the building-up of an articulated sense of self through progressively differentiated introjections, while the gradual separation from the matrix of parental dependence is accomplished through the progressive projective modification and delineation of object-representations.

The major threat to the separation-individuation process is separation anxiety. Separation is an inherent aspect of development arising not only from the natural developmental impulse in the child and his burgeoning wishes for autonomous self-determination and expression, but also can be reinforced and intensified by the reactions of the maternal figure. If the mother reacts to the child's bids for autonomy by excessive rejection and precipitant pushing away from the comforting support of his dependence on her, the child is forced into a premature posture of self-sufficiency. On the other hand, if the mother is excessively threatened by loss of the child as a dependent appendage, her efforts will be directed toward forestalling bids for relative autonomy and a prolonging symbiotic dependence.

These maladaptive ways of emerging from maternal dependence can affect the interaction of projection and introjection in a variety of ways. These distortions create pressures for the child to rely excessively on these mechanisms for defensive rather than developmental purposes. Thus, excessive separation anxiety can lead the child to resort to regressive and more global introjection of the parental image as a defensive means for preserving contact with the need-satisfying, dependency-gratifying object and preserving narcissistic integrity. The basic threat, after all, of separation anxiety at this level is loss of the object, which is, in turn, essential for preserving the infant's sense of narcissistic integrity and omnipotence. If the infant is allowed to make the separation from the maternal orbit without excessive stirring of separation anxiety, introjection will take place, but without the pressures of narcissistic need and defensive exigency.

As development advances, progressive modification of infantile narcissism and increasing differentiation of the sense of self gradually modifies the introjections and correspondingly changes the quality of defensive organization. At each phase of separation-individuation, the capacity for autonomous existence increases and the intensity of the child's dependence on need-satisfying objects diminishes. As the respective differentiation and stability of object- and self-representations gradually increases, the enlarging capacity for toleration of the separateness of objects increases. The capacity to tolerate the separateness of objects is one of the primary goals of the development in object relationships. It implies that the object-representation has been sufficiently developed so that the realistic qualities of the object are recognized and acknowledged, with a minimal complement of projective distortion, so that the discrimination between one's self and the object is clearly established and maintained.

In fact, the capacity to relate to objects in realistic terms and to tolerate their separateness and autonomous independence is intimately related to the stability and cohesiveness of the self. The capacity for realistic object relationships depends upon the organization of a sense of self that has at its core the internalization of a good and loving parent, which serves as the focal point for the integration of successively positive introjective elements. Modell (1968) has expressed this relationship succinctly in the following terms:

> The cohesive sense of identity in the adult is a sign that there has been a "good enough" object relationship in the earliest period of

life. Something has been taken in from the environment that has led to the core of the earliest sense of identity, a core which permits further ego maturation. . . . it is a fact that these individuals who have the capacity to accept the separateness of objects are those who have a distinct, at least in part, beloved sense of self. If one can be a loving parent to oneself, one can more readily accept the separateness of objects. This is a momentous step in psychic development (p. 59).

At the same time, correlative to the emergence and integration of increasing self-cohesion and identity, integration and consolidation take place in the organization of object-representations leading toward object constancy (McDevitt 1975; Meissner 1974). This process involves not only perceptual object constancy, allowing for consistency and persistence of perceptual experience under varying stimulus conditions, but also more complex forms of libidinal object constancy contributing to stable and relatively consistent and mature object relationships. Thus, the differentiation and consolidation of object-representations play their parts, along with the development of self-cohesiveness, in the articulation of important capacities to know and respond to external reality.

The influence of paranoid mechanisms in the oedipal period is particularly vital in shaping the individual's capacity for social engagement. Oedipal involvement provides the initial point of engagement for the young child in more complex social involvement than previously on pregenital levels of interaction. The child's oedipal involvement forces him to begin to grapple with the complexities of relating to others in triadic social relationships. Paranoid mechanisms are called into play in the service of resolving the inherent ambivalence of such involvements (Meissner 1986b).

Development in Groups

This view of the essentially paranoid dynamics in the developmental sequence is expressed in Pinderhughes' (1986) differential bonding hypothesis. His hypothesis links sociocultural processes to the dynamics of these paranoid process mechanisms. He argues that group behavior is characterized by affiliation and attachment to group structures, ideals, values, belief systems, religions, schools of thought, principles, etc.—all related to the paranoid construction. Such affiliative or bonding behavior is either positive or negative, similar to the way in which the child may affiliatively idealize one parent and aggressively compete with the other in the oedipal alignment. Human beings are thus both social and antisocial creatures; they develop affectionate and affiliative bonds to friends and loved ones, but also aggressive, hostile, and disaffiliative bonds to enemies, the objects of hatred and aversion. Bonding behavior involves both approach-affiliative-affectionate behavior on one hand and avoidance-differentiative-aggressive behavior on the other. Acknowledged aspects of the self are associated with affiliative bonds (the introjective component), while renounced and rejected aspects are associated with differentiative bonds (the projective component). The object of affiliative bonding is idealized and aggrandized, the object of differentiative bonding devalued through the operation of the paranoid process. Affiliative bonding takes place between the members of the ingroup, differentiative-aggressive bonding toward certain outgroups. Illusive beliefs are maintained regarding the ingroup and devaluing illusions regarding the outgroup or enemies.

Differential-aggressive bonding involves projective and paranoid processes that we tend to deny. The more adversarial and aggressive our interaction, the stronger the paranoia and projection onto the enemy. The extremes of such differentiative bonding result in devaluation and dehumanization of the enemy, the process of pseudospeciation by which the adversary becomes something inhuman or less than human (Erikson 1966). Such tactics are evident in the treatment of concentration camp inmates, POWs, the treatment of enemies in war, in forms of racial and ethnic prejudice, in religious conflicts and controversies, and so on. Erikson (1978) pondered whether mankind was ". . . destined to remained divided into 'pseudo-species' forever playing out one (necessarily incomplete) version of mankind against all the others until, in the dubious glory of the nuclear age, one version will have the power and the luck to destroy all the others just moments before it perishes itself?" (p. 47).

The oedipal situation itself is an expression of such mechanisms and is to that extent brought into being by the workings of the mechanisms of introjection and projection (Meissner 1986b). The need to resolve ambivalence and the manner of its accomplishment suggest that the loved object can only be protected from destructive impulses by diversion of such impulses to alternate objects which are then assigned a negative status. The conflict inherent in all ambivalence, namely the impulse to destroy that which one also loves and wishes to preserve, can be resolved only to the extent that these conflicting impulses can be distributed between different objects. Thus the use of the familiar mechanisms of splitting and projection to resolve ambivalence leads to a situation in which the loved object is preserved by projecting destructive impulses to a relatively devalued object, leaving the preserved object relatively idealized. Where the object of the displaced destructive impulses is part of one's self, the outcome is potentially toxic and self-destructive. This is the course followed in many forms of depressive illness, in which the value of the ambivalently held object is sustained by means of the devaluation of the self (Rochlin 1965). Clinical depression is one alternative to a paranoid resolution.

However, as Pinderhughes (1970, 1971) pointed out, the destructive impulses are ultimately a part of the self and can only successfully be gotten rid of and projected insofar as they are linked associatively with those components of one's own person which lend themselves readily to devaluation and expulsion. Thus the object of destructive impulses must be linked to representations of expendable body parts or products so that it can be successfully utilized as an object for projection. Thus a variety of processes of riddance of devalued body products can come into play as the symbolic equivalents of the projective displacement of negative and destructive attitudes. The most striking and powerful such bodily process of devaluation and riddance is obviously the anal one. Pinderhughes (1971) commented:

> Mental representations associated with excreted body products are invested with a denigrating false belief system as they are ejected, projected upon, and attacked. Mental representations of persons or groups may be invested with denigrating false belief systems, often by linkages with excreted body products through relationships in the body image. Idealized persons, groups, and body parts are invested with an aggrandizing false belief system. Both patterns are employed normally and consistently in the resolution of ambivalence by a non-pathological but nevertheless paranoid mechanism which projects negative components of ambivalent feelings toward a renounced outside object, and positive components toward an object one associates with oneself. Each individual achieves thereby an outward expression of destructive aggression without endangering any acknowledged parts of the self (pp. 680–81).

Thus, in the context of oedipal relationships, the ambivalence in the relationship with each parent is reduced by distributing ambivalent feelings between them. Classically, in the positive resolution of the oedipal constellation, it is the opposite-sex parent who is consciously idealized and sought after, while the same-sex parent becomes the object of aggressive and negative impulses. However in the negative resolution of the oedipal configuration, the opposite tendency obtains —namely that the same sex parent becomes the object of positive and idealized strivings while the opposite sex parent becomes the recipient of negative projections. Thus the libidinal bond with the one parent and the aggressive bond with the other serves to protect from the threat of psychic loss of these significant objects involved in the destructive components of the underlying ambivalence. Protection from the threat of loss and separation depends on the success with which this process can be worked through and the paranoid mechanisms successfully employed in the interests of diverting destructive feelings and resolving ambivalence. They accomplish this by the use of displacements, projections, introjections, and the institution of a form of false belief system in which one object is relatively idealized and the other devalued (the paranoid construction). We will see this pattern repeated again and again in the subsequent pages of this study.

2

The Cultic Process

Dynamics

The dynamics of the paranoid process, as discussed in chapter 1, are not confined to pathological expressions that might find their way to the psychiatrist's consulting room, but can assert themselves in many divergent contexts of human interaction. My purpose here is to delineate the role of these processes in the formation and evolution of religious groups. This will involve a twofold shift—from the pathological to the nonpathological and from individual psychic mechanisms and processes to the analogous application of these concepts to group and social processes, specifically religious group processes. The elaboration of the mechanisms of the paranoid process in the context of the religious group or community is what I refer to as the cultic process. How does this cultic process come into being and express itself? How, then, do these characteristics of the paranoid process find expression in the cultic process?

The expression "cultic process" designates a general tendency in all religious groups to form factions or subgroupings that set elements of belief at variance from or even in opposition to more generally accepted belief systems. As I envision it, the cultic process finds application in a wide variety of religious movements spanning a broad historical spectrum. My focus in the present work on early Judaic and Christian sectarian religious movements—from early Palestinian movements to the emergence of a more or less unified Christian church—seeks to discern, within the manifest social, cultural, economic, and historical details of these emerging and interacting religious initiatives, an underlying psychologically embedded dynamic, that plays a role in these contending religious formations and I would conjecture further finds expression and realization in all religious group contexts. These psychodynamic forces not only have a powerful influence on the rise of new religious groups and movements, but continue to shape the pattern of religious life within the community of believers beyond the formative stage as powerful forces determining the progressive evolution and course of group development.

The cultic process shares in the diversity, complexity and uniqueness of religious phenomena, and embraces a complex array of both psychological and sociological influences. While this study will emphasize the mechanisms, motives, and processes in the inner world of the believer, these psychological elements of the cultic process are continually and inexorably influenced by social, cultural, economic, and political aspects of the surrounding environment. One of the purposes of the ensuing study is to gain some understanding of the complex interplay of such extrinsic factors and the manner in which they impinge on and shape the course of the cultic process.

The mechanisms and forces of the "cultic process" remain consistent from context to context, but are molded by specific contingencies in each setting. Ultimately, we will have to dig below the surface to reveal the presence and activity of those psychological forces in individual believers contributing to group formation, underlying group adhesion, and accounting for the intensity and vitality of convictions in religious creeds or belief systems. These same psychic processes are at work in the patterns of sectarian divisiveness that lead frequently to schism and heterodoxy, and lay the ground for the development of new religious movements. My argument is that these processes can be identified in the broad history of religious systems, even major religious systems.

The Role of the Paranoid Process

The cultic process operates as an integral part of the group process, but has its roots and draws its dynamic power from underlying psychological and motivational processes of the paranoid process (Meissner 1978b). Our task is to connect the available evidences—essentially historical, social, and cultural—with the largely unconscious and implicit motivational forces driving these processes and providing them with their inherent psychic impact and significance. In terms of the "paranoid" iceberg, described in the previous chapter, identical mechanisms of the paranoid process can be identified in broad segments of the population in forms that are not in themselves pathological but share a close affinity with pathological states. Clinically paranoid traits represent the tip of the iceberg and nonpathological expressions of the paranoid process the hidden mass. Large segments of the population are afflicted with such basically paranoid-like attitudes without ever coming to clinical attention. In fact, our social fabric is such that we entertain a high degree of tolerance of such attitudes without feeling it necessary to regard them or react to them as forms of pathology (Meissner 1978b).

The paranoid iceberg is definable, not merely in terms of identifiable pathology remaining within socially acceptable and nonclinical limits, but also in terms of certain areas of socially acceptable, constructive and adaptive processes, serving to sustain the functioning of the individual human personality on one level, and contributing significantly to the development and functioning of social processes and institutions on another level. The dynamics of the formation and organization of religious movements is one of the primary areas of social and cultural application of the paranoid process. My basic argument, then, is that the social organism finds ways to exploit and channel the potentialities of the paranoid process in the forming of social groupings and institutionalized structures. Such social structures both sustain the fabric of society and provide a matrix, within which individuals find support for maintaining a sense of identity. At this level the mechanisms of ingroup formation, based on introjection (by which members assimilate their sense of self and identity with group ideologies, beliefs and values), and separation from the outgroup through projection, are fully operative. But the concept can be applied to broader fields of social relationships and provide basic insights into the nature of social processes, the formation of social groups, and problems of social conflict.

Such socially attuned attitudes may not be pathological at all. The question is whether social processes can organize themselves so as to absorb significant degrees of paranoid potential and thus turn them to more constructive implementation of important social functions. In emphasizing the paranoid propensities within social and specifically religious structures, the paranoid dimensions are often recognizable as matters of style rather than substance. In discussing the paranoid style in political settings, Hofstadter (1967) offered the following description:

> In the paranoid style . . . the feeling of persecution is central, and it is indeed systematized in grandiose theories of conspiracy. But

there is a vital difference between the paranoid spokesman in politics and the clinical paranoiac: although they both tend to be overheated, oversuspicious, overaggressive, grandiose, and apocalyptic in expression, the clinical paranoid sees the hostile and conspiratorial world in which he feels himself to be living as directed specifically *against him;* whereas the spokesman of the paranoid style finds it directed against a nation, a culture, a way of life whose fate affects not himself alone but millions of others. Insofar as he does not usually see himself singled out as the individual victim of a personal conspiracy, he is somewhat more rational and much more disinterested. His sense that his political passions are unselfish and patriotic, in fact, goes far to intensify his feeling of righteousness and his moral indignation (p. 4).

The description applies analogously to cultic movements and cult leaders, especially millennarian or salvationist cults, that tend to demonize outgroups and divide the world into the good and the bad, the saved and the damned. The common fears and anxieties of such religious groups are discharged by projection onto stereotypical objects threatening the security of the group. Evil may be personified in the form of Satan, Antichrist, the evil archons or demiurge. And the relation of persecuted and persecutor becomes reciprocal; as Trevor-Roper (1969) wrote of the witch-craze in medieval Europe, "Just as psychopathic individuals, in those years, centered their separate fantasies . . . on the Devil, and thus gave an apparent objective identity to their subjective experiences, so societies in fear articulated their collective neuroses about the same obsessive figure, and found a scapegoat for their fears in his agents, the witches" (pp. 165–66).

Nature of the Cultic Process

The cultic process can be meaningfully identified in all religious settings and in each we can expect to find a degree of tension between the divisive aspects of the cultic process and the positive aspects leading toward persistence, continuity, increasing stability and reinforcement within the religious system. The paranoid process is intended to focus and articulate the mechanisms and motivations contributing to and driving those tendencies of religious movements toward divisiveness and the development of deviant belief systems on one hand, and the forces lending internal coherence, stability, and credal adherence of ingroup believers on the other.

The more or less traditional perspective on the nature and structure of cults and other sectarian movements provided a somewhat uncertain, but useful, categorization that served the uses of description and discussion, but only up to a point. These prevailing views have come under severe and telling criticism, which I will address further on. One must begin somewhere, and insofar as my interest is discussion of the processes involved without prejudice, I will use the traditional terminology for no more than descriptive purposes.

In terms of these traditional categorizations, then, the basic characteristics of sectarian and cult movements were held to be exclusivism, responsiveness to and determination by individual needs, resistance to hierarchical structure, separation and isolation from the dominant social environment, a high degree of tension between such deviant movements and the prevailing social institutions, divisiveness and anarchy. These characteristics would certainly manifest the operation of the paranoid process, based in individual dynamic patterns and reflected derivatively in group processes. The cultic process would also find expression in the development of ingroup processes delineating the boundaries of the group from the surrounding milieu and fostering those attitudes which make the ingroup the repository of truth, virtue and salvation, while outgroups are rejected as misguided, false, and untrustworthy.

Accordingly, sect formation was regarded as representing a pattern of revolt on any of a number of grounds. For lower-cast sects, the revolt would represent a rebellion of the underprivileged, the powerless, the disenfranchised—with reference to meaningful religious participation and influence. Individual needs would thus not have been met by the existing religious structure and revolution followed. The revolution would express itself in withdrawal, isolation and the integration of a set of values and beliefs in opposition to the prevailing values of the existing society or the system of beliefs of the existing religious traditions. In the formation of cults, according to this appraisal, these tendencies would be often carried to an extreme—with minimal structure, searching for and valuing of mystical experiences (at times drug induced), attachment to a charismatic leader, and a sharp oppositional break with religious traditions.

Cast in these terms, such developments reflect underlying psychological processes and motivations. Within the perspective offered by these formulations, I propose the hypothesis that sectarian developments, and thereby the cultic process, are motivated by basic needs to bolster the individual's faltering sense of identity or self-esteem and thus answer to internal issues of vulnerability and powerlessness. In terms of the paranoid process, these aspects of the individual's self-structure would, then, be organized around internalized intrapsychic configurations of the sense of self in respect to which the person feels and experiences himself as weak, powerless, victimized, disadvantaged, inadequate, inferior.[1] The paranoid process dissociates and externalizes these aspects of the individual's self-system by way of projection, thus relieving the individual of feeling afflicted by such shortcomings, and providing the means by which these limitations and deficiencies can be ascribed to the outside world. The projective system is then bolstered and consolidated by a paranoid construction, a cognitive elaboration, more or less systematic, that rationalizes, defends, and justifies the projections. The paranoid construction may take the form of a deviant belief system, supporting and lending meaningful coherence to the projective elements.

By adherence to the belief system, whether as a group ideology or in the personified form of adherence and commitment to a charismatic leader, the individual resolves certain core narcissistic issues, secures a means for bolstering and sustaining self-esteem, and gains a vehicle offering meaningful participation and purposefulness to his sense of self and identity. The idealizing tendencies of the ingroup formation, dispelling by projection undesirable or shameful attributes, create a context of self-enhancement and justification. Since truth and virtue reside within the group and are achieved through adherence to the group values and the leader, discomforting and disabling negative attitudes (particularly toward oneself) can be disregarded and submerged. The motivating force behind these processes is the need to establish a coherent and acceptable sense of self that will salvage self-esteem and achieve a sense of meaningfulness and purpose through adherence to and participation in the religious group. In this more or less stereotypical view, salvation is sought at the sacrifice of independence and autonomy.

The basic needs reflected in these dynamics can be satisfied effectively either through adherence to established and traditional religions or can be diverted through channels made available by the cultic process. The cultic process comes into play when the basic need to sustain a sufficient degree of narcissistic balance and integrity remain unanswered and unattended. When traditional religious structures no longer fulfill that need, other resources are sought and come into being. The cultic process can thus be envisioned as deriving from basic human motivations and psychological processes. From the point of view of understanding the relationship of social structures and human dynamics, social processes arise out of individual dynamics in some fundamental sense, and provide the meaningful context not only for the satisfaction of individual needs but for individual dynamics undergirding both social integration and deviance.

---

[1] In clinical terms, these characteristics are readily recognized as aspects of pathogenic introjects (Meissner 1978b, 1981, 1986c). See chapter 1.

Role of the Cultic Process

In all of these instances and many more, society organizes itself into a variety of groupings and structures organized around discriminable differences bringing the paranoid process into play. The paranoid process not only defines and consolidates such groupings, but provides the basic psychic conditions in terms of which the group processes work themselves out and through which the interaction between groups on various levels is determined and qualified. Thus the functioning of the paranoid process in its various manifestations becomes an essential dimension in the organization and maintenance of such social groupings.

Group participation often offers the basis for a degree of inner healing and restitution. Embracing the group ideology and commitment to the belief system carries with it the potential for a meaningful degree of self-integration and consolidation of a sense of identity. In many cases, the fragile narcissism of the member is the locus of this restitution. This narcissistic restitution is accomplished through the integration of ego and ego ideal. As Chasseguet-Smirgel (1985) observes:

> Groups often offer a much shorter route to the long-standing wish for the union of ego and ideal. Such groups are based upon an ideology which may be defined, psychoanalytically, as a system that appears to have a more or less rational basis, corresponding to the outward appearance of dreams and to secondary elaboration. An ideology always contains within it a phantasy of narcissistic assumption linked to a return to a state of primary fusion, which equally excludes conflict and castration and thus operates within the order of illusion (p. 193).

If such social organization serves the interests of sustaining and integrating individual identities, we must also not lose sight of the fact that such groupings and the working through of social processes have an important role to play in the maintaining of social order and in the working out of social adaptations. Social processes are by no means fixed or static in nature. They are rather processes of dynamic tension and change, in which progressive social adaptations and structural modifications are continually being elaborated and worked through by means of the oppositional tension created between relevant social groupings. In contexts of dynamic and changing social structure, a reasonable and manageable degree of confrontation and social struggle is not only unavoidable, but is indeed a necessary and optimal condition for the adaptive integration of social processes.

The paranoid process provides the dynamic underpinning and motivating force maintaining social processes in a state of continual tension and dynamic opposition. The dynamic operation of such processes and their contribution to the working through of social problems can be seen perhaps most vividly in our own time in the civil rights confrontations of past and present decades. Paranoid mechanisms not only promoted and sustained a sense of black identity and purposeful striving, thus making a significant contribution to the enhancement of black self-esteem, but also brought into conflict the tension of rights and values that remains a much broader and significant social issue for the society to face, work through and resolve. Thus these mechanisms make a significant contribution to continuing social adaptation.

The danger of such paranoid dynamics is that the same mechanisms serving adaptive purposes can also be turned to the uses of destructive interference with social structures, or to the extent that they take a destructive turn can end in individual, if not social, disaster. Thus the working of such processes in the political and social orders can lead, for example, to revolution, which may serve the purposes of destruction rather than adaptation. However, even when the revolutionary process is destructive, it may have an adaptive outcome. One could argue, it seems to me, that in some degree, in the French or Russian revolutions for example, important adaptive functions were served by the revolutionary outcome. In any case, in all such instances, we have ample evidence of the operation of the paranoid process. In the case of revolutionary upheavals, it is striking that such outcomes may be the product not only of paranoid mechanisms on the side of those perpetrating the revolution, but it is met by and responded to by equally distorting and destructive manifestations of the paranoid process on the part of the establishment. Potential destructiveness emerges in the clash of these paranoid propensities. These dynamics are unmistakable in revolutionary millennarian movements, but are by no means restricted to these more flagrant and dramatically explosive expressions of the cultic process (Barkun 1974; Cohn 1970a; Worsley 1968). In one degree or other, and in one manner or other, these observations are pertinent for the origins and evolution of all religious movements.

Cult Characteristics

The cultic process, as I envision it, has a role at all levels of religious organization and finds its unique expression in various contexts of ideology and value orientation. In all forms of religious grouping, the divisive dynamics of the cultic process are in constant tension and interaction with contrary consolidative tendencies drawing toward integration, social organization, and cohesion and vying with forces tending toward division and sectarian opposition. These integrative forces exercise their influence in those circumstances in which cultic or sectarian groupings tend to shift progressively toward more consolidated, more socially acceptable, and better socially integrated forms of religious organization, i.e., that of the established sect, denomination or church (Yinger 1957). The cultic process also comes into play in the origin of sects or cults or other forms of schismatic or deviant religious organization. We can conclude, at least tentatively, that the divisive aspects of the cultic process and the countervailing integrative pressures toward greater social and organizational integration persist in a state of tension and continual interaction in all forms of religious organization. The normal expectation is that resolution of such tensions is necessary for any new religious movement to endure. As Robbins and Anthony (1990) expressed this view, "Many denominations have experienced tension between those who criticize society and those who accommodate to it, but in the long run, the latter are more likely to prevail if the group itself is to endure. The sociological distinction between church and sect revolves around a dynamic in which minority religious sects move from an adversarial to an accepting stance toward their cultural environment, thus joining the ranks of the churches and spawning new sectarian splinter movements of their own" (p. 442). But, of course, one does not have to look far to find examples of minority sects that remain adversarial and show no signs of caving in—Adventists and Jehovah's Witnesses for starters.

The cultic process can assume many forms and appear in many guises. Cultic groups differ in lifestyle, ideology, and modes of existence. For some apocalyptic renewal and salvation predominate: they live in communities, follow a leader who is attributed godlike qualities, utilize thought reform techniques, demand unquestioning loyalty and obedience, and tend to exploit the energies and resources of the members. While these characteristics of the cult leader are frequently identifiable, they are not always evident as a dominating facet of cult organization and can easily lend themselves to caricature and prejudicial distortion.[2] Other cult formations emphasize personal psychological

[2] This may be one problem with Singer's (1995) depiction of cult dynamics as centered on the role of the leader. She writes: "I will use *cult* and *cultic group* to refer to any one of a large number of groups that have sprung up in our society and that are similar in the way they originate, their power structure, and their governance. Cults range from the relatively benign to those that exercise extraordinary control over members' lives and use thought-reform processes to influence and control members. . . . It denotes a group that forms around a person who claims he or she has a special mission or knowledge, which will be shared with those who turn over most of their decision making to that self-appointed leader. . . . In my study of cults, I find that the personality, preferences, and desires of the leader are central in

growth, without demanding communal living or engaging in thought control; leaders may be idealized, but not to the point of deification (Cushman 1986). The variations on these themes throughout religious history are countless, but, fairly consistently, the elements in the process, by which such religious movements are generated, assume a characteristic shape, run their historical course, and finally undergo transformation or dispersal, only to be replaced by other religious constellations that in turn express the same compositional elements with new emphases and nuances, remain similar. Behind or beneath these historical and more or less sociological dynamics involved in the coming-to-be, evolution and dispersal of religious groupings lies the cultic process in its manifold articulations contributing to the evolving pattern of religious group experience. The cultic process can claim at least a partial role in the splits, divisions, and partitions adorning the chronicle of religious history.

Sects and Cults

The most significant and dramatic expressions of the cultic process take place in religious cults and sects. It will help to clarify our understanding of the nature of these religious groups. The traditional understanding of sect goes back to the distinction between church and sect in the work of Max Weber and Ernst Troeltsch. Church organization was viewed as hierocratic, bureaucratic and hierarchical. The essential note is that a church is a natural social grouping, similar to the family or the nation, and was thus distinguished from a sect, which was regarded as a form of voluntary association of religious believers, similar in nature to more secular versions, such as fraternal organizations or clubs. Thus, members were born into a church, but must join a sect. The church would tend to emphasize the universalism of the gospel message in contrast to the exclusivism of the sect, which tended to emphasize the individual over the group (Gerth and Mills 1946).

As Niebuhr (1929) observed, these differences in structure also tended to be associated with differences in ethical emphasis and doctrine. The institutional church attached a high degree of importance to

---

the evolution of any of these groups. Cults are truly *personality cults*. Because cult structure is basically authoritarian, the personality of the leader is all important. Cults come to reflect the ideas, style, and whims of the leader and become extensions of the leader" (pp. xix–xx). While this description can be approached in varying degrees in many cult groups, it is by no means universal and is readily drawn into stereotypical application. The description has to remain more empirical within the context of individual cults rather than apriori theoretical.

sacramental means of grace, doctrinal orthodoxy, observance of proper ritual in the administration of sacraments, and orthodoxy in doctrinal teaching by an official clergy. In contrast, the sect emphasis fell on the religious experience of the members prior to their joining the group. It espoused the priesthood of all believers, denying any disparity between an official clergy and the laity, and tended to regard the sacramental aspects of religious practice as mere symbols of fellowship or pledges of allegiance. Lay inspiration was preferred to any form of theological or liturgical expertness, as might be found in an officially designated and trained clergy.

As an inclusive social group, the church tended to be closely associated with extant national, economic and cultural interests. The nature of its organization involved a certain accommodation of its ethical norms to the ethics of the civilization in which it endured. Its morality was that of the respectable majority rather than of any heroic or radical minority. In contrast, the sect was always a minority group maintaining a relatively separatist and semi-ascetic attitude toward the world. Such isolating attitudes were reinforced by persecution. The members of the sect tended to hold to their unique interpretation of ethics with great tenacity, often preferring isolation to compromise. Focusing on issues of reconciliation with the world, Niebuhr (1929) argued that a sect was essentially a relatively unstable form of religious organization that over time would become gradually transformed into a church, a more stable and enduring form of religious organization. The failure of the new church structure to meet the needs of many of its members continued a process of cyclic evolution, sewing the seeds of discontent and leading to further schism and progressive splitting off of new sect formations. In this way, Niebuhr envisioned an endless cycle of birth, transformation, splitting and rebirth of religious movements in a constant process of division and cyclic reorganization.

In these terms, sects were distinguished on the basis of the need underlying their origin and the pattern of response to that need. Response to unfulfilled or unsatisfied needs could take the form of acceptance, aggressive opposition or avoidance. Middle class sects were more likely to accept the existing social order without significant challenge, ascribing difficulties to religious failures rather than to the social order as such. In contrast, lower class sects tended to react more strongly to problems of poverty and powerlessness, interpreting the Christian message in more radical and ethically provocative terms. In their view, society was inherently evil and only true religion had the power to revitalize the social order. Such radical opposition tended almost predictably to failure so that such groups tended either to disintegrate or transform into some other more persistent type.

Sects might also originate in a pattern of avoidance, expressing it-self in devaluation of the importance of this life and attempts to salvage one's hopes in the supernatural world or the after-life. In the mean-while, the problem in facing the world could be mitigated by forming a fellowship of like-minded sufferers. This form of sectarian protest con-fronted the hard facts of life, particularly as they afflicted lower classes in the form of poverty, injustice and impotence. Adventist, Pentecostal and even other forms of utopian or millennarian sects would qualify as forms of avoidance groups, since their beliefs and practices seemed to manage the struggle with life's problems and difficulties by trans-formation of the meaning of life and substitution of some form of reli-gious status for the lack of social status.[3]

The *cult* was attributed somewhat different connotations, including small size, a yearning for mystical experience, minimal organizational structure and the presence of a charismatic leader. These groups repre-sented an even sharper break from the dominant religious tradition than sects. Cults tended to be short-lived, usually local in extent, and frequently centered on the teaching and charismatic influence of a dominant leader—a tendency that sets the cult apart from the sect, in which reliance is placed on a broader distribution of lay participation. Because of their small size and dependence on the leader, it was un-likely that a cult would develop into any form of more established sect or denomination. The emphasis was almost exclusively on individual needs with little regard or interest in questions of social order and so-cial integration. Cults were regarded as religious mutants or extreme variations in the spectrum of processes by which men try to solve the problems of existence by religious means.

This early classification had the advantage of bringing order to a confusing body of data and facilitated discussion and theorizing. But as time passed and the understanding of the complexity and range of variation in religious movements grew, the categories became increas-ingly problematic and the typology increasingly limited and constrict-ing. Not only have the categories become obsolete, but the whole field has been contaminated by prejudicial attitudes that tend to devalue marginal religious groups and their members and often provoke hostil-ity and attempts at various forms of social control that can have delete-rious social consequences and at times catastrophic results. Wright (1995) has recently commented on "the powerful yet indirect effects of the meaning and construction of the term 'cult' as a disparaging label which imposes a crippling stigma on any religious group unfortunate

---

[3] We will recognize this form of utopian belief as a strong component of pre-Christian Palestinian sects and early Christian conviction. See Section II below.

enough to be so maligned. Traditionally linked to racial, ethnic, or sexual minorities, the usage of a stereotype can incite deep-seated prejudices and function as a scapegoating mechanism for societal fears and anxieties" (p. xx). Or again, Hall (1995), "The term 'cult' has a variety of meanings. But whatever the possible dictionary definitions, in the late twentieth-century United States, the term has become almost universally recognized as a stigmatic label for countercultural religious groups" (p. 206). These comments point directly to the effects of the paranoid process as I am presenting it here; needless to say it calls for caution that in the discussion of "cult" dynamics we do not allow ourselves to be drawn into such embroilments. This trend to disparage and stereotype marginal religious groups has persisted despite the efforts of students of the cult phenomenon to support not only the inherent values of sectarian religious movements in terms of cultural innovation and social change (Weber 1922, 1968) but also as providing effective channels for resistant and even rebellious pressures reacting to restrictive or oppressive dynamics in the society at large (Tracy 1987).

In addition, many of the suppositions on which earlier classifications were erected have proven untrustworthy or difficult to maintain in the face of the variety and divergence of characteristics of religious groups. Niebuhr's (1929) view of cults and sects as inherently unstable has proven unreliable and too often contrary to the demonstrated history of certain sects. The development of sectarian movements from the initial stages of charismatic inspiration to more enduring and relatively institutionalized structure, particularly after the death of the charismatic leader and his coterie of charter disciples, seems to follow a variety of patterns contingent on circumstance and the dynamics evolving within the group.[4] The effort to define the vitality of such marginal religious groups in terms of attachment to a charismatic leader has had to yield to more complex perspectives involving broader and diversified perspectives on the function of the leader and his interaction with other group members. Even the understanding of "charisma" itself has undergone revision.

Yinger's definition of "cult" was challenged almost as soon as it appeared, particularly on the grounds that cult groups could not only be quite sizable in terms of membership but more than a few demonstrated

---

[4] The evidence pertaining to the extended evolution of a variety of religious groups has been gathered in Miller (1991). Contributors to this volume recount the course of development of a number of such sects, including the Shakers, the Amana community, American Indian cult movements, the Church of the Latter Day Saints (Mormons), the Hutterites, the Christian Science Church, the Unification Church, and others.

a capacity to persist over significant time spans. Also the distinguishing note of their radical break with the dominant culture has come under fire. This has led Melton (1991), for example, to point out that these approaches to establishing a typology of religious groups have served only to confuse matters, and have led to ignoring "the important theological-ideological dimension that most precisely defines the nature of 'cult.' That is to say, a cult is a religious body with a distinctive religious pattern. It does more than simply vary somewhat more from dominant religious patterns than do sects. It offers a completely different religious gestalt" (p. 3).

Social Environment

Another classification of religious groups is based on a single attribute, namely, the relationship of the religious group to its social environment (Johnson 1963). In these terms, a church differs from a sect by accepting and adapting to the social environment, which the sect essentially rejects, reflecting the degree to which a given group may be in tension with its surrounding social environment. Not only established churches, but also a variety of other religious institutions occupy a more stable sector of the social environment, providing a cluster of roles, norms, values, activities and beliefs that contribute to and maintain the stability of social structure. According to Johnson's axis of tension, established religious institutions tend to occupy the low tension end of the axis, while new or deviant religious movements occupy the area of high tension. The degree of tension often associated with sect or cult formation is equivalent to a form of subcultural deviance marked by difference, antagonism, and separation (Stark and Bainbridge 1979).

We can broaden the implications of the term "sect" to refer to any religious protest against situations in which individual religious needs have become obscured or overridden by an emphasis on social and ecclesial order. This draws the analysis of church and sect more strongly into the psychological sector and away from more strictly sociological implications. The religious sect comes to mean a religious movement in which the primary emphasis falls on the satisfaction by religious means of a variety of basic human and individual needs. It emerges as a form of revolt against a previously existing religious system in which these needs have been inadequately responded to (Yinger 1957).

Consequently, sect organization carries the seeds of divisiveness and ultimately anarchy, just as the organization of church structures might tend toward authoritarianism and rigidity. Yinger (1957) observed:

> In the logical extreme, the sect emphasis on religious beliefs and practices that are efforts to deal with individual needs—with a minimum attention to the function of social integration—leads to anarchy. The sectarian associates order with the disliked order of the church and society in which he feels his needs are smothered. This may lead to the avoidance of any political claims over him, the rejection of some of the moral standards of society (note the various experiments of extreme sectarians, with new patterns of sexual morals or forms of marriage), and the repudiation of other aspects of the supposed wicked society—learning and art, for example. Seldom is this potentiality for anarchy carried to the extreme, but the tendencies are there, just as the tendencies for authoritarian rigidity are present in the church (p. 147).

Stark and Bainbridge (1979) have noted that Niebuhr's analysis of the formation of sects applies almost exclusively to schismatic religious movements originating as an internal faction within another previously existing religious body. But this obviously is not the only form of religious movement existing in high state of tension with the surrounding sociocultural environment. Such religious movements may have no prior history of organizational affiliation to another religious group and may, in fact, lack any close cultural continuity or similarity to such groups. These nonschismatic deviant religious groups may represent either a form of cultural innovation, to the extent that they add some distinctive feature to the more familiar characteristics of religious groups in the culture, or may represent a form of cultural importation as an extension of a religious body already established in some other cultural setting.

Consequently, both cults and sects may be regarded as deviant religious bodies existing in a high state of tension with the surrounding sociocultural environment. But while sects are specifically schismatic movements breaking off from previously existing religious organizations, cults may or may not have such prior ties with previously existing religious bodies. The cult may be imported from an alien religious context, or it may have originated in the host society by way of innovation rather than by schism. In any case, the cult comes to represent something new in relationship to the existing religious movements in a given society. If it arises by innovation, it brings to that culture a new revelation or insight. Usually, imported cults have little in common culturally with the already existing faiths. Consequently, while they may be ancient in their society of origin, they present themselves to the new social context as something new and different.

Ideology

Cults differ with respect to their ideological orientation to the environment. In his analysis of Protestant sect development, Wilson (1959) described four types of sects, characterized in ideological terms regarding the inherent values and patterns of social relationships.[5] *Conversionist* sects seek to alter the world through the conversion of mankind. *Adventist* sects tend to predict a drastic alteration of the world, but rather than promoting this final dispensation seek to prepare themselves for the inevitable change. *Introversionist* sects tend to reject the world's values and replace them with higher ethical values of their own. And finally, *Gnostic* sects tend largely to reject the goals of the world, but seek to find new and esoteric means to transformation of the world and salvation.

The implications and correlates of each of these ideological approaches can be spelled out in the following terms. The conversionist sect centers its teaching and activity on evangelism, typically in a fundamentalist or pentecostal fashion. In the contemporary setting, the Bible is taken as the sole guide to the good life, and is accepted in more or less literal terms. The test of fellowship to the communion is a conversion experience and the acceptance of Jesus Christ as one's personal savior. Individual guilt for personal sin and the need for redemption through Christ hold a central place in the doctrine of such sects. No one is excluded from potential salvation, and the techniques for obtaining conversion and commitment are generally revivalist. Conversionist sects are generally distrustful or indifferent toward other denominations and churches, which they see as having diluted or betrayed the Christian message. They are hostile to clericalism, to any forms of special clerical learning, and particularly toward any modernist tendencies. Modern science, especially geology or evolutionary theories, are anathema.

Adventist sects may also be regarded as revolutionary, emphasizing a future transformation of the present world order and institution of a new, pure and more sanctified dispensation. Emphasis is placed on the role of the Bible, particularly on those passages in which the time and circumstance of the second coming of Christ is predicted. Christ is not only savior but divine leader who exacts a high moral standard from his followers. A share in the new dispensation and in Christ's new

---

[5] While Wilson's analysis was based on more or less contemporary sects, the descriptive details can be regarded as relevant to sect typology in any historical context. In practice, actual religious movements may combine aspects of all of these different types.

kingdom will be limited only to those who have maintained doctrinal and moral purity. Established churches represent the anti-Christ, and clerical learning is devalued. Such sects are hostile to the wider society, emphasizing separation from the world and anticipating the overthrow of the present order.

Introversionist sects tend to be pietistic and to direct their followers away from the world, focusing more intently on the life within the community and particularly to possession of the spirit. Reliance is placed on the inner illumination, regarded either as the voice of conscience or of the Holy Spirit. The Bible serves as a source of inner inspiration and ethical insight. The letter has submitted to the domination of the spirit, so that doctrine is de-emphasized, and the deepening of the experience of the spirit assumes a central position. The members of the sect regard themselves as an enlightened elect with a strong sense of in-group morality. Evangelism has little or no place, and the tendency of the sect is to withdraw from the world or to allow its members only that degree of activity in the world that is consistent with human betterment. There are no spiritual guides or official clergy.

Gnostic sects tend to hold to a special body of esoteric teaching, usually involving a revised interpretation of some essential Christian teaching. The position of the Bible is more or less secondary or subsidiary to the sect's own religious gnosis. Christ is viewed more as a guide or exemplar of the truth rather than a savior. Doctrinal teachings are often replaced by more exclusive and esoteric forms of mysticism, which can only gradually be understood. Secular scientific teachings are replaced by forms of cosmology, anthropology or psychology reflecting elements of the religious system. While conversion does not play a significant role in such sects, instruction and guidance will be offered to the outsider, hopefully leading him along various stages in deepening understanding and enlightenment. Often, there is a charismatic leader or succession of such leaders who express the enlightened teaching of the sect. Other religious groups will be regarded with indifference or as ignorant or backward. Secular knowledge or scientific learning is generally acknowledged as valid and useful, except where it comes into opposition with sect doctrine. The Gnostic sectarian tends less to withdraw from the world than to try to exploit his special gnosis for either changing the world or improving his own position in it.[6]

---

[6] These characteristics of Gnostic sects can be discerned in the historical Gnostic movement in the early centuries of this era. See the more developed treatment in section IV on Gnosticism.

Patterns of Change

In his elaboration of the church-sect typology, Niebuhr (1929) had emphasized the minority status of the sect in contrast to the more established and socially integrated position of the church. Sects and cults necessarily hold themselves in isolation from and hostility toward the social environment. They prefer isolation to compromise, often refuse to engage in political or social efforts, or to participate in government, and in general seek to cut ties as much as possible with the common life of the society and culture. Thus, the sect has usually been the offspring of an outcast minority, taking root in the religious revolts of the poor and of those who found no meaningful place in church or state.

But social forces come to play upon this rebellious outcast with seemingly inexorable effect. Sectarianism is almost always altered in the course of time by the processes of birth and death and the shifting configuration of social pressures that tend to draw the outcast sect closer to the mainstream. Niebuhr (1929) wrote:

> By its very nature the sectarian type of organization is valid only for one generation. The children born to the voluntary members of the first generation begin to make the sect a church long before they have arrived at the years of discretion. For with their coming the sect must take on the character of an educational and disciplinary institution, with the purpose of bringing the new generation into conformity with ideals and customs which have become traditional (pp. 19–20).

The new generation rarely holds the degree of conviction or fervor that characterized the original founders of the sect. Convictions tempered in the white heat of conflict, persecution and martyrdom, give way to gentler sentiments and the need for accommodation. Isolation from the surrounding social order becomes increasingly difficult. Even the frequently observed discipline of hard work and spartan living contributes to the economic well-being of the sect, and with the increase of wealth opportunities for cultural enrichment and greater involvement in the economic life of the surrounding society become possible and less easily avoided. Compromise and accommodation begin to take hold. The spartan and idiosyncratic ethics of the sect begin to shift gradually and to assume a more churchly form. Even the place of lay leadership in the sect begins to give way to a more theologically educated and ritually sophisticated clergy. Children are born and infant baptism once again takes its place as the means of incorporation and salvation. In short, the sect is transformed into a church.

Along the same line, sectarian tendencies, riding on the current of the paranoid process, carry the potential for anarchy and for the negation and avoidance of social claims or pressures. But in fact the sect cannot exist outside of the social order and consequently cannot avoid the problem. Even in the most isolated cultic communities, the problem of establishing and maintaining some form of order to insure the continued existence and functioning of the group begins to assert itself. The original needs for forming the sect or cult may evolve over time, particularly if the socio-economic context in which the sect members live improves. Leadership has a tendency to want to continue itself and to find ways to assure the continuity of power. Particularly in mobile societies where problems of maintaining social order and the pressure of individual human needs constantly impinges on social structures to generate continuous change, the dialectic between church and sect has fertile ground in which to flourish.

The Internal Structure of Sects and Cults

The internal structure of both sects and cults can vary along a number of significant dimensions. The distribution of these factors can influence the degree to which centralizing or divisive tendencies of the cultic process determine the development and evolution of the religious movement. Important points of conflict include a variety of needs: pressure from the surrounding society for conformity, for example, in education, payment of taxes, or military service, external threats to sect values, whether those who assume centralized responsibility become professional public functionaries with specifiable functions that become institutionally differentiated and lead to specialization of roles, whether religious leaders receive special training or not. Schism tends to focus on questions of doctrinal or ritual purity and successful separation usually finds a charismatic leader in the inner elite of the movement.

(1) *The Degree of Separateness from the World*

The sect is usually committed in some degree to keeping itself isolated from the world and to maintaining its distinctness, both to members and nonmembers. This is achieved by two mechanisms: isolation and insulation (Wilson 1959). The isolation may be geographic or local, but usually requires some form of community organization. Generally, sects aspiring to this form of social isolation and avoidance of alien influences tend to be introversionist in type. Insulation involves setting up behavioral rules to protect sect values by reducing external influences when contact must occur or is permitted, or distinctive dress, as in the Mennonites, Hutterites, and some early Quakers. Group endogamy is also an effective means of isolation as in many adventist and introversionist sects.

(2) *Coherence of Sect Values*

Sects also vary in the degree of coherence of sect values. Clearly, the maintenance of separation from the world is one device for maintaining a particular constellation of values. One could anticipate a degree of tension from the conflict between the ideals and values of the sect or cult and the ideals inherent in the wider society. The desire for separateness and the associated values creates certain distinct tensions for the sect and its members. Wilson (1959) described a point of optimal tension at which any greater degree of hostility toward the world would imply direct conflict, and any less accommodation to worldly values. He lists the typical issues in which conflicts of this sort arise: convictions as to what constitutes true knowledge, often leading to conflicts concerning the manner of education; refusal to recognize legitimate social and legal prescriptions and to accept conventional pseudo-sacral practices such as oath-swearing; withdrawal from political participation, e.g., refusing to vote, refusing to salute the flag, or recite the oath of allegiance, etc.; conscientious objection to military service; refusal to recognize marital and family regulations imposed by civil authority; objection to and resistance against state required medical procedures; disregard of economic institutions as in the refusal to register land ownership or to join labor unions. Even in a flexible and pluralistic order, there are limits to which the sect can go in its efforts to depart from accepted moral norms. Beyond a certain limit, a sect inevitably comes into conflict with society.

(3) *Group Commitments*

In some degree a significant commitment to the sect, either general and ideological, or involving acceptance and submission to a charismatic leader, is required for group membership (Ahlstrom 1972). In Gnostic sects, commitment may be simply to the leader or to the ideological position of the movement. The member gains no advantage from the special gnosis of the sect unless he accepts the implicit world view (Wilson 1959). There may be moral correlates, for example, injunctions to abstain from certain foods, drugs, tobacco, alcohol, or sex. Introversionist sects may or may not have recognized leaders or a distinctive charisma, but require a specific moral commitment. Certain forms of behavior are prescribed, along with a strong commitment to the fellowship itself. Adventist groups require a strong commitment to specific doctrines and moral practices. But conversionist sects tend to be less sharply exclusive in their demands, even extending the conditions of fellowship somewhat elastically to any born-again believer.

The quality of social organization plays an important role. Introversionist and adventist sects tend to be *Gemeinschaften* in which fellowship itself becomes an important value. Group relationships tend to be primary and face-to-face, and the individual's role as a sect member takes predominance. Membership tends to be patterned along family lines, and the sect values are often mediated by the kingroup. Conversionist sects share these general characteristics only partially in that the concept of brotherhood for them extends beyond sect boundaries, and its standards tend to be more inclusive and less rigorous. Acceptance into the sect is easier, socialization less intense, and the loss of membership more frequent. In contrast, Gnostic sects tend to be structured more along *Gesellschaft* lines. Personal relationships are more or less secondary, and commitment to the sect ideology and the leadership takes precedence. Impersonality of relationships may even be preferred, since it is the occult gnosis, the ideology, that is important. Sect affiliation may often be easily concealed so that the member can withhold his membership from the judgment and potential disapproval of the outside world.

The Cultic Process vs. Cultic Processes

The delineation of these multiple aspects of religious typologies makes it abundantly clear that any discussion or investigation into the cultic process must take into account multiple dimensions of the phenomenon and must be prepared to find its subject matter displayed in a variety of heterogeneous and divergent contexts. We will not be able to fix on a simple or unequivocal understanding of the cultic process that would allow us to deductively comprehend the full scope its concrete and vital expression. Our approach will have to be predominantly inductive, guided in part by the initial assessment of the lines of force in our potential field of observation provided in the present overview.

At this point, however, we can assume that the cultic process can meaningfully be identified in all religious settings and that in each of these settings there will exist a degree of tension and interaction between the divisive and exclusionary aspects of the cultic process and the more constructive and integrative forces tending toward the persistence, continuity, and increasing stability and reinforcement of social integration within the religious system. The manner, form, and style of this interaction, and particularly the motivational patterns, based in individual psychological needs and intrapsychic dynamics, form the substance of our quest.

Pre-Christian Context

3

Pre-Christian Origins—
Historical and Sociological Background

My purpose in this chapter is to trace the influence of the cultic process in the origins of Christianity. The Jesus movement struck roots in the rich soil of first-century Palestinian sectarian religious struggles. Not only do many of the scriptural and doctrinal elements of early Christianity reflect these Palestinian origins, but I will argue that the impulse that gave rise to the heterodox religious movement around the figure of Jesus owed its dynamic power and motivation to the mechanisms of the cultic process undergirding these sectarian divisions and contentions. The dramatic interplay of these forces was cast against the vast tapestry of socioeconomic and political events in Palestine and the Middle East of the first centuries B.C. and A.D.

Palestinian Background

In the wake of the Alexandrian conquest of Palestine (332 B.C.), the Egyptian Ptolemies and later their Seleucid successors brought with them a burden of oppression and exploitation the likes of which the Judean peasantry had never known before. The Ptolemies wisely interfered little with Palestinian life beyond the payment of taxes; the internal government remained largely in the hands of the high priest and his council. But the subsequent Seleucid conquest brought a gradual process of Hellenization, introducing important social and cultural changes into the fabric of Palestinian life.

The conquerors created an efficient imperial bureaucracy for collecting the hated taxes and imposed Hellenizing measures as the need for funds increased and their position became more tenuous. The Judean high priesthood, already established as a virtual dynasty, were enlisted in collecting taxes. As Horsley and Hanson (1985) observe: "The ruling priestly elite, who maintained their privileged social position, attracted by the glories of Hellenistic civilization, began to compromise themselves culturally, religiously, and politically. The result in Judean society was a widening gulf between the priestly elite and the peasantry, one that finally provoked a popular revolt and set the tone for the next 300 years of Jewish social and religious history" (p. 10). The portrayal of the Seleucids in the book of Daniel is graphic enough: the fourth beast, representing the Hellenistic empire was "terrible and dreadful and exceedingly strong, and it had great iron teeth; it devoured and broke in pieces, and stamped the residue with its feet" (7:7). This program of increasing economic exploitation, repression, and cultural imperialism threatened traditional ways of Jewish life.

The effect was to deprive the vast majority of the people of their civil rights and property. Further, religious leaders, particularly the priestly aristocracy, had lost their legitimacy in the eyes of the people. In the Maccabean revolt, the Pharisees and Essenes regarded the usurping Hasmoneans as illegitimate high priests. The outcome was a bloody civil war between the Pharisees and the Hasmoneans, resulting in withdrawal of the Essenes into their desert strongholds. Herod arbitrarily appointed devotees of Hellenistic philosophy and culture, no longer drawn from the traditional priestly families, as high priests. The Pharisees accordingly refused to accept these creatures of Herod and swear allegiance to him and the emperor. Herod resorted to violence to maintain his control (Saldarini 1988). The refusal to remove the high priest after the death of Herod led to a massive insurrection against the entire ruling structure—Romans, king and priestly aristocracy together (Horsley 1989). The people had been abandoned by traditional mediators between God and his people; the crisis was as much religious as political. As Horsley (1989) comments:

> This recognition of the long history of "radical theocratic movements" prior to the rise of the Jesus movement suggests that they were the result of a "socio-cultural cause" as well. . . . For several generations prior to Jesus, dreams of theocracy in radical form had been cultivated in the wilderness at Qumran—and therefore probably elsewhere in Jewish society—and before that in the Danielic and Enochic apocalyptic literature. The "cause" of the rise of radical theocratic movements would therefore appear to be the intolerable discrepancy between the ideal of God's rule of justice and the

oppressive rule of native high priests in collaboration with imperial regimes (pp. 57–58).

The demise of the Herodian line left the governance of Palestine exclusively in the hands of Roman governors. For the first time in the period of the second temple, Palestinian Jews were governed directly by a
foreign power, something they had not experienced since the Babylonian and Persian conquests; previous occupying powers had exercised
control through the priestly aristocracy or client kings (Herod and
sons) who acted as buffers between the populace and the foreign over-
lords. During this period of Roman and Herodian domination, the
priestly aristocracy became increasingly rapacious and greedy. Horsley
and Hanson (1985) comment:

> Indeed, the actions of the Jewish governing groups compounded
> the alienation and conflict already exacerbated by the intransi-
> gence and repressive measures taken by the Roman governors. The
> high priestly families, Herodians, and much of the wealthy aristoc-
> racy, of course, were engaged in mutually beneficial collaboration
> with the Roman imperial system in maintaining control in Jewish
> Palestine. As the social order began to crumble, the ruling elite not
> only made no attempt to represent the interests of the people, but
> contributed to the breakdown of the society in a violently preda-
> tory manner, yielding virtual "class warfare" (pp. 41–42).

The Jews resented and at times actively opposed Roman rule, and
the Romans responded with authoritarian, often high-handed, and
even cruel repression. Roman rule also brought with it the construction
of cities, roads, and aqueducts produced for the most part by forced
labor. These developments served the interests of the imperial over-
lords and their aristocratic collaborators, but were supported by heavy
taxes and tributes levied on farmers and landholders. Political structures were devoted to economic exploitation and had to be maintained
by military power (Borg 1987; Horsley 1987).

Economic Crisis

The political decay under the Herodians reflected the crisis imposed by the extended political domination of a subjugated people. Imperial exploitation eroded the traditional socio-economic infrastructure
of the society. Economic pressures imposed by taxation led to heavy indebtedness of the peasants, loss of ownership of land, loss of the basis
of economic subsistence, and a radical dislocation in traditional social
structures. The coming of the Romans and the lavish and expensive

building projects, along with the munificence of Herod's court and palaces, imposed additional economic burdens that the people and the society could not sustain (Horsley 1987).

The Jewish people were deprived of any legitimate political participation and suffered severely from conditions of lack and deprivation—poverty, hunger and despair prevailed. Many peasants, forced off their land, had no recourse but to become day laborers or join bands of robbers and bandits prowling the countryside. The priestly aristocracy and the Romans colluded in exploiting the masses and traditional priestly privileges were reinforced and supported by oppressive imperial measures (Horsley 1987), practices especially irksome to the common people whose collective memory was steeped in biblical recollections of freedom from oppression and foreign domination under the rule of YHWH.

Oppression and Banditry

The phenomenon of social banditry in peasant societies has been described as a form of prerebellion, arising when government and landowners exploit the peasants beyond their capacity to endure. Banditry might increase in periods of economic crisis or social disruption. Popular legends of the Robin Hood type frequently proclaim such bandits as champions of justice for the poor and oppressed (Hobsbawm 1981). Often enough, the populace will support and protect such brigands, since they symbolize a common sense of justice and religious commitment. In certain circumstances, such social banditry can lead to more widespread peasant revolt. In Palestine, the surge of banditry toward the middle of the first century was probably abetted by the severe famine around A.D. 46–48 (Horsley and Hanson 1985), and also probably linked to escalating apocalyptic expectations, consistent with the observation that social banditry and millennarianism often go hand in hand (Hobsbawm 1981).

Palestinian society of the time was steeped in violence. Horsley (1987), following Camara (1971), describes a "spiral of violence" in three stages: first, injustice works its basic violence against men and women and their rights; second, revolution of the oppressed seeking greater justice and humanity; and finally, the reaction of the established authorities, who use force to preserve public order. Repressive measures may take many forms, from studied inaction to outright brutality, physical violence, torture and murder. The Roman procurators ruled with a heavy hand and with little concern for Jewish opinion or sensibility. The Jews never regarded the Roman occupation as legitimate. Roman taxes were regarded as robbery, tax collectors as hated extortioners (Neusner 1984). The result was a succession of minor revolts.

The outcome of such repression is rarely to eliminate conflict and unrest—it is more likely to heighten the tension and increase the pressures towards outright rebellion and violent insurrection. In the pressure-cooker of social repression, the pressure can build to the point of explosion—in the form of popular uprisings, revolutionary outbursts, and social upheaval resulting in the overthrow of the repressive government (Borg 1987). As Horsley and Hanson (1985) observe:

> One is forced to ask why so many hundreds, even thousands, of Jewish peasants were prepared to abandon their homes to pursue some prophet into the wilderness, or to rise in rebellion against their Jewish and Roman overlords when the signal was given by some charismatic "king," or to flee to the hills to join some brigand band. Peasants generally do not take such drastic action unless conditions have become such that they can no longer simply pursue the traditional patterns of life (p. 50).

The protests against imperial oppression often took the form of prophetic movements that tended to burst to the surface during the Passover celebrations when throngs of peasants and farmers from the countryside flooded Jerusalem. These peasant movements were usually messianic in character and incorporated many of the brigand bands that on such occasions coalesced in the messianic cause. Jesus' entrance into Jerusalem on Palm Sunday (Matt 21:1-11; Mark 11:1-11; Luke 19:28-40; John 12:12-19) may have been just such a prophetic outburst.

Early Christianity

In this maelstrom of political and religious turmoil the religious movement centered around the figure of Jesus came into being. It drew its roots from the currents of religious ferment pervading the Palestinian terrain. Within Palestine it remained little more than a Judaic splinter group, tied more or less to Judaic religious traditions and practices; outside of Palestine, however, it took on a different character strongly influenced by the Hellenistic culture of the Mediterranean basin and by the widespread cultural influences of the syncretistic melting pot of that world.

After the destruction of the temple in A.D. 70, traditional pharisaic and sacerdotal Judaism was in shambles, and the Jesus movement was transformed into the form of Jewish Christianity that became the basis for the nascent Christian church in the first century A.D. As rabbinical Judaism evolved after the Jerusalem catastrophe and established itself around the new Sanhedrin at Jamnia, the boundaries of pharisaic

Judaism began to be more stringently drawn, and over the course of the ensuing years increasing numbers of Jewish Christians were gradually excommunicated and extruded from the synagogue. The hardening of these lines of separation indicate the operation of the cultic process, reflecting the effects of the Judaic catastrophe and the competition for religious hegemony. The Jesus movement that had contended for space with other heterodox renewal movements in Palestine between A.D. 30–70 became more decisively delineated from traditional Judaism (Theissen 1978).

Wandering Charismatics

The character of the original Palestinian movement was different from that of the later development of early Christianity. The guiding figures of the early movement were apostles, disciples and prophets who traveled the roads of Palestine to preach the good news to small groups of sympathetic listeners. Theissen (1982) has suggested that the missionaries of the early church were

> . . . homeless, roving propagandists without roots or means of livelihood. They embodied a form of socially divergent behavior which was estranged from society's fundamental norms and necessities. One need only recall the demands on the disciples to forsake home, possessions, security, and family. By doing so they preached and lived a freedom from basic social responsibilities of a sort which could be put into practice only by those who had removed themselves from the stabilizing and domesticating effects of a continuing life of work (p. 27).

In this view, the primitive church would have embraced two entirely different brands of preacher: on the one hand the itinerant charismatics, drawn out of the social and economic conditions of Palestine and closely resembling the above description, and on the other the community organizers, represented by Paul and Barnabas, whose mission was to preach to the Hellenistic world. Each group solved the problem of subsistence in different ways that brought them into conflict.

A variety of social, economic, ecological, and cultural factors influenced the religious mission of the itinerant charismatics[1] who thought of themselves as Jews and remained by and large within the framework of Judaism. These "wandering charismatics" supposedly handed

---

[1] Horsley (1987, 1989) questions the suppositions of Theissen's argument, even that such a class of itinerant charismatics existed, yet alone formed a religious movement. See the further discussion below.

on the oral accounts of the early witnesses that provided the basis for the written gospel accounts. Gradually the more informal and unstructured mode of the early preaching mission took on a more institutionalized and organized form as the cult of Jesus became transformed into a *bona fide* religious movement and moved increasingly toward the development of local churches and finally a universal church. The tensions between these groups may have been reflected in the Jerusalem Council in the summer of A.D. 49.[2] The issue was the question of the adherence of Gentile converts to Jewish traditions, particularly the question of circumcision and the observance of Mosaic laws (Acts 15:2-12).

The early Jerusalem church centered around the leadership of the apostles, among whom James became the predominant figure. Theissen (1978) argues that the rest of the apostles were off on the mission given them by Christ to preach and cast out devils (Mark 3:13-14). These early disciples would have fit the model of wandering charismatics who embraced an ethical attitude marked by willingness to surrender home, property, family, and self-interest. They had left home and family behind to follow Jesus—the ideal of the wandering preacher with nowhere to lay his head persisted even after Jesus' departure. They had also abandoned family ties and obligations—dedication to the work of the kingdom did not allow family obligations that would tie the preacher down to specific places and people. The words in Luke 14:26 sound harsh and uncompromising: "If any man comes to me without hating his father, mother, wife, children, brothers, sisters, yes and his own life too, he cannot be my disciple. Anyone who does not carry his cross and come after me cannot be my disciple."

They espoused an ideal of poverty and lack of possessions, traveling the roads without money or provisions, without extra clothing—only one who despised wealth and possessions and had actually given away his own possessions could be free to criticize the attachment to possessions in others. Theissen (1978) summarizes this view of the early Christians:

> The ethical radicalism of the synoptic tradition is connected with this pattern of wandering, which could be carried on only under extreme and marginal conditions. Such an ethos could only be practised and handed down with any degree of credibility by those who had been released from the everyday ties of the world, who had left hearth and home, wife and children, who had let the dead bury their dead, and who took the lilies and the birds as their

---

[2] If this council actually occurred, and it may not have, Paul's letters make it abundantly clear that he did not abide by the dictates set forth in Acts 15.

model. . . . The vivid eschatological expectations of these early
Christian wandering charismatics went along with their role as
outsiders; they lived as those who expected the end of the world.
The more they detached themselves from this world in their everyday actions, the more they kept destroying this world in their
mythical fantasies, as if they had to work off their rejection by this
world (pp. 15–16).

The pattern of activity followed by the wandering charismatics was
modeled in large measure after the gospel portrait of Jesus in his years
of wandering and preaching. These christological images served important social functions in defining the role of the charismatics themselves, and in meeting the needs of the emerging church. Within the
small groups of followers, the charismatics were the authorities who
established new rules and norms for participation in the emergent
church. But in the outside society they were despised and persecuted—
a conflict in social roles and self-images reflected in the themes of exaltation and humiliation regarding the Son of Man (Theissen 1978). We
can recognize here the influence of an ideology defining the ingroup
characteristics and to some extent setting the terms for group membership. It also set the dividing lines between adherents of these views and
other groupings in the early Christian church. Even at this early stage
of development, the Jesus movement was caught up in the process of
creating ingroup cohesion by separation from and opposition to heterodox outgroups. Integrity of the emergent Christian communities was in
part a function of separation and divergence from alienated outgroups,
particularly extant Jewish sects but also other groupings within the
Christian movement.

Social Conditions

Socio-economic factors in the Palestinian background played a role
too. Jesus and his followers left families and homes behind, breaking with
established social norms. The situation was not unlike that found in
other renewal movements of the time—Qumran, the bands of displaced
brigands, and other prophetic movements—all characterized by a certain social rootlessness expressed in social withdrawal, dependency, or
more aggressive resistance. Many of the brigands and robbers, of whom
Josephus wrote, had been driven from their farms and occupations by
economic hardship or excessive taxes and Roman exploitation and had
taken up arms in defiance of the Roman military might in a kind of
guerilla warfare. One can make a case that these lawless bands grew in
size and power during the middle years of the century and finally
emerged as a religious and political movement in the climactic events

of the Jewish revolt and the war of resistance in 66 B.C. Growing numbers of socially rootless people might become beggars, or possessed, or might resort to banditry, or turn to some hopeful messianic movement. The disciples of Jesus may have been among the latter (Theissen 1978).

Critique

Theissen's (1978) portrayal of the early Jesus movement in Palestine has been criticized as somewhat overdrawn and romanticized. This view of the first disciples has come under severe criticism, especially by Horsley (1989). The factual basis for this reconstruction, he argues, is at best shaky and uncertain—a romanticized view of the early followers of Jesus with little textual support. Some of the apostles and disciples were land and property owners. The basis of Jesus' preaching mission was the village rather than the open countryside. The distances between villages were not very great, a matter of a few miles, so that the wandering of the little band was not a matter of long hours spent on the open roads, but rather short walks consuming a modest amount of time. It is also difficult to know the degree to which the view of the wandering charismatics might reflect a style developed later in the evolution of the movement, or in what sense it might have reflected a retrospective idealization for theologizing purposes.

Horsley's (1989) criticisms focus on the application of a functionalist sociological analysis to Palestinian society without respecting the limitations of such analysis (Harrington 1980). The analysis of Palestinian social structure proceeds as though it was a self-contained entity rather than a society torn by sharp conflicts precipitated by Roman rule and Hellenistic culture. The effort to dissociate certain movements as political or religious runs afoul of the fact that radical theocratic movements were not exclusively religious, but religious-cultural-economic-political without distinction. The conservative functionalist approach domesticates the gospel accounts, muting the sharp challenges of the Jesus movement to existing authorities and transforming them into socially conservative postures aimed at maintaining the *status quo*. If the challenging statements of Jesus were addressed to a small band of wandering charismatics, the ideology of itinerant radicalism did not amount to an ethic for an extended religious movement. In other words, the challenging statements in the gospel tradition do not pertain to the ordinary structure of community relations.

A basic criticism is that evidence for Theissen's reconstruction is either lacking or of doubtful relevance. Substantiation of the picture of the wandering charismatics rests on a few questionable texts—the passages on the calling of the disciples in Mark (Mark 1:16, 20) or the commis-

sioning of the disciples in Luke do not support the rather strong conclusion of an ethic of rootlessness, homelessness, and the lack of family
connections and possessions. Appeal to the model of the wandering
Cynic philosophers runs afoul of obvious differences in the calling and
involvements of these groups. The Cynics professed an individual
model of ethical radicalism, living without home, family or possessions, but the followers of Jesus were commissioned to preach to small
communities and their mission was based in the investment of local
communities. Leaving behind family, home and possessions was a secondary and transient side effect of their commitment to this mission.
The thesis of itinerant radicalism cannot be documented in the gospel
tradition. While it seems reasonable to assume that the role of wandering charismatic played some part in the Jesus movement (i.e., it might
apply to a small subgroup of devoted followers), there is no evidence
that it represented the core of the movement or that it accounted for a
significant component of the membership of the Jesus movement
(Horsley, 1989).

Social Deterioration

The social crisis afflicting Palestinian society in this first century
was in some measure due to deteriorating social and economic conditions, including recurrent famine, a series of natural catastrophes that
brought great hardship and resulted in increased deprivation, economic failures, and an increase in robbery and brigandry. The situation
was complicated by a more or less chronic overpopulation in Palestine,
especially in Galilee, the shortage of arable land, struggles over the distribution of wealth, the excessive tax burden, confiscation of land for
failure to pay the taxes and tributes, as well as maldistribution of
wealth—the rich got richer and the poor poorer. The collaboration between the hated Romans and the priestly aristocracy, particularly in
their exploitation of the common masses, created a crisis of confidence
and of trust in religious leaders and traditional forms of worship—a
breeding ground for radical theocratic movements, of which the Jesus
movement was one. It proclaimed the establishment of the kingdom of
God, and however you sliced it, this could mean little else than the
overthrow of the existing regime. Like other theocratic and messianic
movements, the Jesus movement was a threat to priestly and imperial
power, and after the murder of Jesus, the priests were not slow to persecute his followers. The religious movements[3] in Palestine responded
to these conditions in different ways. The Essenes lived apart without

---

[3] These sectarian movements will be described in greater detail in chapter 4.

earthly wealth or possessions. The Zealots choose robbery and plunder, raising them to the level of social protest. The Christian movement resorted to begging, its missionaries receiving their sustenance in return for preaching and healing, a form of charismatic begging that trusted in God for one's daily bread.

Social Protest

The various religious movements of the time would seem to represent forms of social protest devoted to an attempt to preserve the Jewish sense of cultural identity in the face of foreign oppression and the imminent destruction of any sense of religious and cultural independence. This independence was rooted in the Law with its complex of traditions, institutions, and ethical norms. Each of the religious groups sought ways to sustain and validate the Law. The Sadducees emphasized adherence to priestly prerogatives and preservation of the temple worship. For the Pharisees, it was through an interpretive adjustment to the prevailing circumstances; for the Essenes, it was through the preservation of the Law in an isolated and disciplined community; and for the Zealots, it was through authorizing acts of terrorism and plunder. Each movement undertook an intensification of the Law which ends in the ultimate distortion of the Law. Rather than achieving a common cultural and religious identity, the attempts become divisive and destructive, each group claiming for itself the prerogatives of the true Israel.

With the entrance of John the Baptist onto this scene of inner contradictions, a new force was born that sought to strike out in a different direction in the face of the same constellation of cultural and religious perils. John was an ascetic and prophet in his own right; as Eliade (1982) observes: "In fact, he was a true prophet, illuminated, irascible, and vehement, in open rebellion against the Jewish political and religious hierarchies. Leader of a millenarianistic sect, John the Baptist announced the imminence of the kingdom, but without claiming the title of its Messiah" (p. 331). Theissen (1982) comments: "It is no accident that this movement found approval particularly among the socially despised, those very people whose means of earning a living dictated that they compromise themselves in regard to the Law. Such are obviously the tax collectors and prostitutes, but also all the other 'sinners,' that is, all who found it impossible to honor the norms of Jewish society" (p. 33). It was precisely this appeal to the common man, the lower and oppressed strata of the community, that provided the context for the casting of Christ's mission as a challenge and a contradiction to the established Jewish authorities. If Christ came to bring a sword, it was not directed against his more humble fellowmen.

Similar factors were at work in the rise of the group of community organizers. While the economy of Palestine was withering, the rest of the Mediterranean world was in the midst of an economic boom. The Christian mission to the Gentile world had to penetrate the upper social classes quickly if it was to exercise any significant influence. Paul and Barnabas, for example, were not merely poor itinerant beggars. Paul earned his bread by leatherworking, not a particularly lofty occupation, but he also enjoyed dual citizenship (of Judea and Rome), an honor not often reserved for leatherworkers, suggesting that Paul enjoyed a privileged status. Barnabas was able to bring large donations to the Jerusalem church. Presumably they had some influence with more affluent members of the community.

Charismatic begging would not have been suitable in such a context. In terms of the values of such higher social strata, particularly the values attached to work for one's bread, the importance of home and family, the stability of economic resources and commitments, it were better for Paul and Barnabas that they present themselves as craftsmen. Family and work values clearly ran counter to the ethos of roving charismatic beggars, who had no means of support other than their preaching and who disavowed earthly possessions and their importance. To become itinerant preachers, the fishermen and farmers of Galilee had to give up their means of support. Peter could accept the privilege of support, while Paul the tentmaker could renounce it (Theissen 1982).

Messianic Revolt

All of these movements sought escape from the oppressive domination of Rome and to return Israel to the autonomous rule promised in the messianic vision—restitution of the rule of God by miraculous means. The claim of miraculous divine intervention on behalf of Israel against the Romans was by no means rare in the first century. Josephus lists the various episodes, but in each the Romans intervened to crush the revolt by arresting the leaders and slaughtering any who resisted. John's call to repentance in the desert may have posed the threat of rebellion to Herod Antipas, and would have provided a reason for John's decapitation. The resistance movement of the followers of Judas of Galilee (loosely associated with "the Zealots") sought rebellion as the path to the renewal of Israel, thus making hostility to the ruling authorities explicit and posing a corresponding threat.

These forms of imminent eschatology identified the beginning of the reign of God with the overthrow of the Romans. This vision and hope was inherent in the ideologies of the Essenes and Zealots, and possibly other prophetic movements that we know little about. None of these idealized expectations were connected with a continuance of the priestly aristocracy. They were to be bypassed in the new era by the glorious reign of the Messiah. For some of the followers of Jesus, the new era had already begun in the development of the church. When they took possession of the Temple, the Zealots were quick to depose the reigning high priest and replace him by a son of Zadok. The Essenes continued to hope for both a new king and a new high priest. They solved the dilemma by postulating two messiahs—the kingly messiah would be subordinate to the priestly messiah. The extent to which such messianic expectations were alive during Jesus' ministry, outside of the Essene circles, is uncertain, as well as the extent to which they may have been transformed and transposed to the figure of Christ (Meissner 1995). Whether the implications were messianic or not, Jesus was certainly the center of a popular following that, in itself, would have challenged the authorities and prompted the events surrounding Jesus' trial and death.

Part of the problem lay in traditional Jewish attitudes of xenophobia that dictated to some degree the pattern of Jewish interaction with alien cultures. Jewish identity and the sense of religious commitment focused on the observance and preservation of the Mosaic Law. These attitudes were more clearly etched in certain identifiable movements like the Sadducees, the Pharisees or the Essenes, but the extent to which they permeated the society at large is questionable. Certainly the norms of dietary and ritual purity were not as solidly established in the time of Jesus as in later centuries. The ideology, where it was in effect, nonetheless carried the idea that they were God's chosen people, so that other nations would be regarded as inferior, unclean, alien, and hostile—expressions of an underlying cultic process. Anxieties about defilement from contact with anything alien or Gentile played a part in Jewish religious attitudes and the exercise of daily life. Marriage to non-Jews was forbidden and frowned upon. The stringent food regulations inhibited social contact with outsiders—they ate their own food, often at separate tables. They tended to live in their own districts in the great cities where they could minimize the contamination from the surrounding foreign influences. Theissen (1978) comments:

> All these phobias about contact can be interpreted as anxiety over a loss of self-identity in Judaism projected on to people and things. The baptist movement which emerged at the end of the first century B.C. is incomprehensible apart from this anxiety. John the Baptist appealed to anxiety over a loss of self-identity when he questioned whether being a child of Abraham was a guarantee of

salvation (Matt 3:9). Jesus, too, came from this baptist movement (p. 92).

The Cultic Process

The workings of these processes in Palestinian society of this period reflects dynamics of the cultic process. The in-group dynamic of traditional Judaic religious groups dictated a view of themselves as special, chosen, privileged, and as the inheritors of the true religion of the one true God. The mingling of this intensely religiously oriented culture with the alien and dominant influences of the Hellenistic world created conditions of internal crisis—a crisis that permeated Israel in the first century A.D. especially. The crisis, abetted by the conditions of oppression and burdensome Roman domination, was accompanied by self-doubt and the failure of identity that saw the precariousness of Jewish life as punishment for their own failures and sinfulness. The failure of the forces of Jewish integrity and preservation set the stage for the intensification of eschatological expectations. The more desperate the situation in the present, the more the hopes for future restoration became accentuated and meaningful. The tightening of in-group norms and regulations produced increasingly the conditions for internal purification, splitting off of marginal groups, and internal schism, leading to even more profound crisis.

After the death of Jesus, the tensions became more acute and intense. The efforts of Emperor Caligula to substitute Roman religious symbols for traditional Jewish ones, the crisis conditions created by recurrent famines and overly burdensome taxation, and the general conditions of oppressive and repressive domination by the Romans, increased the level of tension and defensive counteraction. In the face of Roman incursions, the traditional religious practices and treasures were all the more intensely and fanatically invested. Along with these developments, the need to find appropriate scapegoats grew apace; the Christians became the likely target for this displaced aggression in the form of increasing persecution at the hands of Jewish authorities. The Christians became a persecuted minority in Palestine and their existence there became increasingly precarious. In addition, the contrasting success of the early Christian preaching outside of Palestine increasingly identified the movement as divorced from its Palestinian moorings and thus antithetical to traditional Judaism.

The intensification and purification of norms within Judaism reached a point where even the best intentioned of the faithful remnant would have great difficulty in living up to the standards of the true Israelite. The breakthrough and disruption of these forces came in the

Jesus movement whose claim it was that birth and descent no longer established the claim to religious superiority and truth, but faith in God and His grace. Gentile and Jew alike could enter the kingdom of heaven. A new in-group dynamic was thereby set in motion. As Theissen (1978) observes: "Traditional ethnocentrism was not, however, finally superseded, but transformed into a new factor: the claim of the church to absoluteness was a metamorphosis of ethnocentrism. Now it was the church which understood itself as the chosen people and all outsiders were treated as Gentiles. An ethnocentrically tinged conception of all foreigners was taken over from Judaism" (pp. 93–94). All of these developments bear the trademark of the cultic process.

4

Pre-Christian Origins—
Religious Background

Apocalyptic Expectations

Violent repression of Jewish resistance to Hellenizing reforms under the Seleucid Antiochus Epiphanes (175–164 B.C.) created a crisis of faith among Palestinian Jews. Acceptance of the reforms would have been equivalent to turning their backs on traditional covenants and the Torah. Resistance meant persecution and even death. In the face of this impossible dilemma, apocalyptic desires intensified. Faithful Jews turned to hope in a divine plan to deliver them from their agony. It was in this period that the great apocalyptic literature arose, including the *Assumption of Moses* and parts of *1 Enoch*, as well as the book of Daniel. The apocalyptic impulse offered consolation in the face of overwhelming difficulties along with the conviction that divine deliverance was close at hand (Horsley and Hanson 1985). In this matrix of seething resentment, oppression, and apocalyptic expectation, Christianity came into existence. Certainly, the preaching of John the Baptist, Jesus, and the early Christians was not unique in its eschatological emphasis and in its apocalyptic expectation of the imminence of God's kingdom (Meissner 1995).

The Context

The origins of Christianity reflect these elements amply, but leave us with a series of significant questions. What is the historical, social and cultural context within which the cultic impulse embedded in the rise of Christianity came about? What was the religious context of its emergence, specifically in terms of other extant religious groups and movements that might have provided a framework within which Christianity arose, either as a countervailing movement arising in opposition to these other groups, or in some part by way of assimilation and integration of religious elements already at work within this historical context?

The prophet and central figure of the new movement was Jesus Christ. As religious leader, Christ undoubtedly fulfilled in one or other aspect of his mission all dimensions of religious leadership (see, for example, Wach 1944). For our present purposes, we can focus on the charismatic and prophetic aspects of Christ's mission. In Weber's (1947) analysis, charism is almost synonymous with the prophetic role; the prophet is a charismatic religious leader. His charism involves a quality of his personality somehow setting him apart from ordinary men and allowing him to be regarded as endowed with exceptional powers or qualities, even capacities that are supernatural or superhuman. In the Gospels, Christ's mission was cast in more specifically theological terms, that is, Christ's religious leadership was viewed as the result of divine intention and inspiration.

The quality and conviction of divine ordination is predominant in the gospel accounts of Christ's initial call to his disciples. But these same phenomena can be viewed in more human terms as reflecting influences both in the social environment, in which the call and response to the ministry of Christ took place, and in terms of inner psychological forces that must have come into play in interaction with them. In these terms, even the prophetic charism of Christ would tend to run its course. Weber (1947) argued that the prophetic leader is most influential in the beginning of his mission, but that initial adoration among his followers is gradually followed by a period of cooling off and progressive institutionalization of his religious inspiration. As the prophetic message spreads through the religious group, it is inexorably processed and modified in terms of divergent interests and needs of the members—"routinization of charisma," as Weber called it (1947, p. 364).

The Cultic Process

The question then, is whether we can find the cultic process operating at the roots of the early Christian movement. Certainly, ground for fertile religious inspiration had been well prepared. The Jews were an oppressed people who had lived for centuries under the domination and threat of powerful neighboring nations. They had been carried into captivity and had their hopes for realization of earthly power and kingdom utterly crushed in the Babylonian captivity. Their lot was that of oppression and suffering, rationalized as punishment for evil and for infidelity to God. The prophets so declared and called for renewal and for a rebirth of righteousness and justice. But the suffering did not abate in ensuing centuries. There was no alternative but that the later prophetic movement had to find meaning and value in the continued suffering of the people of Israel. Israel became the Suffering Servant, the Man of Sorrows who was acquainted with grief (Isa 53:2-5).[1] If there was to be a victory of Israel over her enemies, it had either to be a victory of the spirit or take place through dramatic divine intervention that would create a new world.

Certainly, the origins of Christianity cannot be adequately understood without reference to the Jewish background from which it emerged. Increasingly, in the last score of years, biblical and archeological research has brought into gradually clearer focus the picture of the origins of Christianity as a form of religious synthesis emerging out of the complex Judaic and Hellenistic background of the first century. As Christianity grew from a small Jewish cult into a dominant religious movement, it gradually incorporated doctrines and practices extant in the religious world of the ancient Middle East and synthesized these into a new religious perspective. Elements of the Christian cult had long been familiar as, for example, the notion of a resurrected god, virgin birth, the eucharistic meal, and particularly belief in miraculous powers. Even many of the Christian holy days and feasts represent transformations of earlier pagan feasts that were simply drawn into Christian cult and ritual in a form adopted for new religious purposes. Elements were drawn from ancient mystery cults, from Greek philosophy, particularly Stoicism, and from Judaism. Data derived from study of the Dead Sea Scrolls give significance to the concept of the pre-Christian existence of many Christian ideas and practices in Palestine. We can turn now to try to delineate some of these elements and forces as they must have come into play in influencing the pattern of the emergent Christian cult as that cult advanced toward more complex and evolved forms of religious organization.

Religious Movements

Despite Jewish opposition against the Romans and Hellenizing influences,[2] there was little sense of national or religious unity or solidarity. Religious points of difference regarding the law or the cult of the

---

[1] We should note here the characteristic identification of the entire people or nation in the form of a personification; in Isaiah, the entire people of God are represented in the singular form of the Servant or the Man of Sorrows.

[2] See chapter 3 above.

temple were complicated by varying political alliances and intrigues among various religious groups. Each of these religious movements—Sadducees, Pharisees, Essenes and Zealots—the four "philosophies" cited by Josephus—can be regarded as expressing variant responses to the crisis caused by subjection to foreign imperial domination and exploitation. Despite historical uncertainties and ambiguities, four reasonably well-defined religious sects can be identified.[3]

Sadducees

The Sadducees were a priestly and aristocratic sect, claiming descent from Zadok (1 Kgs 1:26) and tracing the origin of their priestly tradition from the period of Samuel and Kings. As the "Sons of Zadok," the Sadducees were the party of the high priests and leading sacerdotal families, who laid claim to the office of high priest and control of the temple cult and continued to exercise political and religious dominance over the Jerusalem Sanhedrin. They first entered the stage of history as an already formed group in the second century B.C. as allied with the Hasmonean priest-kings (Saldarini 1988).

As a "party," the Sadducees were conservative and guarded prerogatives of the priestly position jealously. They stood for strict adherence to written laws, acknowledging the Scriptures as the only true religious authority and themselves as the only legitimate interpreters. They were violently opposed to the Pharisees' oral interpretations of the Torah, particularly views of life after death and resurrection of the body, primarily because they resented the apparent lay intrusion upon priestly privilege. They rejected any doctrinal development or modernization of the Torah, insisting on a conservative and traditional approach. Only the letter of the Mosaic Law held any authority for them.

In the time of Jesus, the high priest was spiritual leader of the Jews but was maintained in power by the Romans. The Sadducees were wise in the ways of power and politics. They clung to a delicate balance between their role as religious authorities and their need to maintain the balance of power with Rome. Any disturbance, as for example the popular apocalyptic and antireligious (i.e., anti-temple establishment)

---

[3] Description of these movements as "sects" requires a word of caution. The analysis of church-sect structure in more modern terms, as in the Weber-Troeltsch tradition, implies a more differentiated relation between religious and other social institutions than obtained in ancient Palestine—the Temple and its priesthood were a religious, political and economic entity. With varying degrees of articulation and organization, these interest-groups were reactant to and participant in the social and cultural turmoil of the period; their sectarian aspects can be thought of in no more than analogous terms.

movement possibly led by Jesus, would have caused them great anxiety and called for the most vigorous suppression. They lived in fear of Roman reprisals for any show of Jewish resistance or strength (Lohfink 1984). After destruction of the Temple in A.D. 70, they seemed to disappear from the stage of history. Their claim to be the legitimate bearers of the faith of Israel was so closely tied to their priestly functions and temple worship that without the physical presence of that temple they had no social structure or institution to support them.

Pharisees

The Pharisees, in contrast, constituted essentially a lay religious movement, advocating rigorous observance of the Law, based not only on the written Torah but also on oral interpretations of the law, propounded by scribes since the time of Ezra—the so-called "oral Torah." The name "Pharisee" probably reflected the exclusiveness of the sect and their maintenance of separation from the common people as a way of preserving a more rigorous observance of the law (Neusner 1984). Leading figures were the scribes,[4] who were reputed for their learning and knowledge of the Law and were held in high esteem by the common people. The Pharisees first appear as an organized movement in the mid-second century B.C., probably related to the Hasideans, the *Hasidim* or "pious ones," who supported the Maccabean revolt until it shifted from an essentially religious movement to a more political one.

The Pharisees regarded knowledge of the Law as the safeguard of religious inspiration. Knowledge and observance of the law was the essence of their religious devotion. It is not difficult to understand how Jesus' flaunting of the Law would have roused their ire and hostility (Lohfink 1984). They were particularly zealous in matters of dietary observance, tithing and ritual purity, requiring continuous and obsessive attention to minute details. Their insistence on payment of tithes commanded by the Torah added to the excessive burden created by the hated Roman taxes (Borg 1987). With regard to temple worship, the

---

[4] The association between the scribes and Pharisees was loosely formulated and historically uncertain. The scribes may have been no more than a trained and learned group involved in efforts of Pharisees or Sadducees as occasion or opportunity required. They functioned more or less as retainers in the service of rulers or ruling institutions; in the gospels they appear as high-level officials in the service of the priestly aristocracy. It is doubtful that they formed a separate religious group. In Mark they are associated with the chief priests as holding official governing positions. In Matthew they seem aligned with the Pharisees as having common interests and learning. Also in Luke-Acts they seem to be an appendage to the Pharisees, particularly in belief in the resurrection (Saldarini 1988).

Temple was the center of their religious universe—the holy mountain, where the anointed of God would appear. Temple sacrifice was the primary worship of God, but they felt that the priests should follow the oral tradition God revealed to Moses on Mt. Sinai (Neusner 1984).

Despite this burdensome approach to legal observance, the Pharisees exerted considerable influence on other Jews through their learning and piety. They espoused beliefs in human freedom under divine providence, in resurrection of the body, in angels, in coming of the Messiah, and in reconstitution of Israel in the final times. Their basic religious outlook was rooted in the Old Testament as bedrock for their belief. This staunch commitment to tradition, both oral and written, served them well after the destruction of Jerusalem when temple cult came to an end. It provided a rallying point for believing Jews, so that the subsequent course of rabbinic Judaism was largely molded by the pharisaic tradition that ultimately has found its way into more modern orthodox Judaism.

Zealots

A third Jewish movement of the period was thought to be more openly aggressive and revolutionary. They are called the "Zealots," but knowledge of their existence and religious influence is somewhat confused. There is doubt whether they can be regarded as a "sect" at all, since they did not emerge on the pages of history with any degree of delineation until the Jewish revolt of A.D. 66. They have been depicted as a widespread nationalistic religious movement (Horsley 1987) that finally burst into recognizable form as a movement of fanatical advocates of violent overthrow of the hated Romans in the first Judean revolt (Horsley and Hanson 1985; Horsley 1989). Our knowledge of this sect in the New Testament period is limited to accounts of Josephus who attributed the catastrophe of A.D. 70 to Zealot fanaticism, and regarded them as robbers and murderers, condemning them as brigands and outlaws. He wrote of them:

> They agree with the views of the Pharisees in everything except their unconquerable passion for freedom, since they take God as their only leader and master. They shrug off submitting to unusual forms of death and stand firm in the face of torture of relatives and friends, all for refusing to call any man master. Since most people have seen their unwavering conviction under such circumstances, I can omit further comment. . . . The real problem would be that the report about them would understate their contempt for suffering pain.[5]

---

[5] *Jewish Antiquities*, 18.23–25, cited in Horsley and Hanson (1985) pp. 191–92.

Their ranks may have been swelled by disenchanted peasants who had been deprived of their property or suffered some other injustice at the hands of the hated Romans and turned to outlawry rather than submission. Josephus' slanted apologetic and the complete silence of Christian sources about the Zealot movement make any reconstruction highly tentative and conjectural. Nonetheless the possibility remains that the Zealot movement may have played an important role in the mission of Christ and the beginnings of Christianity. They probably did not constitute any kind of organized movement; it is also possible that the label "Zealot" may often have been used as no more than a general term referring to a loose collection of a variety of revolutionary movements.[6]

Another identifiable group among the diversity of revolutionary movements, possibly related to the Zealot movement, were known as "Sicarii" from the fact that they carried short daggers *(sicae)* under their cloaks with which they assassinated leaders of the opposition. It is worth noting that these terrorist attacks were never directed against the Romans, in contrast to bands of brigands that roamed the countryside and often fell on Roman supply trains in search of food and weapons. Rather the Sicarii zeroed in on Jewish collaborators with the Romans, members of the ruling classes who colluded with the hated Romans in exploiting and terrorizing the masses. The terrorist activities of the Sicarii increased over the decades of the 50s and 60s, and attempts of Roman governors to suppress these outlaws drove increasing numbers of the peasantry into active resistance. In the midst of this politico-religious turmoil, the boy Jesus grew to manhood, since we can presume that these movements were in some degree extant in the early decades of the century.

Various religious sects of the period were distinguished less by theological and eschatological concepts than by programs of action for implementing socio-economic objectives. Opposition to Roman oppression may have been much more diffuse and spontaneous in Palestinian society, especially in popular movements led by prophets or messiahs of liberation; it was not the province of a single group of fanatical Zealots. Popular prophetic and messianic movements were

---

[6] The more or less unified view of the Zealots as constituting a "party" or "sect" in any continuous and organized sense may be an historical fiction, a construction in the service of a religious vision more than an historical reality. Horsley (1987, 1989) and Horsley and Hanson (1985) suggest that linkage between the fourth philosophy of Judas of Galilee, the "sicarii," and the Zealots was tenuous and unsupported by evidence, but that it provided "a convenient foil over against which to portray Jesus of Nazareth as a sober prophet of pacifist love of one's enemies" (Horsley and Hanson 1985, p. xiv).

frequent developments, and the phenomenon of social banditry was a chronic symptom of social displacement that rose to a desperate pitch preceding the revolt of A.D. 66–70 (Horsley and Hanson 1985).

Zealot ideology seems to have been short and sweet: there is only one God, and therefore no tribute should be paid to the emperor of Rome. The Zealot ideal embraced two principles: absolute sovereignty of YHWH over Israel and the freedom of Israel. Their mission was delivery of Israel from subjugation and servitude to any foreign power. Resistance to Roman rule and overthrow of Roman power was a religious duty. The revolt of A.D. 66 may well have been influenced by the same vision that lie behind the *Scroll of the War of the Sons of Light against the Sons of Darkness* discovered at Qumran. It envisioned an Armageddon, the final struggle between the forces of Israel and the hated *Kittim* (Romans) and the ultimate intervention of God on the side of the sons of light. While the document is Essene in origin, connections between the Essene and Zealot movements are still open to conjecture, especially in the light of the discovery of Essene materials at Masada. One speculation is that belief in the final confrontation and God's divine intervention may have influenced the Zealot uprising and the final cataclysm. Their fanatical resistance to Rome resulted in the mass suicide at Masada in A.D. 74.

Essenes

Perhaps the most interesting sect to occupy the Palestinian stage in the pre-Christian era was the movement of religious and national reformation known as the Essenes, probably connected with the *Hassidim,* the pious ones, who joined forces with Judas Maccabeus. The sect lasted for more than two centuries, until "the coming of the rulers of the Kittim." The origins of the sect in the Maccabean revolt had to do with outrage of the Hasideans *(Hassidim)* at the religious blasphemies of Hellenistic Jews favorable to the cause of Antiochus. Particularly galling was removal of the high priest in favor of someone not descended from the legitimate priestly line of Zadok. The Essenes abandoned temple worship, regarding it as corrupt and its calendar erroneous (Neusner 1984). Many withdrew into the desert where they established a community in which they could prepare themselves for the coming of the kingdom of God. The Hasmonean period was riddled with political, social, and religious conflict. The *Hasidim* and Hasmoneans had joined forces against Seleucid oppression, but when the Hasmoneans replaced the traditional Zadokite priesthood, the *Hasidim* parted company.

The Qumran literature from that period is polemical and bursting with invective. Adversaries condemned for their crimes included the wicked priest, the man of lies, the man of scorn, the lion of wrath, and the seekers after smooth things. These are undoubtedly references to the strife that flourished in the second century B.C. under the Seleucids. The "lion of wrath" probably refers to Alexander Janneus who crucified his opponents. The "seekers after smooth things" may refer to the Pharisees (Saldarini 1988). Hasidean support for the Maccabees was essentially religious in inspiration and intent, but as the Maccabean revolt evolved, it became increasingly less religious and more political. The Damascus Covenant described this period of lukewarm alliance with the Maccabees as "twenty years in which they were like blind men groping their way." At this point the Teacher of Righteousness entered the picture to guide them on the paths of truth (Horsley 1987).

Beliefs of this sect centered on the doctrine of the Teacher of Righteousness, but hardly anything is known about his identity except that he was a priest of the Zadokite line and probably a man of great personal piety. The break between the Righteous Teacher and the Maccabees probably came in 152 B.C., when Jonathan was appointed high priest by the Syrian king. Assumption of the high priesthood by a Maccabee who was not a legitimate Zadokite successor was an unforgivable transgression. There are references to the "wicked priest" who opposed and even persecuted the Teacher of Righteousness; the wicked priest was very likely either Jonathan himself or his brother, Simon Maccabee.

About this time the sect retired to Qumran and began their desert settlement. The men who gathered there sought a better, purer life, removed from the evil and corruption of the world. They believed that this impure age would come to an end, and that those who remained faithful to the God of Israel had to prepare themselves for a holy war at the end of time (Neusner 1984). They formed an eschatological community, based on the new revelations of the Teacher about the meaning of Scripture. They believed that traditional prophecies were being fulfilled in their own time, and that they alone represented the faithful remnant, the true Israel destined to be saved in the final times. They kept themselves in constant readiness for the imminent battle between the demonic forces of darkness and God.

After death of the Teacher of Righteousness, the Qumran community flourished and increased significantly in size, possibly resulting from persecution of the Pharisees by Hyrcanus, forcing many of these disillusioned Pharisees to join forces with the Essenes. Opposition between the Essenes and the Hasmonean priest-rulers of Jerusalem continued unabated, to be later replaced by fear and hatred of the Romans. References to the coming of the terrible *Kittim*, the Roman legions representing God's judgment against the Hasmonean corruption, were presumably written after Pompey's entrance into Jerusalem (63 B.C.).

Archeological remains point to a violent end to the first phase of the Qumran settlement, probably by fire and earthquake. After many years in ruins, the Qumran settlement was reconstructed at the beginning of the Christian era and entered on a new life that lasted for decades (until A.D. 68). The new sectarians were now anti-Roman rather than anti-Hasmonean. The *Kittim* now represented forces of darkness in the eschatological war between the sons of light and the sons of darkness. As the Romans tightened their hold on Palestine and gradually crushed pockets of resistance, the Qumran settlement felt the crushing power of Roman might in A.D. 68. Prior to the destruction, a large number of manuscripts were deposited in the caves of Khirbet Qumran, presumably for protection from Roman destruction. The Romans established a military encampment on the ruins of Qumran and apparently found some of the manuscript hordes, brutally mutilating many of them. But some also escaped detection, only to be rediscovered in recent years. After destruction of the Qumran community, some of Essenes may have fled south to join the Zealots in the stronghold of Masada.

Religious Ideas

From the time of the Babylonian captivity, the idea of the new covenant entered Jewish religious thought, referring to inner spiritual transformation of the individual Jew, so that God's law became an interior law written in the heart of every Jewish believer. This same covenant theology was the basis for the belief system of the Qumran community. They were the faithful, and in fact, final remnant. The Teacher of Righteousness had come to establish the new covenant, the only valid vehicle for the bond between God and Israel. The new covenant could be preserved only by absolute faithfulness to its precepts.

Major emphasis fell on study of the Scriptures, not only as guides to morality, but also as revealing deeper understanding of eschatological verities. But, as with the Law, Scripture was full of pitfalls for the naive and ignorant. Only the wisdom of the community could understand the Scriptures correctly, so that the proper path could be followed into the final cataclysm. Only the inspired interpretation of the Teacher of Righteousness could find this deeper meaning and the path to truth and salvation. Biblical commentaries are largely concerned with the struggle between the righteous and the wicked and the ultimate destiny and triumph of the House of Judah and defeat and annihilation of those who had rebelled against God. The Teacher of Righteousness had received a special revelation concerning all the mysteries of the prophets and the scriptures. The view from Qumran saw the entire history of

Israel as preparation for this final community of the new covenant. The law and teachings of the Righteous Teacher were essential guides to the right way. The extent of the influence of Essene ideas on the New Testament, as we shall see, particularly on Paul and John, is not only probable but more than likely to be extensive. But again there is question of direct influences versus the more pervasive impact of the general cultural matrix.

In any case, for the sake of our overall understanding of the dynamic aspects of the rise of the Jesus movement, we can note both the sectarian and divisive dimension of the configuration of these religious groups, functioning within the pressured and oppressive strains of Roman occupation, and with the fact that the theological positions staked out by these respective movements can be read as preformed expressions of viewpoints and attitudes that will find their way into the Christian ideology, integrated and transformed by the dynamics operative within that emerging community or communities. The cultic process was detectable even in this pre-Christian setting in which dynamic processes were ostensibly at work in defining and shaping the character and history of these Palestinian religious groupings.

5

Sectarian Influences

As the Jesus movement emerged from the Palestinian background, it was confronted with the challenge of defining itself as a separate religious movement and determining its relations with pre-existing religious groups. The task involved establishing the identifying characteristics of the group and determining the degree and manner of influence and interaction with other religious groups and the surrounding sociocultural environment. This development relied on the mechanisms of the cultic process. Relations with the Sadducees and Pharisees were generally more straightforward and oppositional, however the connection with both the Zealot movement and the Essenes of Qumran were more complex.

The Zealot Connection

The Jesus movement saw itself as a way of revitalizing Israel society in the throes of a severe crisis. As one of the revitalizing movements extant in Palestine, it would have intersected with, overlapped, and even to some extent found common cause with other revitalization movements. It was a charismatic movement, rooted in the power of the Spirit, and centered on the person of Jesus as its prophet (Borg 1987). Among the powerful currents of renewal provoked by the years of oppression and Roman domination and exploitation was that represented by the Zealots.

The problem of the possible connections of the Zealot movement with the origins of Christianity is perplexing to say the least. The view of the Zealots as a movement of national liberation, the fanatical advocates of violent revolution against the power of Rome, provided a contrasting background for portrayal of Jesus as a prophet of peace and the love of enemies. However, there does not seem to be much historical basis for this view of the Zealot cause (Horsley 1987). In contrast to the violent and fanatical portrayal of the militant Zealots, the gospels present Jesus as the prophet of nonviolence, love of enemies, and turning the other cheek. He is even pictured as the friend of tax collectors (viewed as collaborators with the enemy by the Zealots), and as recommending payment of the tribute to Rome ("Render unto Caesar. . . ."). His execution as a political criminal is ignored or glossed over by a spiritualized interpretation. Yet it can be argued that, as a charismatic prophet, Jesus was deeply involved in the sociopolitical life of his time, such that he became a national figure who undertook a mission of revitalization of his people in a time of great cultural crisis (Borg 1987).

Brandon (1967) argued on rather conjectural grounds that the apostle James, the leader of the Jerusalem church, along with other Jewish Christians, may have been in sympathy with the aspirations of the lower orders of the clergy and the Zealots, and thus opposed to the sacerdotal aristocracy and their Roman backers. James stands out in the history of the early church as holding to the strict observance of the Torah and devotion to traditional ritual practices. The argument with Paul over circumcision reflected James' insistence that converts be required to submit to the Jewish Law. Thus James and his followers were committed to a view of themselves as part of the destiny of Israel and to a belief in the crucified Messiah who would restore the kingdom of Israel.

To this extent the early church was a deviant Jewish messianic sect —a fact which must have set the stage for James' execution by stoning on the order of the high priest Ananus. This action added oil to the flames of resentment against Ananus, who represented the Sadducean aristocracy and was hated for his persecution of the lower orders of clergy. Many of these priests, who became members of the Jerusalem church—so the argument goes—were infected with Zealot aspirations. Their resistance to the imposition of imperial sacrifices set off the revolt of A.D. 66. These connections may have contributed to the execution of James, just as they may have played a part in the crucifixion of his brother and Master.

Jewish Christians and the Zealots both emphasized the divine sovereignty and the restoration of the kingdom of Israel by divine intervention. The Roman imposition of a divine emperor and the repeated Roman violations of both temple and Torah were intolerable. The leaders of both movements had died on the cross at the hands of the Romans, and the threat of crucifixion was a constant anxiety. The resistance of Judas of Galilee, in the early stage of the Zealot movement, to Roman rule shared with Jesus' proclamation of the kingdom of God the principle of the absolute sovereignty of the God of Israel. Their respective movements were both religious and political (Grant 1970), both hated and opposed the pro-Roman higher priesthood, and both drew their strength from the "people of the land." They shared an antipathy to the rich and powerful. The differences, however, are also striking: the Zealots sought revolution by violent means, the Christians preferred more peaceful means.

Brandon (1967) saw the two groups as bound by common sympathies and united in their opposition to the sacerdotal authorities and the hated Romans. The essential difference was the Christian belief that the restoration of Israel would be accomplished by the return of Christ as the Messiah. Brandon's analysis has been criticized, particularly in its highly conjectural status and its overemphasis on the strong links between the Christians of Jerusalem and the Zealots (Yoder 1972; Edwards 1972). While the Christian movement may not have been involved in the violence of the Zealot cause, there seems to have been sufficient ground to justify the claim that Christ's mission was in part political in its origins and that strong sympathies existed between the early Christian church and the Zealot cause (Yoder 1972; Cullmann 1956). In other respects the two groups may have found common cause in their political alliance and destiny.

Jesus and the Zealots

The possible linkage of the mission of Christ with the Zealots rests on little more than a tissue of probabilities. First, there is reason, however tenuous, to think that some of the twelve disciples were Zealot adherents—Simon, one of the twelve, was called "Zealotes" (Luke 6:15; Acts 1:13). Cullmann (1962) suggested that Judas Iscariot may have had some connection with the *sicarii*. And Peter himself, the prince of the apostles, is called *bar-yônâ* (Matt 16:17)—one variant of the Aramaic expression is "terrorist," leading to the suggestion that Peter may have been one of the Zealots.[1] Second, Christ was not slow to attack the priestly aristocracy. His cleansing of the Temple would have been an

---

[1] Cullman (1956) even suggested that as many as half of the twelve were recruited from among the Zealots. It remains unclear, however, what the term "zealot" means in this context. There does not seem to have been a clearcut political or religious movement extant at the time of Jesus that could have been denominated

attack on the temple-trading system highly profitable to the temple priests. Such behavior could hardly have been viewed as anything but subversive by both the Jewish and Roman authorities—a form of revolutionary activity.

The gospel accounts picture this attack as the work of Jesus alone. The likelihood that such an effort could have been carried off by one man is small, regardless of his strength of purpose and personality. In addition the temple police would have put a stop to such business in short order. But if the cleansing episode followed hard on the heels of the triumphal entry (probably the next day, Mark 11:11), Christ would have had with him his disciples and a large following (Brandon 1967). Both Mark (15:7) and Luke (23:19, 25) mention a bloody insurrection in the city about the same time. Was Christ's attack on the temple trade and the authority of the priestly aristocracy merely an isolated prophetic gesture, or was it linked to a more extensive and serious insurrection (Cullmann 1970)?

The possibility remains that the seizure of the Temple may have been an expression of deeper-lying social and political conflicts, however cloaked in the guise of religious ideology. Oppression of the poorer classes had set up an antipathy between them and the temple hierarchy; the movement instigated by Jesus, to the extent that it was allied with these groups, would have set its course toward a dangerous collision not only with the Romans but also with the temple priests. Jesus' challenge, as part of a larger seditious challenge to Roman power and authority, may have triggered the events that led to his trial and crucifixion. The power and popularity of his teaching may have been enough to threaten the authorities with political consequences—without any direct revolutionary threat. In this sense, his execution as a rebel against Roman rule may have not been a mistake at all. As far as the Romans were concerned, Jesus would have fit the mold of Hebrew secular messiahs, would-be kings of the Davidic line; they would have seen nothing unusual about hanging him between two Zealot resistance fighters (LaBarre 1970). In one sense he was innocent of the charge—he was neither a Zealot nor a Zealot sympathizer; but in another sense he was guilty, for his allegiance was neither to Rome or any kingdom of this world (Borg 1987).

---

by this term. The Zealot movement only emerged onto the pages of history at the time of Jewish revolt in A.D. 66. However, Gamaliel (Acts 5:36ff), cautioning his fellow rabbis, connected the disciples with previous Zealot leaders Theudas and Judas the Galilean (Cullmann 1970). Could the term apply only loosely to displaced groups of social bandits at large in the hills and deserts of Judea? See Horsley and Hanson (1985).

If such were the case, Jesus might have had much closer ties to the Zealots than the tradition has conveyed. However, the conclusion that Jesus was on a Zealot inspired mission of violent revolution would strain the imagination, if not the sources. Yoder (1972) observes that the events in the temple court and the trial might not have convicted Jesus of revolutionary action, but they also did not reflect an effort to avoid an impression of an insurrectionary vision. The Jewish and Roman authorities were defending against a real threat, not of armed revolt, but of nonviolent tactics of real political significance sufficient to justify such strong punitive action. But the theme of violence cannot be ignored. Jesus' cherished herald met a violent end at the hands of Salome and Herod. And later, in his eulogy of John, Jesus sounds the cadence of violence:

> What did you go out into the wilderness to behold? A reed shaken by the wind? Why then did you go out? To see a man clothed in soft raiment? Behold, those who wear soft raiment are in kings' houses. Why then did you go out? To see a prophet? Yes, I tell you, and more than a prophet. This is he of whom it is written,
>
> > "Behold, I send my messenger before thy face,
> > who shall prepare thy way before thee."
>
> Truly, I say to you, among those born of women there has risen no one greater than John the Baptist; yet he who is least in the kingdom of heaven is greater than he. From the days of John the Baptist until now the kingdom of heaven has suffered violence, and men of violence take it by force (Matt 11:7-12).

A similar note is sounded in Luke (16:16). Is "men of violence" to be taken here as referring to the Zealots who sought to establish a messianic theocracy by violent means? Was John's unfortunate end the result of the political threat raised by his preaching?

Third, the gospel accounts of the passion and death of Christ portray him as the innocent victim of Jewish malice and Roman stupidity. His posture is that of meek acceptance of violence and injustice and the repudiation of resistance or armed force—a theological portrait of an apolitical Christ. Might the possibility that Pilate sentenced Christ to die on positive grounds of political subversion have been suppressed by the tradition? The reasons behind the exacerbated hostility of the Jewish authorities, especially the priests and the members of the Sanhedrin, remain somewhat obscure. If we content ourselves with mere doctrinal differences to explain the events, they seem pallid and hardly proportional to the extremes of the gospel narratives. The possibility remains that Jesus was seen as the head of a powerful and popular movement that threatened the political and religious position of these vested authorities (Lohfink 1984). His attacks on the excesses in temple worship would have earned him the enmity of the temple priests, and his critique of the legalistic interpretations and program of the Pharisees would have gained him their antipathy as well (Sloyan 1973). The account in John adds credibility to such a view:

> Many of the Jews therefore, who had come with Mary and had seen what he did, believed in him; but some of them went to the Pharisees and told them what Jesus had done. So the chief priests and the Pharisees gathered the council, and said, "What are we to do? For this man performs many signs. If we let him go on thus, every one will believe in him, and the Romans will come and destroy both our holy place and our nation." But one of them, Ca'iaphas, who was high priest that year, said to them, "You know nothing at all; you do not understand that it is expedient for you that one man should die for the people, and that the whole nation should not perish." He did not say this of his own accord, but being high priest that year he prophesied that Jesus should die for the nation, and not for the nation only, but to gather into one the children of God who are scattered abroad. So from that day on they took counsel how to put him to death (John 11:45-53).

This account brings the enmity of the temple authorities to the mission of Jesus to a head. Ironically, the fears placed in the mouths of the priests became a reality in the destruction of Jerusalem and the Temple in A.D. 70 at the hands of the Romans. The uprising that brought about the ruin of Jerusalem and the end of temple worship came at the instigation of Zealot fanatics who sought to overthrow the power of Rome by violent means. These words were placed in the mouths of the priests in a kind of postdiction in the wake of the events of A.D. 70. Was a connection implied between the reaction of these bearers of the vested authority of the Temple and the threat of a Zealot revolt, and was the prophet from Galilee, like Judas of Galilee before him, associated with that threatening movement? On his cross he was labeled "King of the Jews." This was the common end of revolutionary Jewish patriots and messianic pretenders.

One of the forms of popular unrest in the troubled period of the second Temple was the forming of groups of revolutionaries around a leader whom they declared king (Horsley and Hanson 1985). Certainly the triumphal entry into Jerusalem and the subsequent cleansing of the Temple would have served as a challenge to the Jewish authorities and would have carried with them a subversive cast. The Romans must have regarded Jesus as a threat to their governance in Judea and would have condemned him on sufficient, if minor, grounds. If the Jewish leaders had arrested Christ and handed him over to the Romans on a charge of sedition, the evidence may have been sufficient to substantiate the charge and justify the death penalty (Cullmann 1970).

While the argument remains highly conjectural, it opens the possibility that the mission of Christ and the origins of the religious movement he headed were more significantly political than traditional views have allowed. While the links to Zealotism do not substantiate any view of the origins of Christianity as a violent revolutionary movement, they underline certain aspects of conjunction and sympathy between them that may contribute another dimension to the antipathy between early Christians and the Jewish authorities and suggest some of the realities behind the gospel accounts of Christ's messianic mission and his execution. Certainly, the failure of Christ's preaching mission sounded the death knell for the hopes of many. Luke recounts:

> And there followed him a great multitude of the people, and of women who bewailed and lamented him. But Jesus turning to them said, "Daughters of Jerusalem, do not weep for me, but weep for yourselves and for your children. For behold, the days are coming when they will say, 'Blessed are the barren, and the wombs that never bore, and the breasts that never gave suck!' Then they will begin to say to the mountains, 'Fall on us'; and to the hills, 'Cover us.' For if they do this when the wood is green, what will happen when it is dry?" (Luke 23:27-31).

Cullmann (1970) suggests that the reference here is to the Zealot uprising that was to come in A.D. 70—if the Romans could do this to one they judged to be a Zealot (the green wood), what will they do to a full-blown Zealot rebellion? These words reflect the destruction that is to come—prophetic from the perspective of the gospel account and post-dictive from the vantage of post-destruction reflection.[2] Was there more here than the outpouring of personal affection for a beloved preacher? or was there also the devastation of revolutionary political, social, and religious dreams—perhaps even messianic expectations?

But for all of the Gospels, the gradual evolution of the doctrine of Christ as divine Savior undermined the notion that he would have been involved in matters of Jewish nationalism and subversion of Roman rule. John has him reassure Pilate that his kingdom is not of this

---

[2] These Lucan texts are prophesies *ex eventu*, cast in the light of the later destruction of Jerusalem. My point in citing them is that they reflect a mind set extant among the first century Christians, and that they probably express a state of affairs continuous with attitudes and feelings associated with the earlier years of the Jesus movement, if not actually extant at those earlier times.

world, that his kingship was no challenge or threat to Rome, but was of another world. Rather than Zealot violence, Jesus brought a "politics of compassion" with him. As Borg (1987) comments:

> The politics of compassion addressed two central issues generated by the crisis in the Jewish social world: the growing internal division within Jewish society, and the deepening of the conflict with Rome. Jesus' emphasis upon compassion as the ethos and politics of the people of God contravened the barriers created by Israel's social world, made up of its blend of conventional wisdom, holiness, exclusivity, and patriarchy. Historically speaking, Jesus sought to transform his social world by creating an alternative community structured around compassion, with norms that moved in the direction of inclusiveness, acceptance, love, and peace. The alternative consciousness he taught as a sage generated a "contrast society," an "alternative community with an alternative consciousness" grounded in the Spirit (p. 142).

Brandon (1967) reminds us, however, that the Christian tradition has preserved another, perhaps more primitive conception of Christ and his mission, that is found in the Apocalypse of John—a vision of a terrible rider on a white horse, whose "eyes are like a flame of fire . . . He is clad in a robe dipped in blood, and the name by which he is called is The Word of God . . . From his mouth issues a sharp sword with which to smite the nations, and he will rule them with a rod of iron; he will tread the wine press of the fury of the wrath of God the Almighty. On his robe and on his thigh he has a name inscribed, King of kings and Lord of lords" (Rev 19:12ff).

The Essene Connection

Our fragmentary knowledge of the Essene movement and particularly the structure and organization of the Qumran community raises many interesting and difficult questions about a possible connection between the Essenes and nascent Christianity. In large measure, the questions remain unanswered, and the implications of possible influences remain speculative. There is no evidence for any direct connections or for any explicit or self-conscious derivations of Christianity from Essenism. But, nonetheless, comparisons, similarities and parallels abound. Both were Jewish apocalyptic sects and parallels between the preaching of Jesus and his followers and Essene usages are apparent. They were both forms of conversion community; for both the transition from a preconversion life of sin to membership in the salvific community was formalized through baptism. Adoption into the community was accomplished through spiritual cleansing, but the baptismal rite at Qumran was less a rite of admission than a daily ablution to maintain the purity of the initiate entering the sect (Segal 1990). One could scarcely imagine that the early followers of Jesus, and even Jesus himself, would have been unaware of the Essene movement, since it provided an important element in the general religious background against which the mission of Jesus played itself out.

Speculation has also been raised about a possible influence of Essenism on Jesus himself, but the Gospels give us no direct evidence for this view. Others have argued that Jesus was in some sense the successor to the Teacher of Righteousness, that the origins of the Christian church were rooted in the Essene movement, and that the early Jewish Christian church borrowed much of its organization, regulations, doctrine and mystical and ethical notions from the Essene movement. The attitude toward Christ in the New Testament bears striking resemblance to the attitude toward the Teacher of Righteousness in the documents of Qumran. Christ's identification of himself as "teacher" (Mark 14:14) during the instructions for the Last Supper points to an understanding of his role along the lines of the Teacher of Righteousness, who was perceived by the Qumran community as serving a central eschatological function linked to the promise of a prophet like Moses (Kee 1987). The Qumran sectarians looked forward to a new and fuller knowledge of God in messianic times. Did this mean a fuller knowledge of the Law, or something more? In the final time, this new understanding would be brought by a prophet, a new Moses, who would bring, if not a new law, at least a new understanding (Davies 1966).

Question has been raised regarding the possible Essene influences on Matthew, e.g., in the Sermon on the Mount (Charlesworth 1987). Like Mark, Matthew pictures Christ as a teacher like the Teacher of Righteousness. After the destruction of the Qumran community in A.D. 68, about the time Matthew wrote his Gospel, the surviving members would have been dispersed and possibly many joined ranks with the Christians. It certainly seems reasonable that under these circumstances contacts between the sectarians and the Christian community would have been intensified and that Matthew may have incorporated some Essene influences into his writing (Davies 1966). Despite the fact that the Essenes do not appear at all as such in the New Testament literature, there may be occasional references to the doctrines of the sect as, for example, when Jesus refers to "eunuchs who had made themselves that way for the sake of the kingdom of heaven" (Matt 19:12), possibly referring to the Essene practice of celibacy. Stendahl (1968) pointed to the so-called "formula quotations" as reflecting a style of exegesis also employed by the sectarians at Qumran. Also Matthew's notion of the church and the organization of church discipline contain certain striking parallels to the organization of the Qumran sect (Davies 1966). The influx of sectarians with their highly articulated and hierarchical model of community structure may have contributed significantly to the emerging notions of the organization of the church in early Christianity.

Essene influence was probably greater on the early development of the Christian church than on the origins of Christianity. Insofar as the Qumran sect was already an established institution by the time the Christian movement came on the scene, the early Christians may have looked to the Essene community as a workable model. The church also had its general assembly, the "whole assembly" of Acts (Acts 6:2, 5), and its special council of the twelve, the intimate followers of Christ. In addition, many aspects of the role and function of the *episkopos* seem to parallel those of the Qumran supervisor. The more or less monarchic pattern of the later Pauline churches, organized under the direction of single leaders, may well have been modeled on the characteristic Essene pattern of a single guardian acting as the director of each individual camp. This pattern was not typical in the ordinary Jewish community structure, which tended to be administered by groups of elders. In addition, the patterns of common life and religious communism found in descriptions of the Jerusalem church in Acts closely mimic the organization of Essene communities. Finally the ideal of celibacy as a way of life was quite foreign to traditional Jewish thinking, so that its place in the Christian value scheme might suggest some adaptation of Essene eschatological asceticism.

Despite the similarities between the Essenes and early Christianity, both movements retain their differentiating characteristics so that there is little danger of confusing or identifying them. Not only do the respective literatures have a distinct character and frame of reference, but none of the cast of characters familiar in the New Testament can be found in the Dead Sea manuscripts. Ritual practices also differed, as, for example, the elaborate custom of ritual purification at Qumran in contrast with the once-and-for-all Christian baptismal rite, explicitly in the name of Jesus Christ. The sacred meals of Qumran served as anticipations of the messianic banquet to come; in contrast, the Eucharistic meals of the Christians were directly connected to the worship of Jesus Christ, the eucharist commemorating his death and celebrating his resurrection. The Jerusalem church was decidedly urban and missionary in its impulse, as opposed to the isolated monastic desert existence observed at Qumran (Vermes 1977). In any case, as Harrington (1982) observes, the decisive difference between the Qumran sect and the early Christian church was the faith in the power of the death and resurrection of Jesus Christ. In the Christian perspective, the process of eschatological realization had been set in motion through the coming of Christ, and the Scriptures had been brought to fulfillment in him.

Qumran and the New Testament

One of the most fascinating areas of Qumran research is in the striking parallels and possible influences of the Qumran literature on the New Testament. The discovery of the Dead Sea scrolls created a new dawn in scriptural studies and cast the whole question of the pre-Christian origins of Christianity in a new light. The traditional emphasis on the Hellenistic background of the New Testament and the early church had to be radically revised in favor of the potential influence of Palestinian Jewish religious traditions and practices. In the light of these recent discoveries, the religious life of pre-Christian Jews in Palestine and the religious literature they developed must be acknowledged as potentially important sources influencing the form and content of the New Testament writings.

Developments in this area have been succinctly summarized by Fitzmyer (1981):

(1) Along with many parallels and influences, the Pauline corpus has interesting parallels to the Qumran literature, particularly Pauline dualisms (light versus darkness, Christ versus Belial), the doctrine of God's righteousness, the rooting of human justification in God's mercy, some of Paul's ideas about angels, and his use of the term *mysterion* ("secret").

Even Paul's teaching about justification through faith may have its antecedents. Possible precedents have been identified in the Essene material at Qumran. A close reading of the Dead Sea Scrolls reveals similarities in the vocabulary of justification used by the Essenes regarding divine justice and apocalyptic endtime. It is entirely possible that Paul was familiar with Essene theology and that some of his ideas bear a close similarity to Essene formulations. He might have come to know their doctrine before his own conversion or during his pharisaic training. Paul, however, says nothing about this connection and it may just be that the similarities are the result of similar sectarian conflicts rather than any direct influence. The Qumran community was itself an apostate and heretical Judaic sect much like Paul and his followers. Nonetheless, the documents of Qumran and the Pauline corpus are the major loci for first-century Jewish theological ideas regarding justification (Segal 1990).

(2) In the Johannine material, there are also dualistic parallels but in a somewhat different fashion than the Pauline texts, as well as the emphasis on divine knowledge and the doctrine of the Spirit. The analogies between the Johannine and Essene theological language has been noted by Eliade (1982):

> The Qumran texts contain a number of specifically Johannine expressions, for example "light of the world" (John 8:12), "sons of light" (John 12:36), "the man who lives by the truth comes out into the light" (John 3:21), "the spirit of truth from the spirit of falsehood" (1 John 4:6). According to the doctrine of the Essenes, the world is the field of battle between two spirits whom God created from the beginning: the Spirit of Truth (called also the Prince of Light and the Angel of Truth) and the Spirit of Wickedness or Perversity; the latter is none other than Belial, the Prince of Darkness, Satan. . . . The Essenian eschatological scenario has been compared to certain Johannine texts. . . . Similarly, the First Epistle of John speaks of "children of God" and "children of the devil" and exhorts believers not to let the devil lead them astray (1 John 3:7-10, 4:1-6). But while the Essenes await the eschatological war, in the Johannine literature, despite the fact that the combat still continues, the crisis has passed, for Jesus Christ has already triumphed over evil (p. 357).

(3) According to the Bultmann interpretation, the christological title "Lord" (in the absolute sense) did not derive from early Palestinian Christian usage, but was borrowed from the Hellenism of the eastern Mediterranean. But the evidence of the scrolls indicates that there was an emerging pattern among pre-Christian Palestinian Jews to refer to God absolutely as "the Lord" in both Hebrew and Aramaic. Thus, the absolute application of the title "Lord" to Christ in the New Testament could well have been an adaptation on the part of Palestinian Christian Jews of an already extant custom of referring to YHWH.

(4) Prior to the Qumran discoveries, the title "Son of God," so ladened with theological import, has never before been identified in any extrabiblical text of pre-Christian Palestine. In view of the Old Testament background for this title, most scholars have shied away from looking for a Hellenistic origin. But the title has now turned up in a Qumran Aramaic text in parallel with "Son of the Most High." The striking similarity to the Lucan infancy narrative (Luke 1:32-35) raises a host of interesting questions about the composition of that narrative.

(5) The passages on divorce in the Dead Sea scrolls make it clear that divorce was prohibited among the Essenes and that one of the forms of fornication designated in these texts was specifically marriage within degrees of kinship forbidden by Leviticus (18:6ff). These texts also support the argument that there was a Palestinian tradition proscribing both polygamy and divorce, and that this usage may well provide the context for the Matthean divorce texts.

(6) A more general aspect of the study of the Scrolls is the light they have shed on the use of the Old Testament in the New Testament. Study of the Qumran material has identified a new literary form, the *pesher,* a type of commentary or *midrash* on the Old Testament. It differs from the classical *midrash* of rabbinical tradition in that it relates the texts of the prophets or psalms to the history or theological beliefs of the sect, applying Old Testament prophecies to current and future events without the ethical expositions or anecdotal explanations of the traditional *midrashim,* and dating for the most part from the latter part of the Qumran period. This usage provides a striking parallel and background for New Testament citations of the Old Testament.

Fitzmyer (1981) summarizes these elements as follows:

> It has been pointed out that, although the Qumran community and the early Christians who produced the New Testament were two types of eschatological communities, both were precisely alike in insisting that they were the Old Testament come alive, the "New Covenant," that they were the true continuity of the People of God. They not only argued this in similar ways, but also based their arguments on authoritative parts of the Old Testament. Both turned back to the exilic period as the rock from which they were hewn; they differed in details and in the passages of the exilic period from which they drew their proofs. Each emphasized certain parts of the Old Testament in its own way. In the Qumran literature, the writers felt that they had been given the key to the understanding of Scripture in the Teacher of Righteousness. Early Christians too argued similarly, insisting that Jesus was the key to the Scriptures. Each community was convinced that its key provided the means to see clearly, through the Scriptures, what God was doing in its day. Each thought of itself as the New Israel, but, admittedly, in a different sense (p. 365).

(7) There are striking similarities in the introductory formulae used to cite Scripture between the Qumran and the New Testament

literature. The similarities between the Qumran usage and the Christian usage are closer than those between Qumran and the mishnaic formulae of the rabbinical tradition. This may simply reflect the later origins of the rabbinical commentaries. The Essene movement remains a silent element in New Testament accounts, possibly because of the isolation of the Essene community in the Judaean desert, but also because the participants in the sect who lived in more populated centers may well have absorbed the pharisaic ideology.

If these connections and their suggestive affiliations have any validity, they may reflect the degree to which the emergent Christian community was active in assimilating conceptual and value orientations from a previously extant and ideologically at least prominent religious community and tradition, transforming these elements as they were absorbed into a new framework articulated around the person and doctrinal direction of Jesus as the charismatic prophet and leader of the Christian sect. It also casts another selective light on the issues confronting the Jesus movement and its evolution into the early Christian community having to do with establishing itself as a separate and independent movement distinct from the Essenes, even though they bore certain similarities. This would have been especially the case insofar as the Essene movement, in addition to the desert communities, involved even larger numbers of adherents who lived in the towns and cities of Judea with whom the early Christians would have been in constant contact and interaction. The challenge to the Christians in accomplishing this work of internal cohesion and transformation of derivative components and increasingly decisive differentiation from associated religious groups such as the Essenes would have called into play the mechanisms of the cultic process as essential constitutive forces.

6

The Cultic Origins of Christianity

Implications for the Cultic Origins of Christianity

It was probably somewhere between A.D. 26–30 that Jesus inaugurated his public ministry. He apparently emerged quickly on the public scene, possibly introduced by events surrounding baptism at the hands of John the Baptist (Matt 3:13-17; Mark 1:9-11; Luke 3:21-22). He quickly gathered a group of disciples and launched his preaching primarily in Galilee, then under the rule of Herod Antipas. Jesus' teaching was a distillation of many elements of contemporary Jewish religious, ethical and eschatological teaching, retaining many of the most basic religious convictions of the Jewish tradition, changing or modifying others, and proclaiming a new path to salvation.

As he gathered disciples and extended his influence, opposition was inevitable. The hostility he encountered from the beginning of his public ministry (Mark 3:6) continued until its climax in Jerusalem (Lohfink 1984). The New Testament reveals a growing pattern of opposition and challenge from more established religious groups, particularly the Pharisees and Sadducees. The oppositional tone is injected from the very beginning of the public ministry. Matthew recounts John's preaching:

> But when he saw many of the Pharisees and Sadducees coming for baptism, he said to them, "You brood of vipers! Who warned you to flee from the wrath to come? Bear fruit that benefits repentance,

and do not presume to say to yourselves, 'We have Abraham as our father'; for I tell you, God is able from these stones to raise up children to Abraham. Even now the axe is laid to the root of the trees; every tree therefore that does not bear good fruit is cut down and thrown into the fire. I baptize you with water for repentance, but he who is coming after me is mightier than I, whose sandals I am not worthy to carry; he will baptize you with the Holy Spirit and with fire. His winnowing fork is in his hand, and he will clear his threshing floor and gather his wheat into the granary, but the chaff he will burn with unquenchable fire" (Matt 3:7-12).

And from Jesus' lips, "For I tell you, unless your righteousness exceeds that of the scribes and Pharisees, you will never enter the kingdom of heaven" (Matt 5:20). It is not clear whether this opposition reflects the state of things in Jesus' lifetime, or whether the derivative context is rather the growing tension and alienation between proto-Christian communities and the parent Jewish religious tradition, particularly post-destruction Jamnian pharisaism that came to dominate Jewish religious interests in late first and second centuries. The hope for the Christian future lay in the direction of the Hellenistic world of the empire, and increasingly away from Palestine and Judaism.[1]

One of the dominant themes permeating the gospel accounts and reflecting some of the most primitive layers of the gospel material is the notion that Jesus was God's special envoy who was rejected by Israel and that those who follow him must expect to experience persecution in much the same manner (de Jonge 1991). The earliest expression is in Paul referring to the Judean persecution:

For you, my brothers, have been like the churches of God in Christ Jesus which are in Judaea, in suffering the same treatment from your own countrymen as they have suffered from the Jews, the people who put the Lord Jesus to death, and the prophets too. And now they have been persecuting us, and acting in a way that cannot please God and makes them the enemies of the whole human race, because they are hindering us from preaching to the pagans and trying to save them (1 Thess 2:14-16).

---

[1] One of the difficulties in this sort of historical reconstruction is the lack of direct evidence concerning the real events in the life and works of Jesus. The evidence we have has all been filtered through the gospel accounts reflecting the selectivity and retrospective distortion of the oral tradition and the primitive sources, and written with an apologetic and theologizing mind set reflecting concrete vicissitudes of the particular Christian communities to whom they were addressed. Beyond the historic (*geschichtlich*) figure of Christ stands the real historical (*historisch*) Jesus whose real words and works we cannot know. See Meier (1990) and de Jonge (1991).

Similar sentiments are found in Q and Mark, among the earliest sources. A Q-passage in Luke links the persecution and killing of the prophets with the judgment against the Jews (Luke 11:49-51), and among the prophets rejected by the current generation were John the Baptist and Jesus (Luke 7:31-35). Mark (12:1-9) provides the parable of the vineyard in which a series of messengers are beaten and killed by the laborers, until the final envoy is sent, the owner's son. But he too is rejected and killed.

Thus in the earliest strata of the tradition the persecution of the Jesus' followers mirrors earlier persecutions of the prophets.[2] As de Jonge (1991) comments: "Jesus was met with unbelief and rejection, as were his disciples. John the Baptist, another messenger of God who came immediately before Jesus and was directly linked with him, had been murdered. It is extremely likely that not only Jesus' followers but also Jesus himself viewed John's fate, the opposition they faced, and the possibility of violent death for themselves, in the light of those passages from Scripture that denounced Israel's violent rejection of messengers sent by God" (p. 37). The pattern of opposition and rejection is a direct expression of the cultic process in action. The efforts of Jesus and his disciples to establish a new religious perspective are met by counterforces from more established groups—in the gospel accounts it is specifically the Sadducees and Pharisees who fill this role—creating a definitive us-vs.-them context of oppositional interaction.

Opposition of the Scribes and Pharisees

The pattern of opposition reached a crescendo in the final journey to Jerusalem, where the messianic elements of Jesus' mission received their most forthright and explicit expression. The preaching of this new approach to the Jewish religion posed a decided threat to those in power, particularly the Sanhedrin, who saw themselves as protectors of traditional religious worship. The story of the final conspiracy of the Pharisees and Sadducees, leaders of the Sanhedrin, and the subsequent crucifixion by the Roman authorities is well known.

The tenor of Jesus' preaching and particularly the setting of his doctrine in opposition to existing religious approaches is consistent with and forms a typical expression of the cultic process and his role as cult leader. These aspects come into clear focus in the diatribes against the scribes and Pharisees recorded in the Synoptic Gospels (Borg 1987). These discourses were probably gathered and composed out of disparate sources and fragmented elements of a basic kerygma characteristic of the whole of Jesus' ministry, and even of the later preaching of

---

[2] The same theme is found in Luke 6:22-23; Matt 5:11-12; Acts 7:51-53.

the primitive church, rather than being concentrated at a particular point in time in the context of the Jerusalem ministry. In Luke, for example, the discourse against the Pharisees is introduced by the discussion of the "sign of Jonah" (11:29-32)—the generation to which Jesus preaches is an evil generation that seeks a sign but shall not be given one. The only sign it shall receive is the sign of Jonah, for as Jonah became a sign to the men of Nineveh, so the Son of Man will become a sign to this generation.

This is followed by an attack on the Pharisees and scribes (Luke 11:37-54): externally they practice cleanliness and purity, but within they are full of extortion and wickedness. They observe and demand observance of the minutiae of the Law, but neglect justice and charity. They burden men with legalistic demands, but they persecute and kill the prophets. Jesus' watchword to his disciples was "Be on your guard against the yeast of the Pharisees—that is, their hypocrisy" (Luke 12:1). Little wonder that Luke records: "When he left the house, the scribes and the Pharisees began a furious attack on him and tried to force answers from him on innumerable questions, setting traps to catch him out in something he might say" (11:53-54).

In Mark, the messianic overtones of Jesus' entry into Jerusalem are unmistakable: "Blessings on the coming kingdom of our father David! Hosannah in the highest heavens!" (11:10). The motif of opposition and rejection by the leaders of Israel is stated from the beginning. The curse that he places on the fig tree (11:12-14) expresses the sense of alienation between Jesus' religious mission and the religious establishment. The confrontation reaches a violent outburst as Jesus enters the temple precincts, drives out the vendors and money changers, proclaiming not only that it is his house but that it should be a house of prayer, while the priests who control the Temple have turned it into a den of robbers. Mark comments: "This came to the ears of the chief priests and the scribes, and they tried to find some way of doing away with him; they were afraid of him because the people were carried away by his teaching" (11:18).[3] It was, in effect, an indictment of the priests and pharisees, as well as a challenge to their power and position (Borg 1987).

The chief priests, scribes, and elders confronted him, demanding to know by what authority he acted. In Mark's account, Jesus answers by

---

[3] Horsley (1989) calls attention to the tendency of modern biblical scholarship to play down the conflict between the Jesus movement and ruling institutions: "As long as the Temple and high priesthood are viewed as only religious and Jesus' action in the Temple, for example, understood as a 'cleansing' or, at most, an attack on certain 'abuses,' it is possible to avoid serious implications of substantive social-structural conflict" (pp. 130–1).

confronting them with a dilemma: "John's baptism: did it come from heaven, or from man?" (Mark 11:30). They would either have to admit their own failure to recognize and accept John's preaching, or would have to face the wrath of the people who regarded John as a real prophet. The following parable of the vineyard (Mark 12:1-12) allegorically connects rejection of the prophets with the forthcoming murder of Jesus. Mark adds: "And they would have liked to arrest him, because they realized that the parable was aimed at them, but they were afraid of the crowds. So they left him alone and went away" (12:12).

The following episodes clearly reflect the continuing theme of opposition and attempts on the part of the authorities to trap Christ into some self-condemning position. The confrontation by Pharisees and Herodeans regarding payment of the census tax to the emperor (Mark 12:13-17) reflects the background of subjection to Rome and the resentment of the Jews in having to pay in silver coins bearing the emperor's image. Confrontation by the Sadducees on the question of the resurrection (12:18-27) reflects Sadducean rejection of the oral Torah and beliefs in immortality and resurrection. Jesus' answer again confounds the religious leaders and avoids the trap. The idea that after death men will share in the beatitude of the angels was not a universal Jewish doctrine, but is found in the Qumran scrolls. Even in the discussion of the Messiah as son of David, Jesus' preaching places him in opposition to the traditional Jewish view of the Messiah as descended from David. The implication is that the messiah is not merely a son of David but something more exalted, more transcendent in origin, than even David himself. The title "Lord" with which David addresses his supposed son is one that is otherwise reserved for reference to YHWH himself.

Mark finishes this section with the condemnation of the pharisaic leaders echoing the condemnation in Luke and probably from the same source: "Beware of the scribes, who like to walk about in long robes, to be greeted obsequiously in the market squares, to take the front seats in the synagogues and the places of honor at banquets; these are the men who swallow the property of widows, while making a show of lengthy prayers. The more severe will be the sentence they receive" (Mark 12:38-40).

In Matthew, perhaps the most Jewish of the Gospels, the same events are recounted with relatively the same emphases, but with addition of the discourse, or better invective, against the scribes and Pharisees, summarizing and synthesizing elements of Jesus' attack upon established Jewish religion. A major emphasis in the Matthean redaction of the gospel account is the identification of Christ as the fulfillment of the messianic expectation of the Jewish people. The diatribe against this sectarian opposition rises to an apogee in the twenty-third chapter of

Matthew, which serves not only as a diatribe against the religious teaching and practice of the scribes and Pharisees, but also makes it clear that the messianic kingdom Jesus propounds is not at all congruent with pharisaic expectations. It is difficult to know how much of this text came from the teaching of Jesus himself and how much reflects later struggles of the Jewish Christian community in Jerusalem in the face of persecution by Jewish authorities.

Matthew's Gospel was written for a community of predominantly Jewish-Christian converts who joined the nascent Christian church in the wake of the terrible destruction of the temple in A.D. 70. The most significant development in post-war Judaism was establishment of Jamnian pharisaism. The central problem for the Matthean community was how to relate to these current developments within Judaism. The reorganization of the pharisaic movement under Johannan ben Zakkai was to assume exclusive authority setting up the Jamnia assembly as the replacement for the Great Sanhedrin of Jerusalem. While the shift took several centuries to accomplish, in time these Pharisees took measures to control and discredit the traditionally powerful priesthood of the Sadducees and to gain control of the calendar and associated religious observance of the Law. Gradually they assumed authority over liturgical functions, transferred parts of the temple ritual to the synagogues, and legislated regulation of gifts and offerings. Interpretations of the Law were gradually codified, and measures instituted to bring about unification of synagogue worship by standardizing traditional services. More to the point, as this reform movement gradually took shape within pharisaism, it moved increasingly to confront and deal with the threat posed by the rising significance of the Christian sect.

These changes in Judaism had profound implications for the Christian community. Their sense of religious conviction and identity had been rooted in their Jewish origins, but as Jamnian pharisaism grew in power and influence, it forced upon them questions and doubts about their connection with Judaism and their own sense of religious attachment. The issues focused on questions regarding their place as a sect within Judaism, the nature of their connection with and mission to the Jews, and problems relevant to observance of the Law. Matthew wrote his Gospel in an attempt to establish and consolidate a sense of Christian identity in the face of these changing influences. Matthew's answer was that his community was no longer a sectarian subdivision within Judaism, but an independent religious movement, still Jewish, but separate from the Jamnian Pharisees and drawing its inspiration from Jesus Christ. He accomplished this by portraying Jesus as the expected Messiah whose message and mission was in opposition to the scribes and Pharisees. In the recurrent debates between Jesus and the

Pharisees, Matthew's readers could readily recognize the contemporary context (LaVerdiere and Thompson 1976).

The Matthean polemic (Matt 23) and other texts make it clear that the antipathy against the temple, the high priests, and against the Pharisees and their lawyers, was marked and strong—members of the Jesus movement did not acknowledge the authority of these establishment figures. The indictments in the Q source material and the Marcan pronouncement stories are more pointed, declaring judgment on the scribes and Pharisees. These texts speak with the voice of an oppressed people, proclaiming against the extortion and greed of their leaders, who tax and tithe them into destitution. They have become blind guides who ignore matters of justice and charity and lay intolerable burdens on the people (Horsley 1989).

The Cultic Process

We can conclude that elements of the cultic process played their meaningful part in the origins of Christianity. The Christian movement arose out of a situation of social, cultural and economic distress in which contending forces had created a political and religious crisis. Palestine lived under the conquering heel of Rome. Contending cultural forces brought with them progressive Hellenization and undermining of traditional values. The outcome was a religious crisis marked by decline in traditional religious convictions and heightened cultic adherence.

The different extant religious movements struggled to find their respective viable solutions to these contending elements. The response of the Sadducees was essentially conservative, falling back on traditional religion, particularly on the elements of privilege and status they claimed as the aristocratic and priestly class. The Pharisees would reflect a more achievement-oriented movement more open to external influences but holding somewhat rigidly to prerequisites of knowledge and observance of the Law. To a certain degree both of these sects represent movements that accepted the current situation, each in its way tried to find an adaptive path that would preserve the traditional religion without overly compromising with or capitulating to the onslaught of Roman and Hellenizing influences.

The Zealots seem to have occupied the opposite end of the spectrum. Theirs was a position of no compromise, of violent rebellion and revolutionary confrontation. Their reaction probably represents one course of response in the middle and lower strata of Jewish society. The other significant group, the Essenes, reflect similar social influences, but chose the path of withdrawal and quietistic reflection. Nonetheless, Essenes and Zealots must have had some aspects of their religious orientation in common, if only in terms of their common enemy, the hated Romans or *"Kittim."* It would not be surprising, then, that the Romans would raze the Qumran settlement, and that subsequently some of the survivors of the Qumran holocaust would have fled south and made common cause with the Zealots at Masada.

The Christian movement followed a quite distinct and different path. As a movement, it was both accommodative and revolutionary. It assimilated elements from extant religious currents, as the early Christian kerygma is reflected in the gospel accounts. But it placed itself decisively and confrontationally in opposition to established religious authorities. The Gospel reconstructs a story of gradual and increasing opposition between the new prophet and his followers on one side, and the chief priests, Pharisees and scribes on the other. The extent to which this opposition reflects pre-existing currents of opposition between Essene and Zealot factions and aristocratic and priestly classes whose sympathies and political destiny were tied to the hated Romans, is a matter of conjecture. Certainly Christian attitudes, even those placed in the mouth of Jesus, were in sympathy with what we know of Essene and Zealot views. The unanswered question is whether the movement inaugurated by Jesus was one of social and political protest, even rebellion, in addition to its call to repentance and redemption.

This fundamental conflict continued to play itself out in the subsequent history of early Christianity. The death of Christ was followed, according to the record of Acts,[4] by confrontations between the apostles and the Jewish authorities, and even further by outright persecution. The challenge to Rome and the record of persecution and martyrdom that followed was a later story, but only extended the process that had marked the origins of Christianity from the beginning.

At the same time, the Jesus movement had to articulate its own ideology and program for response to and redemption of the powerful forces awash in Palestine of the first century. Horsley (1989) comments on the social and psychological role of the Jesus movement:

> It seems impossible to separate analysis of the Jesus movement's characteristics and activities in Jewish Palestine from that of the conditions of and for its emergence. Many of the features of the Jesus movement are also aspects of how the movement was interacting with and affecting the society which it was apparently at-

---

[4] It is worth mentioning that Acts cannot be taken unequivocally as verifiable history, since it was written within the context of the struggles of the Christian church to establish itself and addressed the needs of a specific Christian community. The purposes of its author were, in addition to recording the facts and deeds of the early church, at the same time propagandizing and theologizing in some degree.

tempting to "renew." Thus, in response to illness, self-blame, and possession by alien spiritual forces, for example, the Jesus movement continued the healing, forgiveness of sin, and exorcism initiated by Jesus. In attempting to deal with the heavy indebtedness, poverty, and despair that plagued many of the people, the Jesus movement advocated mutual forgiveness of debts, socio-economic cooperation, and other forms of reciprocity in local communities. In reaction to the disintegration of local village communities and the decline of patriarchal authority, the Jesus movement apparently revitalized local life in terms of egalitarian nonpatriarchal familial communities. In response to despair over declining and disintegrating conditions of life, finally, the Jesus movement appears to have generated a renewal of individual and group spirits, one that could motivate some of the other aspects of the revitalization of social life (pp. 127–28).

As Theissen (1982) has commented, Christianity was basically a messianic-chiliastic or millennarian movement. It shared the characteristics common to such movements, e.g., expectation that the end of the world was to come soon, unfulfilled hopes of a *parousia* in which the present order would be overthrown and replaced by an idealized and utopian existence, belief in miraculous and ecstatic phenomena, and exaltation of messianic prophets and leaders. He concluded: "Thus, messianic-chiliastic movements are frequently reactions of an oppressed people to a politically imposed foreign culture in which the injured sense of self-esteem within the dominated culture seeks to assert itself" (p. 194). The charismatic prophet on whom these hopes hinged was Jesus, the promised Messiah. His role in the Christian community paralleled the function of the Teacher of Righteousness in the Qumran community, and like the Qumran community, the Christian movement responded to death of the messianic leader by emphasizing eschatological rewards. When faced with death of the prophet and disappointment of hopes for the imminent coming of the kingdom, the cult did not wither and die, but renewed its hope in the resurrection and threw itself into proselytizing and conversion of the multitudes. Particularly important in the coherence of the church in the face of these vicissitudes was the sense of inner community and adherence to belief in the mission of Jesus, and the pressures toward a joining of ranks in the face of common enemies—the Jews, the world, and the power of Rome.

Psychodynamic Roots

Behind the swirl of historical and cultural events, powerful psychological forces were at work playing themselves out in conflictual and oppositional terms leading to Christ's crucifixion and exploding in the next generation into religio-political revolution and the second destruction of the Temple and Jerusalem. I would argue that such patterns of conflict, opposition, and rebellion are undergirded psychologically by the paranoid process (Meissner 1978b).[5] External events and psychological forces come into convergence to create the dynamic of historical process. Persecution and domination, at first by the Seleucids and later the Romans, imposed a pattern of victimization and narcissistic assault on the Jewish community and called into play restitutive mechanisms. Actual victimization and degradation impinges on the inner sense of victimhood and narcissistic inferiority built into individual introjective configurations that contribute significantly to the individual's sense of self and identity, particularly in this instance as members of the people of God, chosen by God as the vehicle of the messianic restitution, bearers of great religious tradition with its inherent beliefs and values, but continually ground into the dust under the conquering heel of those who destroy not only the fabric of social and economic life but destroy the very religious institutions that have provided the essentials of Jewish life and identity. This external reinforcement of inner psychological patterns elicits a paranoid response through which destructive hostility and powerful superiority are projected onto the oppressive enemy. The reality is compounded by the projective elaboration and the enemy becomes more than an attacker and oppressor; he becomes a hated and feared paranoid object.

This dimension of the process serves to reinforce the intrapsychic sense of victimhood and oppression. But restitutive mechanisms are summoned to action to reverse and overcome the dire inner state. Aggressive and destructive capacities are mobilized to turn the psychic tables and make the powerful and feared enemy the victim. The capacity to translate this dynamic into effective rebellious action confirms the intrapsychic gain. Paranoid fears are countered by the destruction of the paranoid objects. In the case of Christianity, there were also called into play a series of defensive reactions modulating and displacing the intensity and potential destructiveness of these underlying dynamics and converting them into an ethic of universal love—especially love of one's enemies. These intersecting forces, creating a situation of considerable ambiguity and ambivalence, left the Christian community pulled in conflicting directions eventuating in polarizations and further splintering of the faithful.

---

[5] See the discussion of the paranoid process and its relation to the cultic process in chapters 1 and 2 above.

Narcissistic dynamics were played out in a similar fashion. Narcissistic defeat and degradation are countered by mechanisms of narcissistic enhancement and restitution. This most frequently takes the form of the genesis of a revolutionary ideal or utopian vision of the shape of reality—political, social, cultural, or religious—to be triumphantly realized after the oppressor has been destroyed. The Essene mythology dictated defeat and destruction of the hated Romans and establishment of an eschatological kingdom. The Essene ideology tended to be primarily conversionist (Wilson 1959), much like the Christian, but took on an adventist coloration in terms of the ultimate eschatological confrontation in which God brings victory to the sons of light. The Zealots likewise looked forward to a glorious reign of the victorious Messiah, but their ideology was more forthrightly adventist in their espousal of armed struggle and revolution as the royal road to the new kingdom. These idealized and utopian belief systems served to salvage the narcissistic disillusionment imposed by Roman domination and the desecration of sacred Jewish beliefs and institutions. Such beliefs take the form of paranoid constructions that offer a sustaining context for concrete projections and lend a sense of purposeful belonging and inspiration.

The inevitable outcome of these processes is the generation of groupings based on the opposition of those who are with us against those who are against us, of those who belong to the group against those who are its enemies, of those who embrace the ideals and objectives of the group against those who oppose them. Truth and right exist within the group; falsehood, evil and deceit are located in the outgroup. Thus lines of opposition are drawn and enemy faces enemy. On both sides of the line paranoid processes are at work reinforcing differences and increasing the titration of hatred and fear. And unfortunately, as in all such situations, hatred begets hatred, fear begets fear, paranoia begets paranoia.

Behind the currents of opposition and conflict endemic to the Palestinian context at the time of the origins of the Christian movement, these paranoid mechanisms were brought into play and wove themselves into the emerging pattern of events. Christianity emerged as a Palestinian messianic cult whose driving psychological power drew its strength from these intrapsychic processes. Whatever else it may have been or done, early Palestinian Christianity provided a myth, a messianic vision, and a sense of purposeful belonging and mission answering to the deep psychological needs of many, particularly those who were dispossessed, oppressed, and victimized by the dire political realities of the time.

In conclusion, whatever its divine inspiration and impetus, Christianity can be understood as a religious movement that arose in a specific political, cultural and religious context, and served as the distillation and channel of expression of decisive social and psychological forces that gave it impetus as a religious innovation. These dynamic forces are elements that express aspects of the cultic process and derive their power to move, convert and convince from powerful psychodynamic motivations that undergird and complement the cult dynamics.

SECTION III

Early Christianity

7

Cultic Elements in Early Christianity

Introduction

In previous chapters, we have defined some of the contending forces in the political, cultural and religious background in pre-Christian Palestine that formed the context for the prophetic mission of Christ. The Christian movement, as it emerged out of that background, assimilated in varying degrees important dimensions of the extant religious traditions. Certainly, the influence of Jewish Palestinian traditions came into play most intensely in the emergence of the early Jerusalem church, and also came to bear on Paul and his mission to the Gentiles. However, as the influence of the church grew and extended itself slowly through the Mediterranean world, it came increasingly into contact with and fell under the influence of Hellenizing influences representing powerful cultural currents in the Roman Empire.

Traditional Jewish religion was under constant threat from tendencies toward cultural assimilation from superior and alien cultures crowding the borders of Palestine and penetrating the core of Palestinian society. The Essenes and Pharisees emerged from the struggle with Hellenizing influences and the efforts of the Ptolemies and Seleucids to turn Judea into a Greek enclave and Jerusalem into a city-state. Resistance in the first century A.D. was against the foreign and Hellenizing influence of the Roman occupation, a clash of two cultures, "one of which reacts to the claims of the other with ethnocentric attitudes, whether of antisemitism or xenophobia" (Theissen 1978, p. 87).

Sectarian Tendencies

These contending forces did not find peaceful resolution within the Christian inspiration, but continued to exercise a conflictual and divisive influence. The story of the interplay of these contending forces, and their effects on various groups within the early church, provides an additional context for the study of the influence of the cultic process in the emerging patterns of church organization and doctrine, and in drawing lines between orthodoxy and heterodoxy.

In addition, the prophetic mission of Christ entered the existing world of traditional religious structures as one of a number of challenging new forces, setting itself in opposition to existing religious groups and challenging them in almost revolutionary fashion. Efforts on the part of postdestruction rabbinical Judaism to establish norms of the Law and consolidate the boundaries of belonging to the faith of the Fathers led to increasing delineation and extrusion of deviant groups. Various renewal groups, including the Christians, were pressured to the periphery and beyond of Judaism. In this connection, the Pharisee Saul played his role as one of the persecutors of the Jesus movement.

Consequently, as Christianity entered the Jewish Palestinian religious world, it was seen as a threat to be defended against and crushed. Persecution was not slow to follow, as the accounts of Acts and Paul's epistles make clear. As the mission to the Gentiles spread the teachings of Christianity to the rest of the Mediterranean world, the seeds of persecution were spread as well. In large measure, Christianity set itself up in conflictual opposition to the world it sought to influence and convert. In this sense, the adherents of Christianity proposed themselves as the true believers, bearers of the only true religious inspiration and belief, centered on their conviction that the death and resurrection of Jesus Christ proclaiming him to be the Son of God. The epistles attributed to Paul, reflecting the dynamics of the cultic process, are larded with in-group terms to designate the members and consolidate their sense of community and correspondingly distinguish them from nonbelievers. As Meeks (1983) observes:

> Repetitive use of such special terms for the group and its members plays a role in the process of resocialization by which an individual's identity is revised and knit together with the identity of the group, especially when it is accompanied by special terms also for "the outsiders," "the world." By this kind of talk members are taught to conceive of only two classes of humanity: the sect and the outsiders. To the extent that this process is effective, each should think of himself in every activity in terms of the new typification: "I am a believer" or "I am in Christ." Stigmatization by outsiders in

the same or equivalent terms—"He is a Christian"—but with hostile connotations reinforces the self-stigmatization. . . . Especially striking is the language that speaks of the members of the Pauline groups as if they were a family. They are children of God and also of the apostle. They are brothers and sisters; they refer to one another as "beloved" (pp. 85–86).

In the second century and after, persecution followed on the refusal of Christians to observe the imperial cult. In these centuries, Christianity was regarded as a *religio illicita*, a secret cult with no official standing or recognition. Septimus Severus published the first decree against the Christians in A.D. 202; finally Decius decreed that all citizens were required to sacrifice to the gods. The Christian refusal was predictable. The subsequent persecution was severe and led to many defections. The last of the Roman persecutions came in A.D. 303–5 under Diocletian, largely motivated by his wish to strengthen imperial authority. For such purposes, an identifiable enemy is always helpful. As Eliade (1982) comments: "For the authorities, Christianity was not only clearly guilty of atheism and *lèse-majesté*, it was suspected of all kinds of crimes, from orgies and incest to infanticide and cannibalism. For the pagan elite, the essence of Christian theology—the incarnation of the Savior, his sufferings and resurrection—was highly unintelligible. In any case, the fanatical intransigence of this new religion of salvation made any hope of peaceful coexistence with the polytheistic religions illusory" (p. 367). Paul himself was not slow to recognize this barrier to communication of the Christian ideology to the surrounding world— "to the Jews a stumbling-block, to the Greeks foolishness" (1 Cor 1:24).

The sectarian aspect of the early Christian movement has been delineated, particularly on the basis of its emergence out of an agrarian protest movement, its rejection of establishment claims (whether they be claims of family origin, religious status, wealth, or theological doctrine), on its egalitarian structure, on its fostering of the qualities of special love and acceptance within the ingroup of sect adherents, on the fact that it was voluntary in organization, that it demanded total commitment from its members, and on the apocalyptic emphasis of its doctrine. The oppositional dimension of the Christian sect emphasized that salvation was to be found only in the church, while the pagans and nonbelievers, who did not accept the divine character and salvific mission of Christ, were doomed. They were not only the enemies of sect adherents, but they had set themselves against God's salvific purposes.

Certainly the Judaic heritage was a salient element—the exclusivity of Jewish monotheism had been a powerful component of the Jewish sense of themselves as the chosen people. The adherents of the Jesus movement had grown up with this conviction as a significant part of their religious orientation. It served to articulate their difference from outsiders and to consolidate a sense of unity within. The new Christian sect departed from this view to the extent that in the new dispensation Jew and Gentile alike were included in the people of God. The emerging sense of Christian identity was also consolidated around the belief in a privileged revelation made only to believers. This was also part of the Jewish heritage, perhaps compounded by later Gnostic elements, related to the Jewish apocalyptic tradition. In apocalyptic, the secret revelation is given to a chosen figure and through him to the faithful. Belief in this privileged revelation increased the boundaries between believing members and nonmembers (Meeks 1983).

The dialectic of in-group–out-group tensions continued to play themselves out as Christianity evolved and gradually separated itself from its Judaic roots. The question remains as to what influences allowed this process to continue and progress, and what inherent needs in the social fabric was this new development responding to that made it possible. Theissen (1978) argues that a central problem was the need to deal with the aggressive forces unleashed by the processes of schismatic division and the resulting social tensions. The Jesus movement capitalized on these factors by providing the means for containing and overcoming this aggression. But we can add that restitutive narcissistic processes played a central role as well.

Social Defenses

The Jesus movement fashioned several devices—patterns of social defense—that served to buffer and transform aggression. First was the capacity to compensate for aggression by reaction formations. The commandment to love one's enemies was given primacy of place—"You have learnt how it was said: you must love your neighbor and hate your enemy. But I say this to you: love your enemies and pray for those who persecute you" (Matt 5:43-44). One might guess that this saying was articulated in a context of ongoing persecution of the early church, but the injunction against aggression, particularly counter-aggression against one's enemies, is clear. The motive of vengeance was proscribed. The need for the defense tells us that the aggressive impulses were by no means dispelled; to the extent that the defense was effective in muting the expression of aggressive impulses, we would expect that they would find some alternate route of expression.

The second line of defense was a combination of displacement and projection. Displacement allowed the aggression to be directed against substitute objects. Aggression against the hated and feared Romans could be displaced to the demons, another class of occupying powers that tormented and oppressed their victims. Those who suffered persecution in the Jesus movement could call upon the forces of eschatological justice to wreak vengeance on their persecutors. When Christ returned in his messianic glory, he would right all wrongs and punish all evildoers. As Theissen says, "By identifying themselves with the Son of man they could project their aggression into an eschatological future and delegate the performance of aggressive actions to the Son of man. . . ." (p. 101).

Another device was the reversal of aggression against the aggressor, not as physical aggression but as a moral reproach and an unspoken appeal to forego the aggressive wish. Aggression is introjected in the form of superego derivatives calling for repentance and the observance of moral norms. Rebelliousness against the Romans was transformed into guilt for one's own rebelliousness and hate, into a form of rebelliousness against the self. Theissen argues, consistent with the cultic process, that the intensification of norms, intended to preserve the nation from assimilation by alien cultures, produced schisms involving the release of aggression against those who did not submit to the accentuated norms of the in-group. The fragmentation into mutually repudiating groups left none with a clear claim to the truth and all with a sense of failure and guilt in the face of divine judgment.

The traditional "eye for an eye" was replaced by the injunction to turn the other cheek. The purpose was to divert aggression and create the conditions for inhibition of aggressive impulses. This is the ethic of nonviolent resistance that Ghandi made a political force in our own time—the appeal to the oppressor by the renunciation of self-defense. As Theissen (1978) observes:

> Of course this appeal comprises a sublimated form of aggression, namely a reproach based on the fact that the other will accept it of his own free will—without compulsion. The hope is that part of his aggression will be directed inwards, so that new aggressive actions call forth shame and an awareness of guilt. We also find this method of dealing with aggression in the symbols of christology. The execution of Jesus was a repressive measure carried out by the Romans. But it did not call forth any rebelliousness against the Romans within the Jesus movement. They accepted defeat. The cross became the sign of salvation. It was a revelation, not of Roman guilt but of their own: Jesus had to die for our sins. The failed Messiah became the bringer of salvation (pp. 107–8).

The failure of messianic expectations became the foundation for a new belief. The impotence of Judaic belief in the face of Roman power was transformed into a system of religious symbolism in terms of which the defenseless victims created an appeal to which the powerful victors and victimizers had ultimately to yield.

The institution of the scapegoat has a long and honorable position in the history of religion (Girard 1979, 1986), serving as a symbolic vehicle for relieving guilt, aggressive conflicts and intragroup tensions. In the Jesus movement, the scapegoat was elevated to a central role that became the touchstone of Christian faith. The unconscious dynamic of the scapegoat is made the explicit focus of christological symbolism. The innocent Lamb of God—the *Agnus Dei*—was led to the sacrificial slaughter to atone for the sins of mankind. The scapegoat takes upon himself the aggressive conflicts of the group, both in its aggressive wishes and impulses and in its conflictual self-directed aggression of guilt and shame. As Theissen (1978) comments: "A good deal of aggression could be transformed into criticism of riches and possessions, Pharisees and priests, temple and tabus, and thus be made to serve the new vision. A good deal of aggression was diverted, transferred, projected, transformed, and symbolized. It was this way of dealing with aggression that made room for the new vision of love and reconciliation at whose centre stood the new commandment to love one's enemy" (p. 110). But, with reference to the cultic process, one has to have an enemy to love.

As the mission to the Gentiles evolved and as the Pauline churches became established, the picture became more complex. On one hand the churches retained the qualities of an eschatological sect with a strong sense of in-group–out-group boundaries. But at the same time their mission called them to a more open stance, seeking adaptation to the outside world and encouraging the flow of converts to their message. Yet the spirit remained sectarian. As Harrington (1982) observes:

> This was an inherently unstable combination, though an enormously creative one. The boundaries between the Pauline churches and the society around them were defined by special language emphasizing separation (the chosen, brothers and sisters, the saints, etc.), rules, the penalty of exclusion from common meals, the creation of autonomous institutions to serve the members, and sanctioned interactions with the society at large (p. 158).

The expressions of the cultic process in the further evolution of Christianity led through a progression of steps leading gradually toward a unified and relatively integrated church structure. The cultic process reflected the interplay of a variety of social and psychological forces, as well as complex economic and cultural processes that played their respective roles in shaping and directing the patterns of religious experience within the church. Part of this process concerned delimitation of the boundaries of orthodoxy, particularly through the operation of identifiable mechanisms that gradually defined and segregated different heretical groups and constellations of belief.

The Historical Context

The evolution of the early Christian church in the first two centuries after the death of Christ was set against the background of the post-resurrection events and the destruction of Jerusalem and the Temple in A.D. 70. After the events of the passion, death and resurrection, and following the Pentecostal experience, the early Christian community set out on a path of active proselytizing. Early success in converting Palestinian Jews, as recorded in Acts, was followed by gradual enlargement of the scope of missionary activity and extension of the influence of the new religion to the major metropolitan centers of the then Roman Empire. These proselytizing activities were directed first to the Jews of the diaspora, and with gradually increasing intensity to their Gentile neighbors.

As for the fate of the Christian church in all this turmoil, little is known for certain. By the second Judean revolt, the break between the synagogue and the church had already taken place in more or less definitive fashion. The Jerusalem church was presided over by Simeon, possibly identified with Simon the "brother" of Jesus (Mark 6:3; Matt 13:55) or Jude, the third bishop of Jerusalem, as another of the "brothers" of Jesus, who was martyred in A.D. 107. The lot of the church was largely one of persecution and martyrdom. Certainly, the proselytizing activity of the early church seems to have been carried on actively, not only in Jerusalem and Judea, but throughout the diaspora.

Sociological Factors

The pattern of structural and doctrinal evolution characterizing the growth of the Christian movement did not take place in a vacuum, but reflected the complex interplay of a variety of social, economic, cultural and psychological forces. The present discussion will aim at bringing into focus certain of these elements as a vehicle for understanding something about the underlying psychological processes. There is no attempt here to be exhaustive or definitive in specifying the nature and variety of these issues.

The view of early Christianity as basically a lower-to-middle class movement has prevailed for some years, based on the writing of the New Testament in colloquial Greek, reflecting the popular origins and nonliterary character of the early Christian inspiration. Other data from papyri and ostraca have supported a somewhat romanticized view of Christianity as a popular movement directed to and reflecting the deepest desires of the common man. This approach has been challenged by Theissen (1982) who points to the role of professional language in the New Testament documents, suggesting that at least some of the writers must have come from a higher social stratum than that suggested by a more vernacular style. Indeed, the evidence indicates that Christian communities in a variety of urban centers included contributions from relatively well-to-do church members. If Corinth can be taken as typical, the Christian communities were dominated by a socially prestigious group, in addition to a broader lower class constituency. This probably also applies to the recipients of Paul's preaching.

There is good evidence, therefore, of a significant degree of social heterogeneity in the composition of the early churches. These social stratifications necessarily had implications for the shaping of emerging Christianity. The economic background in Palestine contributed to political instability and the rise of radical religious movements. Religiously inspired forms of socially divergent behavior tend to arise in contexts of economic and social pressure. Thus the Essenes would take in those who were refugees from a weary life. The Zealots revolted against the levying of Roman taxes and the exacting of debts. Even the Christian movement included a radical critique of worldly wealth and possessions. But such social and economic pressures were not burdens only to the poor. They affected all social strata, the upper classes at times even more severely. The ranks of even the primitive Christian itinerant preachers included representatives of the better classes: the father of James and John had men working for him.

Early Catholicism

The expansion of the church's mission to the Gentile world was simultaneously a transformation of the church from a rural to an urban movement. Paul's world was centered in the great cities of the empire, not in the smaller rural towns. His mission required resources—money for ship passage, for living in the city. One could not simply help oneself or pluck grains of corn from a neighboring field. He and his followers had to rely on the resources of existing congregations, particularly members who enjoyed means and privilege. They had to appeal to people of a different culture and different traditions. The model already extant in the culture was that of the Cynic philosopher, a man of wisdom who accepted no money for his wisdom. Paul deliberately exploited this model, calling his competitors sophists, avaricious imposters, from whom he sought to distinguish himself and his mission (2 Cor 10–13). Thus, Paul's departure from the model and practice of the itinerant charismatics is deliberate and calculated as a means for enhancing the effectiveness of his mission in a new social, economic, and cultural context.

Clearly Paul's mission to the Gentiles created tension and conflict with the itinerant preachers who came out of the Palestinian tradition. This conflict of forces was dealt with by the emergence of Christianity described as "early catholicism" (Kaesemann 1964, 1969). Early catholicism was the government of the church described in Luke-Acts, the pastoral epistles, Ephesians, Jude, and 2 Peter. This phase of the development of Christianity was marked by a fading of messianic expectations of an imminent end of the world and the second coming. Rather than the creation of the Word, the church became the receptacle of truth and the mother of the faithful. This transformation implied a demand for a sacramentally guaranteed clergy and ritual. The hope of eschatological intervention was replaced by salvation history and the universality of the church. Freedom and missionary zeal gave way to uniformity and organization. The church of early catholicism began to reach out to the world, even as it sought internal consolidation along with increasing sociological and ideological differentiation.

Early catholicism represents the beginnings of a transition out of the status of cult or sect, in the traditional terminology, into that of an established sect. A group of official pastors took over the functions of teaching and administration, leading toward emergence of the role of presbyter-bishop. The authority of the institutional ministry was bolstered by tradition and legitimate succession; hierarchical organization became apparent in the form of orders of presbyters, deacons, and widows.

The emergence of early catholicism would represent one expression of the cultic process in emerging church structure. Kaesemann (1964) focuses this transition under the rubric of response to "enthusiasm." The impulse of the Spirit was tied to church organization and office, establishing a continuity of structure that offered stability in the midst of many destabilizing influences. Certainly, other reasons can be entertained for the emergence of this structuralizing tendency in the early church, including the deaths of early guiding charismatic figures, the spread and growth of the church, and the influence of external persecution (Harrington 1982). But it should also not be ignored that the pattern of emerging structure in the case of early Catholicism fits the formula for the routinization of charisma and for the familiar pattern of change experienced generally in the history of the development of cults and sects: in this view they evolve in the direction of increasing structure and centralized authority, or they gradually diffuse and die out. At least such is the conventional wisdom.[1]

Antioch and Jerusalem

The divisive forces of the cultic process came into play almost from the beginning of the church's existence. As the Christian community grew in self-conscious possession of its mission and established itself increasingly outside of Palestine, it came into ever more intense and hostile collision with its Jewish origins and with the Jewish Christians who maintained their attachment to these origins. The Jerusalem Christians came into conflict with the high priests and Sadducees (Acts 4:1-3): Peter and John were brought before the Sanhedrin and later released. The Pharisees were seemingly less hostile—Gamaliel, Saul's mentor, defended them, before the Sanhedrin—but while the attitude toward judaizing Christians was somewhat favorable, the antagonism towards Hellenizing Jewish converts of the diaspora was marked (Eliade 1982). The writers of the Gospels wrote the tensions and conflicts of their own religious milieu into the gospel accounts. A point of crisis was reached in the conquest of Jerusalem and the destruction of the Temple. As Horsley and Hanson (1985) comment:

> The consequent devastation of Palestine, including the destruction of the temple and much of the city of Jerusalem, became a great turning point for both the Jewish and Christian religious traditions. In reaction against the apocalyptic spirit and revolutionary impulse, sobered Pharisaic sages laid the foundation not only of a reconstructed Jewish society, but also of what became Rabbinic Judaism. As a result of the Roman suppression of the Jewish revolt, moreover, the nascent Christian movement turned its orientation away from Jerusalem and the temple as a geographic and symbolic center (p. xi).

The nascent church was hence cut off from its nurturing roots in Judaism and was left to fend for itself in the hostile environment of the Greco-Roman world of the Mediterranean basin.

The story of the increasing tensions involved in the movement away from the Jerusalem and Palestine setting and into the wider world of Hellenistic and pagan influences is told most graphically in the gradual emergence of the church at Antioch, the eastern capitol of the Roman Empire, and the process by which it increasingly segregated and defined itself over against the Jerusalem church.

---

[1] As already noted, there are notable exceptions to this rule.

Contending Groups

The contending interests of four groups of early Christians shaped the pattern of events in the evolution of the primitive Christian church.[2] The first group consisted of Jewish Christians and Gentile converts, who espoused full observance of the Mosaic Law, including circumcision, for all believers. Their conservative perspective demanded that converts had equivalently to become Jews in order to participate in the messianic kingdom promised by Jesus. They were found primarily at Jerusalem, were strongly influenced by pharisaic traditions, and were hardly receptive or enthusiastic about receiving Gentiles into the church. They developed a Jewish Christian missionary force antagonistic to Paul's preaching and tried to establish a form of Jewish Christianity of strict observance, not only in Palestine but in other parts of the diaspora.

The second group of Jewish Christians and Gentile converts did not insist on the rite of circumcision, but required that converted Gentiles keep some of the other traditional Jewish observances. They were moderately conservative and probably included James and Peter, the pillars of the Jerusalem church; James particularly was insistent on the observance of dietary prescriptions of the law (Acts 15:20). In Galatians (2:11-13), the "men from James" created a stir at Antioch over the issue of Jewish Christians eating with Gentiles and thus failing to observe the dietary laws. This group would have, as Meeks (1983) says, "wanted to ensure that the tested, traditionally and biblically sanctioned means by which the Jews had maintained their identity in a pagan culture would continue to serve the community of Messiah Jesus" (p. 81).

A third group also consisted of Jewish Christians, again including Gentile converts, who did not insist either on circumcision or on the observance of the Jewish kosher food laws, nor did they require that Christians abstain from eating food dedicated to idols. Paul himself would be the main spokesman for this relatively liberal attitude. Paul had had to resist the view advocated by James' representatives, and even had to deal with Peter over the issue (Gal 2:11). And Paul's position was adamant and uncompromising—as Segal (1990) comments, "Paul is ready to oppose anyone who dissents from his vision of unity. Even the pillars *(styloi)* of the church in Jerusalem cannot legitimately challenge his authority on this issue. He was ready to stand alone, if necessary, against those who follow James or Peter at Antioch or Jerusalem" (p. 213). The break with Barnabas (Gal 2:13; Acts 15:39) probably was over this same issue. Thus, Paul and his followers would have

---

[2] I am following here the reconstruction offered by Brown and Meier (1983) since it provides an up-to-date reconstruction of the forces at play and the patterns of their conjunction and interaction.

adopted a somewhat more liberal view regarding the obligations of the Law than that taken by James and Peter. Certainly, Paul's own position regarding the observance of the prescriptions of the Mosaic Law was not without a certain degree of ambivalence, but his clear teaching was that the coming of Christ had delivered men from the burden of the Law and that faith in Christ had replaced the Law (Gal 3:10-13, 24-25).

Paul's stand would have seemed offensive to Jews, whether Christian or not—as an apostasy from the faith of the fathers (Segal 1990). He was in continual conflict with Jewish authorities throughout his missionary efforts. According to Acts his life was threatened in Damascus and again in Jerusalem. He was stoned and left for dead at Lystra (Acts 14:19), imprisoned at Philippi (Acts 16:19-24), forced to flee Thessalonica (Acts 17:5-10), persecuted by Hellenists in Jerusalem (Acts 9:29), met constant antagonism from the Jews (Acts 13:50; 14:2, 5, 19; 16:19-24; 17:5-9), and was finally taken as a prisoner to Rome because of charges brought against him by the Jews. He himself complains of his sufferings (1 Cor 4:9; 2 Cor 11:22-29), inflicted for his preaching against the Law—not only his own apostasy but even further for inciting others to abandon Judaism. He might well have appealed to Rome, since the charges against him would have carried a potential sentence of death. He expressed his anxieties about going to Jerusalem to his Roman brethren, seeking prayers that he be delivered from the threats of the unbelievers in Judea (Rom 15:30-33). Those unbelievers may have included not only Jews but more conservative Jewish Christians who were insistent on observance of the Jewish Law for Christians, Gentile as well as Jewish (Segal 1990).

Paul represented a growing minority within the church—an embattled minority facing the antipathy and rejection of the Jewish Christian majority. The chasm between these groups frustrated Paul's efforts to draw them together into the one body of Christ. For Gentile Christians, the distinction between Jew and Gentile came down to the purity of observance of the Law—union with the Jews in one religious community could be purchased only at the price of circumcision and ritual observance. Paul's brand of Christianity without circumcision would have seemed inauthentic to converts tinged with traditional Jewish apocalyptic views proclaiming all those outside the group to be damned. While these sentiments strengthened the internal cohesion of the group of believers, it also erected walls of division with other groups of Christians. The growing strength of the Gentile church in both numbers and influence only served to heighten the tensions and make the divisions more acute.

Paul's insistence on a single unified Christian community did not enjoy much success, and in fact ran into considerable opposition from both Gentiles and Jewish Christians—both were quite content to carry on as separate communities. Paul met strong opposition from the Jerusalem church which saw his antinomian stand as abandoning ancient Judaic traditions. If the issue had simply been freedom from the Law for non-Jewish converts, the antipathy might not have been as intense. But Paul's insistence on a unified church meant that Jewish Christians would have to surrender their attachment to the Law. This was offensive to many Jews and brought forth their hostility against Paul and his mission to the Gentiles. Paul met such hostility from the Jews, not only in Jerusalem and Rome, but elsewhere. The tensions between these groups in the church was to outlast Paul and color the relations between Christian groups for centuries.

Paul's influence became a dominant force in the early church, but soon diversified into a school of Pauline Christianity. It has been established that the Pauline corpus was not the work of a single person—only a few of the letters can be ascribed directly to Paul, the others were written by disciples or associates. Paul was more or less the leader of a group of associates for whom he was the leading figure and charismatic authority. As long as Paul was alive, there might have been a degree of cohesion in this group, but after his death, diffusion and diversity began to assert themselves. The authenticity of the Pastoral Epistles (to Timothy and Titus) and other apocryphal writings ascribed to Paul have been questioned, but may have been the products of a Pauline school that lasted into the second century. Paul would have become, then, the patron not only of a central tradition within the church but of a variety of heretical movements as well—particularly some leaning in a Gnostic direction (Meeks 1983).

However, Paul's position was not the most liberal or extreme. There was a fourth group of Jewish Christians and Gentile converts who like the previous group did not insist on circumcision or observance of the dietary laws, but who in addition saw no abiding significance in observance of the Jewish cult and feasts. This group seems to have been even more radical in their attitude toward Judaism than Paul himself. These were the Hellenists, probably Jewish Christians who had been raised under the influence of Greek culture, even to the point of speaking only Greek rather than one of the semitic languages. Meier (Brown and Meier 1983) suggests that the attitude of Stephen, expressing disdain for temple worship (Acts 7:48; 9:29), may reflect this more extreme position. A later expression of the Hellenist position might be found in the Gospel of John, where the Law is regarded as pertaining only to Jews and not to the followers of Christ (John 10:34; 15:25). Similarly, the Temple was to be destroyed and replaced by the worship of Jesus (John 2:19-21). Thus, this branch of Jewish-Gentile Christianity would have broken more radically with Judaism to become the new religion, the new wine that could not be put into old wineskins.[3]

The Church at Antioch

These groups entered into contention in the Antioch Christian community, and the tensions among them reflected the gradual withdrawal of the Antioch church from the sphere of influence of the Jerusalem church. As Meier (Brown and Meier 1983) describes it, there are three discriminable stages in this evolution. The first stage represents the church of Paul, Barnabas, Peter, and James (somewhere around A.D. 40–70); the second stage is represented in the Gospel of Matthew, probably written at Antioch somewhere in the decade from A.D. 80–90, but representing the Antioch community of the intermediate period (from A.D. 70–100); and a third stage, represented by the more evolved and hierarchically structured church of Ignatius of Antioch (after A.D. 100).

These contending factions came into focus around the Council of Jerusalem (A.D. 49). The issue before the council was whether Gentile converts to the Christian faith would be required to submit to circumcision. The question had presumably arisen in Antioch in the debate between the more liberal and conservative elements. Some of the more conservative Judaizing Christians had created a division by insisting that Gentiles had to be circumcised as a requirement for church membership and salvation. Paul refers to these Judaizing radicals as "false brothers" (Gal 2:4), probably a group of Christian Jews with strong ties to the pharisaic movement.

The decision at Jerusalem was that Gentiles were not bound by the requirement of circumcision. Paul was to carry on with the mission to the Gentiles, while Peter would continue the mission to the Jews. While the issue of circumcision seems to have been satisfactorily resolved, the whole question of the observance of kosher laws remained a thorny issue that came to a head after Paul and Barnabas returned to Antioch. Their missionary partnership fell apart, according to the account in Galatians, by reason of the fact that Barnabas sided with Peter, who had withdrawn from eating at table with Gentile Christians because of pressure from the James faction. Clearly, at this point in the evolution of the Antioch church, the influence of Jerusalem was still decisive, and the Council of Jerusalem elders, including Peter and James, maintained a certain definitive authority over the Antioch church and even over Paul himself.

---

[3] The position of the Johannine community is discussed further in chapter 9.

At issue in these wranglings and contentions was not simply a question of deciding about certain religious practices. Rather, the implications reached far beyond the confines of Antioch and Jerusalem and concerned the ultimate nature and mission of the newly born church. The more liberal Pauline and Gentile Christians sought a more open and universal religious mission, with baptism rather than circumcision as its initiation rite. For them, the teachings of Jesus were to replace the Mosaic Law as the ethical basis of Christian life. These universalistic aspirations and attitudes found their way into Matthew's Gospel, and would have found in Peter a sympathetic ear. But these universalistic ambitions would have been difficult to achieve as long as James' influence remained predominant among the Jewish Christians in the Antioch church; he and his followers represented a right-wing faction providing a natural haven for any judaizing extremists[4] in the Antioch church. This faction may have also been the source of some of the more narrow and particularistic statements on the mission of the church found in Matthew's Gospel (see 10:5-6, 15-24).

While the extremists did not gain the upper hand at Antioch, there seems to have been some reconciliation after the departure of Paul, modifying the breach between Christian Jews and Gentile converts. The compromise was purchased at the price of the imposition of certain kosher laws on the Gentile Christians. As Meier (Brown and Meier 1983) suggests, there may have been a split in the more radically conservative groups, the most radical possibly moving in the direction of the Ebionites[5] and other marginal Jewish-Christian heretical groups, while the less radical contingent found a more comfortable allegiance with the less extreme conservatives.

After the Destruction of Jerusalem

The changes in the Antioch church reflected the influence of a combination of external and internal factors. The most significant external event was the first Jewish revolt (A.D. 66–70), culminating in the destruction of Jerusalem. Another important event was the death of James in Jerusalem somewhere in the sixties, probably around A.D. 62. These events were decisive for the conservative Jewish Christians and their influence at Antioch. The James party had held the upper hand, but once James had been martyred and the Jerusalem church dispersed

[4] See the first group described above.

[5] A later Jewish-Christian heretical sect that espoused an unorthodox christology and rejected the christology preached by Paul. For them Christ was a mere man who had been raised to the position of Lord by God.

in the Roman conquest, all meaningful ties of the Antioch church to its Jewish roots were severed. The more liberal groups of Jews and Gentiles, who were connected with Paul or followed a more Hellenistic persuasion, gained in strength. Some of the members of the more conservative faction may have been willing to compromise with Gentile Christians (group 2 above), but the more extreme conservatives (group one above) may not have been able to come to any compromise with the conditions existing after A.D. 70. They would have moved to preserve their Jewish heritage and remained faithful to the views of James.

The shift of radically conservative groups toward a Gnostic resolution, as for example in the Ebionite heresy, would have drawn support from residues of Palestinian Jewish-Christian communities and even from some of the remaining Essenes who might have been converted to Christianity in the wake of the destruction of the desert community. In fact, some of the later Jewish-Christian heretical writings tend to elevate the position of James, even putting him before Peter, and casting him in opposition to the enemy, Paul. It may even be that some of the attacks on the Jewish leaders in Matthew's Gospel may have been aimed in fact at these proto-Ebionites. These factors underscored the unavoidable conclusion that the conversion of the Jews had proven to be a failure, while the missionary effort directed to the Gentiles and the wider world was increasingly successful. For the Jewish Christians at Antioch and elsewhere, the handwriting was on the wall; after the failure of the Jewish revolt and the destruction of Jerusalem, it was unmistakable that the future of the church lie in the mission to the Gentiles, freed from any of the ritualistic or legalistic encumbrances left over from the Mosaic Law.

There were also changes within the Antioch church. The conflicts between the contending forces representing the Jewish and Gentile groups had reached a level of compromise that re-established in some degree a sense of community and fellowship. The resulting process of mutual assimilation was intensified by the persecution from the side of the synagogues on one hand and from the side of the civil authorities on the other. As the moderate groups were driven closer together, the more extreme right-wing group (group 1 above) could no longer find a home either in the synagogue or in the church and had to find its own way. It was probably in this context that Matthew wrote his Gospel in an effort to synthesize the various tensions and groups which constituted the remnant of the Antioch church.

The Second Century

The church in Antioch was transformed from the relatively loose structure of Matthew's time (ca. A.D. 85) to the church with a more structured and articulated hierarchy, headed by a bishop who enjoyed full authority, in the time of Ignatius of Antioch (ca. A.D. 108–117). Under him a group of presbyters served as a sort of council of elders, and at the lower echelon a group of deacons. Meier (Brown and Meier 1983) argues that some further crisis or series of crises at Antioch stimulated further organization and unification of church structures in order to respond to a common external threat. One plausible source for such a crisis was the early rise of Gnosticism, particularly its docetic form.[6] Since the threat posed by the Gnostics was essentially intellectual and doctrinal, the response of the Christians might be expected to have been a closing of ranks and a unified organization that would counter the Gnostic threat more effectively.

This hierarchical structure was already in place by the time Ignatius was writing (A.D. 108–117). Consequently, the gradual shifts and changes in the development of the Antioch church seem to reflect the pattern of change that is usually found as the original cultic inspiration undergoes gradual transformation, and the primary cult or sect evolves into a church with its greater degree of structure, hierarchical organization and authoritative body of teachers. Meier (Brown and Meier 1983) summarizes this progression in the following terms:

> It is at Antioch that the first organized circumcision-free mission to the Gentiles is undertaken. It is from Antioch, with its embryonic theology, structures, and liturgy, that Paul goes forth on his mission. It is at Antioch that traditions about Peter as the rallying point of church unity are fostered. It is at Antioch that Matthew overcomes a basic crisis in the church's identity and role by drawing together divergent traditions into the masterful theological synthesis of his gospel, the Synoptic Gospel favored by the second-century church. It is at Antioch, in and perhaps before the tenure of Ignatius, that a new challenge to church unity is met with the three-tier hierarchy. It is at Antioch that Ignatius develops a theological synthesis, holding to the unity of the divine and human in Christ and holding to the unity of the local church and of the church catholic. Peter, Matthew, and Ignatius all had to undertake a delicate balancing act between left and right as they struggled for a middle position in what was to become this universal church (p. 85).

The new wine had after all been poured into new wineskins.

---

[6] Docetism was an early Christian heresy that taught that Christ did not really die on the cross, but only seemed to. The gnostic tendency of this view of the incarnation derived from the understanding of Christ as wholly spiritual, not possessing a real physical body. See section IV on gnosticism below.

The emergence of factions, seen here in Antioch in the conflicts between Judaizers and Hellenizers, between Paul and the party of James and Peter, between adherents to the Law of Moses and adherents to the Law of Christ, reflects the workings of the cultic process. Each group had its leader, invested with charismatic authority, who advocated an ideology that was given exclusive claim as the authentic religious truth and the vehicle of salvation. Opposing ideologies were regarded as false and heretical.

Under the influence of persecution, the more moderate elements in the church of Antioch closed ranks and found a common cause in the face of a common enemy. This consolidation had the effect of isolating the more extreme factions, both the radical Judaizers and the protognostic or docetic adherents. The outcome was not only a degree of unification, but following the laws of sectarian evolution, the emergence of an authoritative hierarchical structure that guaranteed consistency, unity, and orthodoxy in the ongoing struggle with the forces of destruction and persecution surrounding the nascent church.

8

Corinth and Rome

Corinth

The rapidly emerging development of the Christian church was articulated around the apostolic mission of Paul to the Gentiles. The church extended its roots into the soil of the Hellenizing pagan world of the empire, and concomitantly, became increasingly dissociated from its ties to its Palestinian origins and to Jewish traditions and practices. Paul's mission carried him on several occasions to Corinth, and finally to his decisive and terminal arrival in Rome in the last act of his tragic drama.

Social stratification and the conflicts and tensions associated with it played an influential role in the Corinthian church. Theissen (1982) has traced these influences in some detail. The social composition of the Corinthian community included a strong, socially dominant group of Christians from higher social levels. The number of wealthy Corinthians was probably due to its thriving commerce and to the fact that it had been largely colonized by freedmen who could build their own aristocracy without the onus of a repressive indigenous social hierarchy (Meeks 1983). While the majority of church members may have come from lower and middle classes, they stand in marked contrast to the more influential members, probably fewer in number, drawn from higher social strata. This pattern of social structure was probably not limited to the Corinthian church, but reflects a more characteristic pattern in churches with considerable numbers of Hellenistic converts (Meeks 1983). Paul himself described some aspects of the social structure as follows:

> Take yourselves for instance, brothers, at the time when you were called: how many of you were wise in the ordinary sense of the word, how many were influential people, or came from noble families? No, it was to shame the wise that God chose what is foolish by human reckoning, and to shame what is strong that he chose what is weak by human reckoning; those whom the world thinks common and contemptible are the ones that God has chosen—those who are nothing at all to show up those who are everything. The human race has nothing to boast about to God, . . . (1 Cor 1:26-29)

Social Stratification

Theissen takes these references to the wise, influential, and noble as referring to a social stratification contrasting this level of social status with those who are lower-born, despised, or dispossessed. If there were not many in the Corinthian church who could be regarded as wise, influential and nobly born, there were some. Their influence must be counted as significant, insofar as Paul seems to feel it necessary to devote the better part of his letter to dealing with their supposed "wisdom."[1] Paul even draws a rather strong contrast with his own circumstances, e.g., that he earns his bread by the work of his hands, experiences hunger, has no permanent home, and is persecuted, whereas those who are powerful and honored occupy the opposite end of the social scale. If the upper-class members of the church constituted a minority, they must have formed at least a prominent and probably influential minority. Certainly the majority of the Corinthians known to us by name seem to have enjoyed such elevated social status and probably represent the more active and important portion of the Corinthian church.

The stratified composition of the Corinthian community probably reflects a more advanced stage in the development of primitive Christianity. The oldest forms of church structure were found in Palestine. The transition from the more rural and structured world of Palestine to the more highly urbanized and Hellenistic world of the Mediterranean basin was accompanied by a social shift, in which the influence of Christianity penetrated more deeply into higher social strata. Paul's

---

[1] The issue of the "wisdom" of this Corinthian elite will surface again in connection with the role of gnostic or protognostic thinking in the Corinthian church. See chapter 11 below.

collections for the poor in Jerusalem were based on support gathered from these more influential and well-to-do classes. As Theissen (1982) comments: "The history of primitive Christianity was thus shaped even in the first generation by a radical social shift which altered important socio-cultural, socio-ecological, and socio-economic factors through the processes of Hellenization, urbanization, and the penetration of society's higher strata. If this is taken into account it can hardly be deemed an accident that the Hellenistic congregations only hesitantly accepted Palestinian traditions, which came from an entirely different social world" (p. 107).

The divisive implications of such social stratification in the Corinthian community focused around the issue of eating meat (Theissen 1982). Meat was relatively rare in the diet of the lower classes, since they in large part depended on the public meat distributions connected with certain official ceremonial occasions. In addition, meat was included as part of pagan religious celebrations, in which lower classes might have had contact with meat, but which also established a close connection between the act of eating meat and the religious worship of idols. In contrast, upper classes would have had much greater access to meat supplies and would have been much more accustomed to consuming it.

The conversion of upper-class Gentiles introduced these social differences into the Christian community, creating difficulties for both Jewish Christians and lower-class Gentile Christians. The resulting conflicts would have created inevitable tensions: former pagans would have difficulty in seeing meat independent of its ritual setting, but they would not have wanted to lose out on the meat offered in the pagan feasts. If they did eat meat, it would have been with a guilty conscience. Converted Jews, who had been liberated from Mosaic dietary restrictions, would also have been tempted to eat the public meats, but would have found difficulty in abandoning old taboos. None of these inhibitions would have had much effect on higher class converts. The result, as Meeks (1983) concludes, was

> to leave the issue of the Christian group's boundaries somewhat ambiguous. On the one hand, social intercourse with outsiders is not discouraged. The mere act of eating meat is desacralized in order to remove a taboo that would prevent such intercourse. It is thus not idolatry. On the other hand, any activity that would imply actual participation in another cult is strictly prohibited. Thus the exclusivity of cult, which had been a unique mark of Judaism difficult for pagans in the Hellenistic cities to understand, would remain characteristic also of the Pauline congregations. The emphasis in Paul's paraenesis, however, is not upon the maintenance

of boundaries, but upon internal cohesion: the mutual responsibility of members, especially that of strong for weak, and the undiluted loyalty of all to the One God and One Lord (p. 100).

Thus, the real issue, in terms of the cultic process, was the internal cohesion of the church and the establishment of the group boundaries defining believers over against nonbelievers.

Paul's Mediation

In the middle of all this, Paul tried to weave a conciliatory course. He did not consistently support the position of the enlightened and affluent, even though he seems to have been in basic agreement with it. He tried to re-evaluate the norms of social rank and dominance, including the aspects of higher knowledge and wisdom, in terms of the preaching of the cross. He appealed for the higher classes to accommodate to the needs of the lower classes, and to allow for the acceptance and tolerance of more than one tradition. While the privileges of higher class status are preserved, for example, in allowing private meals with consecrated meat (1 Cor 10:23ff), he emphasized the undesirable effects of scandalizing the weak by this practice.

In this context of social stratification, the problem was balancing socially differentiated expectations and class-specific demands. The well-to-do in Corinth probably provided the means for the eucharistic feasts, probably following a practice common to their social group of bringing special food consumed separately from the rest of the congregation. Their participation, therefore, included a kind of private meal eaten at a separate table from the others (Meeks 1983). Theissen (1982) summarizes the situation:

> It is worth summarizing once again our reconstruction of the behavior of those Christians who consume their "own meal" in the congregational gathering. Some wealthier Christians have made the meal itself possible through their generosity, providing bread and wine for all. What was distributed is declared by means of the words of institution to be the Lord's and given to the congregation. Thus, in conjunction with this common meal there could have taken place a private meal because the starting point of the Lord's Supper was not regulated, and up to this starting point (that is, until the words of institution) what had been brought and provided was private property. More importantly, this distinction was possible because the wealthier Christians ate other food in addition to the bread and wine, and the words of institution made no provision for sharing this with the fellowship (p. 160).

It is not difficult to see how such a practice would have sown the seeds of division and contention. The obvious danger was that the Lord's Supper, rather than being the point of unity and common sharing in the body of Christ, would become the basis for internal division, envy, and antagonism.

All of these examples reflect the underlying dilemma for these emergent groups of establishing their exclusive identity and drawing boundaries that would distinguish them from the surrounding culture, yet also allow them to interact and adapt with that same culture in constructive terms. Paul and his followers had deliberately abandoned the norms that had maintained the boundaries of Jewish communities; the traditional symbol system, by which the boundaries between the sacred and the profane were drawn, had been discarded. If circumcision and the prohibition of certain foods could no longer serve these purposes, the importance of social functions, such as the sense of unity inherent in the sharing of the eucharistic supper, became all the more salient for maintaining the social cohesion of the in-group in the face of the tensions due to social stratification and economic disparities (Meeks 1983).

The Pauline solution, abrogating the place of the Torah in Christian observance, drew the line between Christianity and Judaism and established Christianity as a Jewish heresy. If the Torah could still be seen as prophetic, it no longer served as the symbol of the community's boundary. The redrawing of the boundaries between Christianity and Judaism would take centuries—but abandoning the Torah was for the Jew an apostasy. Pharisaic Judaism regarded circumcision as essential for conversion. But the difficulty for Paul lay not in the Jewish stand, but rather in the Christian community itself. Conservative Jewish Christians would expect Gentiles to be circumcised in order to join the Christian community. But for Paul, the unifying factor was belief in Christ—the union of Jews and Christians had to be based on their common experience of Christ, receiving the same baptism, embracing the same faith in the crucified Messiah. The identification with Christ had nothing to do with circumcision.

In Galatia, Paul's opponents belonged to a party of circumcising Christians, who had accepted circumcision when they converted, and adherents to the view that conversion to Judaism was prerequisite for church membership. They brought pressure to bear on Paul's converts to undergo the operation. Paul wastes no words, comparing circumcision with castration. The controversy was bitter and intense. Paul's commitment to the mission to the Gentiles stands in stark conflict with the converts to Jewish Christianity with its conviction of the value of ceremonial law (Segal 1990). Compromise was impossible—the issue

extended beyond mere circumcision to the issue of commitment to a
new social structure and the establishment of its self-identity. Commitment and identity for the Jews meant ceremonial observance of the
laws. For Paul and his followers, commitment and identity was a matter of conversion and faith—the presence of the risen Lord and faith in
his kingdom was the basis of the new community that was to replace
the old.

Paul's apocalyptic persuasions led to his insistence on strong delim-
iting boundaries between the community of believers and nonbelievers
(1 Thess 4:12; 1 Cor 5:12; 2 Cor 6:14–7:1). 2 Corinthians draws a firm
line between insiders and outsiders, and Paul makes a forceful argument that Christians should not be fooled by those who do not support
his apostolate—they are outsiders and any who associate with them
will be tainted:

> Do not harness yourselves in an uneven team with unbelievers.
> Virtue is no companion for crime. Light and darkness have nothing
> in common. Christ is not the ally of Beliar, nor has a believer any-
> thing to share with an unbeliever. The temple of God has no com-
> mon ground with idols, and that is what we are—the temple of the
> living God. We have God's word for it: *I will make my home among*
> *them and live with them; I will be their God and they shall be my people.*
> *Then come away from them and keep aloof, says the Lord. Touch nothing*
> *that is unclean, and I will welcome you and be your father, and you shall*
> *be my sons and daughters, says the Almighty Lord.*
>
> With promises like these made to us, dear brothers, let us wash
> off all that can soil either body or spirit, to reach perfection of holi-
> ness in the fear of God (2 Cor 6:14–7:1).

Whether this text came from the hand of Paul or not, the theme of
preservation of the purity and separation of the community is clear
enough. The parallels to Qumran separatism are striking. Paul is relying on material drawn from an apocalyptic background similar to that
of the Essene community in the Judean desert. Christ is placed in the
role of God himself or at least one of angelic messengers of Jewish
apocalyptic lore. The demonic opposition belongs to Belial, just as at
Qumran. The themes of apocalyptic dualism are present—believers vs.
nonbelievers, light vs. darkness, saved vs. damned—and other motifs
found in the Qumran literature—the people as the temple of God, the
need for purification, for example. Unbelievers and outsiders are
treated with contempt and scorn. Paul used a style of invective drawn
from Jewish apocalypticism, implying a highly committed and cohesive group as at Qumran.

Rome

The dominant form of Christianity at Rome in the early days (in the 40s and early 50s) was closer to the Jerusalem and Judaic model. Similar to the Antioch story, the church underwent progressive changes, moving through a phase reflected in Paul's epistle to the Romans (ca. A.D. 58), through an intermediate period, covering most of the last third of the first century, and evolving in the direction of the structures reflected in the letter of Clement, written from Rome to Corinth (ca. 96 A.D.). Thus, Roman Christianity was transplanted originally from Jerusalem and reflected the Jewish-Gentile Christianity associated with the pillars of the Jerusalem church, Peter and James.[2] The story of the development of Roman Christianity then is one of the gradual integration and reconciliation of the Christianity of Paul with a more developed Petrine tradition that allowed the two apostles to join forces in the establishing and consolidating of the Roman church (Brown and Meier 1983).

Petrine and Pauline Traditions

There is good evidence to suggest that the ultraconservative Jewish Christians made life difficult for both Peter and Paul in the decades of the 40s and 50s, especially in Jerusalem. Peter's attitude toward maintaining the Jewish tradition was more moderate and more conservative in tone than Paul. While the majority position in Rome was primarily identified with Peter, a minority of more radically conservative Jewish Christians were also on the scene. Despite his attempts to hold to a moderate line in his epistle to the Romans, Paul repeats his opposition to any demand for circumcision among Gentile converts. Insofar as Jews were exempted from Nero's persecution, Jewish Christians and their circumcised Gentile converts may have represented themselves as Jews to distinguish themselves from the Gentile Christians converted without circumcision. Peter's more moderate position may have forced Paul to moderate his earlier repudiation of the Judaic traditions. Paul's approach to Christian unity did finally prevail, but only when opposition from the conservative Jewish faction had finally diminished sufficiently. As long as the insistence on Jewish Law prevailed, Paul's brand of Christian unity could not find footing; the underlying ideology of unity and universal inclusion were too disparate from prevailing sentiments for any meaningful integration (Segal 1990).

These same polarities were at issue in regard to observance of the laws regarding food. Paul argues for a common table among Christians

---

[2] Essentially group two in chapter 7.

(Rom 14:1-6, 15-20). The weak, primarily conservative Jewish Christians, eat only vegetables, whereas the strong, representing mostly Gentile Christians, eat at the common table without problems. Paul's concern is to preserve the unity of the church in Rome, so that his position seeks to accomplish the same purpose as the Judaic food laws, preserving the unity of the community. Paul's own position is that of the strong—no food is impure of itself—but for the sake of unity he is open to accommodation and urges tolerance and magnanimity on both parties. He would urge the same accommodation to the Corinthians: "Whatever you eat, whatever you drink, whatever you do at all, do it for the glory of God. Never do anything offensive to anyone—to Jews or Greeks or to the Church of God; just as I try to be helpful to everyone at all times, not anxious for my own advantage but for the advantage of everybody else, so that they may be saved" (1 Cor 10:31-33).

At the same time, the direction of Roman thinking did not favor a too radical rejection of the Jewish heritage. The issue surfaced again in the middle of the second century in the teaching of Marcion. While Paul had taught a basic opposition between the Law and the teaching of Christ, he still maintained that the Law came from God. Marcion, however, took an extreme position, declaring that the Law was the creation of a demigod, who was not the true God who had sent us Christ as his emissary. Marcion's adoption of and reliance on Paul as the basis of his teaching did not save him from expulsion from the community of believers (ca. A.D. 144). Thus, the Paul of Romans represents a more moderate and conservative view of the relationship between Christianity and the Jewish heritage than the Paul of Galatians.

The Political Situation

External events must here too have played their part. The fall of Jerusalem and the destruction of the Temple had a profound affect on Roman Jews, who would have witnessed Titus' triumph and the parading of the sacred liturgical vessels from the Temple. The Judaean campaign had been something of an embarrassment to Rome, the Roman military juggernaut having been forced to go to extreme lengths to swat a fly. Propaganda made up the difference, however, so that for many years afterwards coins were struck celebrating the defeat of the Jews—a continuing daily reminder to the Roman Jews of their humiliation. The great arch of Titus portraying the destruction and sacking of the Temple was completed in A.D. 80. In addition, a special "tax" for the support of the Roman temple of Jupiter Capitolinus was imposed.

During the first century Christians were regarded more or less as another Jewish sect. They increasingly felt the burden of differentiating and separating themselves from Judaism and dissociating themselves from any connection with the Jewish rebels who had created such a disturbance in Palestine that Vespasian himself had to go out to crush it. This situation was only made worse by the insurrection of bar Kochba that Hadrian squelched in A.D. 133. Mark tended to play down the role of the Romans in the trial and execution of Jesus, but he was writing for a Roman audience. The inculpation of the Jews, especially in the recounting of the events before the Sanhedrin, may have had a political focus—one that reflected the position of the church in the late first-century Roman Empire.

Clement of Rome's Letter

By the time we reach the end of the first century, the forces of moderation and consolidation had reached a new level, reflected dramatically in the first letter of Clement, addressed to the Corinthians. Despite the controversy over the implications and significance of this epistle, there is general agreement that it profoundly influenced the future directions of church thinking whether for good or ill. Viewed against its historical background, it may well have been the difficulties in the Corinthian church that prompted this consolidation in the Roman church. By the time of its writing, Roman Christians had already felt the sting of persecution in the time of Nero and Domitian. Christianity was regarded as a "foreign superstition." But for Clement the greatest danger was internal disorder, the jealous opposition of Christians against fellow Christians. His remedy was an appeal to order based on the twofold themes of a strong Jewish heritage and respect for imperial authority.

Clement drew on the symbolism of the levitical priesthood to argue in support of the ecclesiastical structure already developed in many of the major churches by the end of the first century—the tripartite structure already identified in the church of Antioch. Clement's claim of divine approval on this hierarchical structure carried with it a demand for solid allegiance with the bishops and presbyters, a call for unity and a closing of ranks in the face of a looming persecution that would last for two hundred years. Clement's admiration of Roman military discipline made him realize that the fortunes of Christianity were limited unless Christians could learn to take advantage of the strengths of its adversary. Rome tolerated a variety of cults without much difficulty as long as they did not challenge the established religious and social order. But Christianity was not destined to be just another oriental mystery religion; it was destined to establish itself as a society with exclusive claims that were basically antithetical to those of the absolute state. Earlier Christian works (Rom 13:1-7; 1 Pet 2:13-17) had demanded obedience to Roman authority, but Clement tried to establish the same claim for church authorities. The future of Christianity depended on the success of the structure and integration of its communities and its ability to retain converts. Its organization and structure would go the empire one better and would provide better motivation for its members. Clement's letter thus offered a formula not only for overcoming persecution, but for defeating the persecutor.

Commenting on this view, Harrington (1982) summarizes the argument as follows:

> . . . orthodoxy or ecclesiastical Christianity represented the type supported by the majority of Christians in Rome at the end of the first century and the beginning of the second century. The Roman church then gradually extended the boundaries of its influence to Corinth (see 1 Clement), Antioch, and other places. . . . Orthodox and heretical groups used similar tactics; e.g., repeating false rumors, not recognizing false believers as fellow believers, not admitting anything good about opponents, emphasizing their weaknesses and inadequacies, and supporting or even falsifying their views. But in the course of the early Christian centuries the so-called heretical groups remained divided and even fought among themselves. They were finally routed, one after another, by so-called orthodox Christians (p. 163).

From Jerusalem to Rome

Brown (Brown and Meier 1983) argues that Clement's letter is in fact continuing a trajectory that has its proper antecedents in earlier Christian attitudes toward the conversion of Rome. The Acts of the Apostles dramatically begins the story of the church in Jerusalem, but closes its account with the establishment of the church in Rome. Even in the account of Acts, the Christian destiny was cast with Rome and with the Gentile world. The church's hopes were centered on Rome, rather than Athens, the great museum of classical antiquity, or Alexandria, the repository of classical learning. These early Christians understood that the power to change the world lay not in the museum or in the library, but in the capitol of political power, the center of the Roman Empire. As Brown comments, "If there was a Christian 'drive toward Rome,' in part it was because centered in that city was the machinery that ruled the known world and through which that world could be claimed for Christ" (p. 181).

The pattern of contending forces, divergent interests and splits that took place between various segments of the primitive Christian church, particularly among Jewish Christians and their Gentile converts, reflects a pattern of gradual withdrawal and separation of the nascent Christian community from its dependence on and ties to the Jerusalem church. At Antioch, the beginnings of the Christian movement saw face-to-face confrontations between Paul and the Hellenists on the one side, and Peter and the followers of James on the other. The strains posed by the issue of the relationship between the Gospel and its Jewish heritage continued even after the destruction of Jerusalem, so that the splits between more conservative and liberal groups continued to exercise a powerful influence in the face of the increasing majority of Gentile Christian converts. Matthew's attempt at a synthesis of the various traditions and positions represents an attempt to mold this *mixtum gatherum* into a consistent Christian identity. His view of the church's mission mediated between the more liberal outlook of Paul and the more conservative exclusionary attitude of the James faction. As a primary figure in the early church, Peter was caught in the middle, pressured from the one side by the followers of James, but also realizing the implications of Paul's mission and the importance of extending the gospel message to the rest of the non-Jewish world.

It was presumably in the face of these persistent tensions and divisions, and probably also partially in response to Jewish persecution (thus creating a common enemy), that the Antioch community evolved in the direction of a more stable, authoritative structure under the headship of a single teacher-bishop. Ignatius of Antioch propounded this structural solution as an effective response to the divisive forces within the Christian community. More liberal factions tended to be more open to Hellenizing influences in the social environment, particularly Gnostic influences, and began to move gradually in the direction of a "high" christology (emphasizing Christ's divine origin) that in its extreme form tended to evacuate the humanity of Christ (docetism). The opposite conservative extreme of the Judaizers maintained a powerful influence, even though their numbers were diminishing. In the time of Ignatius, things had not yet come to a point of schism, but Ignatius found it necessary to find a mediating middle ground for the sake of preserving the integrity of the Christian community.

The situation was roughly similar at Rome where the dominant influence of the Jerusalem church, espoused from the beginning a strong connection to the Judaic traditions advocated by James and to a certain extent Peter. Thus, the early Roman converts would have been more attached to the Jewish heritage than Paul's Gentile converts. Paul's approach to Rome, seeking to gain support for a collection on behalf of the Jerusalem church, was considerably more moderate toward the Judaic question than it had been earlier. The more moderate view of Paul in the late fifties allowed him to be accepted in Rome, but it is possible that his martyrdom may have been the result of a reaction on the part of extremely conservative Jewish Christian zealots. In any case, this more moderate Paul took his place side by side with Peter as one of the pillars of the Roman church.

After the destruction of Jerusalem, the Roman church assumed the rights of pre-eminence that had belonged to the older Jerusalem church and became the leader, guide, and teacher of the other churches. By the end of the first century, Clement had already wedded the levitical heritage to the Roman heritage in an insistence on the authority of the bishop and the necessity of the acceptance of and obedience to his prerogatives based on the model of Roman imperial order and authority. Thus, the organizational and structuralizing tendencies arising in the context of the Antioch controversies found their logical extension in the evolution of a Roman hierarchy and the notion of apostolic succession.

9

Early Christianity—
The Johannine Community

A special case in the evolution of church doctrine and structure is provided by the Johannine church. Questions have arisen regarding the connection of the Johannine community to the rest of the church. The dominant theological force in the first century after Christ was the teaching of the apostle Paul, but the Pauline influence on the Johannine community is easily overestimated. Paul had certainly established the separation of Gentile Christianity from its Judaic roots, thus preparing the way for the Johannine development. Paul's work at Ephesus may have influenced the community within which the Fourth Gospel was written as well as the writer himself (Dodd 1968).

Gospel Origins
Certainly the Gospel of John, representing the main literary remains of the Johannine community, diverges in a variety of ways from the synoptic tradition. Instead of the discourses on the kingdom and the use of proverbs and parables, the Jesus of the Fourth Gospel addresses his followers in symbolic discourses of a more evolved theological tone. There are further differences in chronology and geography. The messianic message is the culmination of the synoptic message; for John it is his point of departure (Perkins 1990b). The Gospel probably reflects independent traditions held in the Johannine community. There

are links to the synoptic tradition and the author of the Fourth Gospel may have drawn material from the other Gospels, most probably Mark. Whatever the contacts and borrowings, the Johannine Gospel embodies a relatively separate tradition preserved in the Johannine churches.

The derivation of the content of the Gospel from religious movements extant in the first century remains uncertain. Scholarly advances are becoming more comfortable with the origin of the Gospel in first-century Judaism. Some expositions are reminiscent of traditions and *midrashim* extant in the first century. The Johannine declaration of Jesus' special relationship with God also reflects a Jewish background. The identification of Jesus with the divine Word, the *Logos,* derives from the traditional view of Wisdom as the agent of divine creation (Prov 8:22-30; Wis 9:1-9). Wisdom and the Word are equated in Philo of Alexandria. Moreover the Johannine Jesus claims for himself the divine "I Am," (John 8:24, 28, 58; 13:19), a title reserved in the Old Testament for God himself (Isa 51:12; 52:6).

The origins of the Johannine community were probably no different than the origins of the Christian movement in general, except that the followers of John were more likely to draw their converts from the Jews who came to Jesus with high messianic expectations and found in him the Messiah of their hopes. Their claim was that "We have found the one Moses wrote about in the Law, the one about whom the prophets wrote" (John 1:45). Brown (1979) argues that the christological developments may also have been triggered by the conversion of a large group of Samaritans—a conjecture supported by the account of the Samaritan converts in John 4:7-42. This integration of the two groups and the acceptance of the new converts by the majority of the Johannine community would have elicited the suspicion and hostility of the synagogue leaders. The Samaritans, as well as the Essenes, looked for a "prophet like Moses," but also expected the eschatological restoration of the true worship on Mt. Gerizim. The conversion of the Samaritans in John 4 marks a turning point, after which the Gospel focuses increasingly on the rejection of Jesus by "the Jews." Whether the new converts consisted entirely of Samaritans or not can be argued, but they probably included Jews of anti-temple views, who had incorporated some aspects of Samaritan teaching, including a christology not based exclusively on the notion of a Davidic Messiah.

Essene and Gnostic Connections

Questions of the influence of the Essenes on the Fourth Gospel find no convincing evidence for direct Qumran influence on John. If there was any influence at all, it had to be indirect, probably through the conversion into the Johannine community of Jewish Essenes who would have brought with them ideas that can be found in the Qumran literature, e.g., the dualisms of light vs. darkness, truth vs. falsehood, spirit vs. flesh, the notion of an angelic Spirit of Truth who leads the sons of light against the sons of darkness, etc. The image of the devil, the adversary, the "ruler of this world," mirrors the accounts of the "angel of darkness" who misleads the children of the light in the Qumran literature. Even the doctrine of the Spirit, the connection of water and the receiving of the Spirit, and the notion of the "Spirit of Truth," echo themes found in the Dead Sea Scrolls. These ideas would have been readily incorporated into the Johannine christology as reinforcing the divine origin of Christ and enriching the theological understanding of the Johannine community. These symbolic similarities suggest the possibility of a derivation from sectarian Jewish sources. However, Perkins (1990b) adds a qualifying note:

> Differences between John and the DSS [Dead Sea Scrolls] make it unlikely that the evangelist forged his theological vision by simply taking over the symbol system of a 1st-cent. Jewish baptismal sect. The life-death antithesis, which is prominent in John (e.g., 5:24; 6:49, 58; 8:51; 11:25), does not play such a striking role in the DSS. Whereas purity and obedience to the law distinguish the "children of light" from those of darkness in the DSS, the Fourth Gospel makes belief in Jesus as the one who has come from God and who reveals God the dividing point. There are, however, enough similarities to support the suggestion that at some time there must have been contact between the Johannine tradition and the type of religious symbolism that had developed in such sectarian Jewish circles (p. 945).

The question of Gnostic influences on the Gospel is much disputed.[1] Most of the Gnostic writings are dated after the Gospel, and so cannot be sources for understanding Johannine views of Jesus and his mission. The "I Am" proclamations of the Gospel have parallels in the Gnostic declarations regarding revealer figures, but, as Perkins (1990b) comments, "Any contacts between the Fourth Gospel and gnosticism would have to be between Johannine traditions and those strands of heterodox Jewish exegesis and pagan myth making and philosophy that were welded together in later gnostic syntheses" (p. 945).[2]

---

[1] See the further discussion of these issues in chapter 11 below.
[2] See also MacRae (1978).

Development

The development of the Johannine community can be traced through a series of phases. The first phase represents the pregospel era, reflecting origins of the community and its close relations to mid-first century Judaism. By the time the Gospel was written, antagonism between Johannine Christians and the synagogues had been exacerbated because of the teachings about Jesus. The post-destruction form of rabbinical Judaism led to expulsion of the Christians from the synagogues. This first pregospel period probably covers several decades, extending from the mid-fifties to the late eighties. The Christian Palestinian community at this juncture consisted primarily of Jews who adhered to a relatively low christology (a view of Christ emphasizing his humanity rather than his divinity). The gradual emergence of a higher christology (emphasizing the divine origin of Christ) brought the Johannine faction into increasingly sharper conflict with the Jews, who would have regarded such a view as blasphemy. The high christology may also have been the bone of contention between factions within the Johannine community.

The second phase involved the situation around the time of the writing of John's Gospel, about A.D. 90. The period was one of continuing persecution and the persistence of deep antagonisms between the Johannine community and "the Jews." These conflicts reinforced the Johannine insistence on a high christology, an emphasis having further implications for relationships between the Johannine faction and other Christian groups not sharing the Johannine christological ideology. It may be that later redactions of the Gospel placed greater emphasis on Jesus' position as equal to God and sharing in God's creative and eschatological power. In this connection, Neyrey (1988) posits a developmental progression in the evolution of the Johannine community: (1) a preliminary stage of missionary preaching and propaganda; (2) a subsequent stage in which Jesus was proclaimed as messianic replacement for the defunct institutions of Israel; (3) the emergence of the high christology, reflecting the conditions of revolt against not only the synagogue but other apostolic communities as well;[3] (4) a final stage articulated in John 21 leading to moderation of earlier divisive tendencies.

To this can be added a subsequent phase reflecting the situation at the time of the writing of the Johannine epistles, probably around the end of the century. Brown (1979) offers the hypothesis that this period

---

[3] Neyrey connects the community in this phase with Douglas' (1970) analysis of group process in terms of "low group, low grid."

was marked by a struggle within the Johannine community between two groups of disciples, interpreting the Gospel in quite divergent ways. The reverberations from these splits in the community are decisive in the epistles.

The last phase was marked by the dissolution of the Johannine church after the writing of the epistles. The more radical secessionists broke off communion with the more conservative faction, and probably drifted in the ensuing years of the second century into Docetism, Gnosticism, Cerinthianism[4] and Montanism.[5] They carried with them the influence and teaching of the Fourth Gospel, which thus came to have a central place in influencing heterodox views. The followers of the author of 1 John seem to have gradually merged with the "church catholic" of Ignatius of Antioch somewhere in the early second century. This shift was marked by a gradually increasing acceptance of the higher Johannine christology, but at the price of the acceptance of the authoritative teaching structure of the church. As Brown (1979) comments:

> Much of this recognition shows a community whose evaluation of Jesus was honed by struggle, and whose elevated appreciation of Jesus' divinity led to antagonisms without and schism within. If the Johannine eagle soared above the earth, it did so with talons bared for the fight; and the last writings that were left us show the eaglets tearing at each other for the possession of the nest. There are moments of tranquil contemplation and inspiring penetration in the Johannine writings, but they also reflect a deep involvement in Christian history. Like Jesus, the word transmitted to the Johannine community lived in the flesh (p. 24).

Sectarian Tendencies

The Johannine community, centered around the figure and the teaching of the author of the Fourth Gospel, revealed definite sect characteristics consistent with the dynamics of the cultic process, particularly in its opposition to various groups of outsiders, whether the

---

[4]Cerinthus was a gnostic heretic who taught that the world was created by a demiurge, not by the supreme God, and that Jesus was a mere mortal on whom the spirit of Christ descended at baptism. Thus, in the crucifixion, only Jesus suffered since the Christ could not suffer.

[5]Montanism was a gnostic, illuminist heresy, originating in the second century, based on the teachings of Montanus, who preached a spiritualist doctrine, calling his followers to a renewal of primitive simplicity to form a spiritual elite under the direct guidance of the Holy Spirit.

"world" or "the Jews," or even other Christians. The term "Jew" in the Fourth Gospel came to represent the world in all its hostility to the God of the Christians. Behind the symbolism lay the social reality of the ostracizing of the Jewish Christians in the Johannine community from the synagogue—a fact that was little forgotten and the source of great rancor (Segal 1987). By the time of the composition of the Fourth Gospel, conversion from Judaism had become past history, and the "Jews" were regarded as outsiders, unbelievers who rejected and opposed Jesus and his mission, in other words a stereotype for Jesus' protagonists; they drew their origin from below, while Jesus came from above (Perkins 1990b).

Brown (1979), following the lead of Scroggs (1975), takes the position that the early Christian movement manifested sectarian characteristics: origin in an agrarian protest movement; opposition, at least in its early stages, to establishment claims (the claims of family ties, of religious institutional affiliation, of wealth, and even of theological intellectuality); egalitarian claims; special acceptance within the community; voluntary character; demands for total commitment from its members; and a basically apocalyptic doctrine—all attributes associated with a cultic movement. Thus the Christian community, as revealed to us through the Fourth Gospel and the Johannine epistles, must be regarded as a sect, but at the same time as part of the larger sectarian movement of Christianity.

The sectarian or cultic quality of early Christianity, at least in its Jewish Palestinian form, set itself in opposition to other groups of Jews who did not believe in Jesus. The critical doctrinal point was Christ's claim to the divine name in John 8:58: the "I am" title was equivalent to the Hebrew YHWH. It was not the claim to be the Messiah that brought down the wrath of the Jews, but the claim to divinity.[6] In Acts (24:5, 14) such nonbelieving Jews were regarded as forming a *hairesis,* the same term used to describe other Jewish sects. Despite these sect characteristics, the further question of the extent to which the Johannine community had actually broken communion with other Christians remains a matter of controversy (Brown 1979). Segal (1987) argues that the Johannine community may have crossed a boundary between what it meant to be Jewish and what it meant to be Christian, a boundary not yet passed by the Synoptics. Consequently the Fourth Gospel may have been the product of a group excluded from the Jewish community and feeling itself persecuted as a result. Such feelings may explain their projection of a dualistic and incipiently Gnostic interpretation on the "Jews."

---

[6] See also John 5:18 and 10:33.

This antagonism toward the Jews and the expulsion from the synagogue probably drove the Johannine community increasingly toward the Gentile world, resulting in adaptation of Johannine thought to make it more intelligible and acceptable to this wider context. In the wake of the expulsion, the missionary intent of the community became focused on the Gentiles. A strain of universalism enters the Gospel, interpreting Christ's mission as divinely ordained to all men who would come to believe in him. But this attitude is qualified by a dualism dividing the human race into those who believe against those who do not believe, into the followers of darkness and the followers of the light, into those who are condemned and those who are saved.

To this extent, then, the Johannine community increasingly defined itself in oppositional terms, establishing its claims to divine truth and salvation by way of opposition to other external groups. The various groups of opposing forces are detailed in the accompanying table (see table I), together with their characteristics and the rationale of rejection. The spectrum of opposition and rejection underlines the inherent sense of specialness, privilege and elitism that permeated the Johannine community.

The increasing rejection by "the Jews" and by the world in general contributed to a major theme of Johannine thought. The theme is consistent: "To his own he came; yet his own people did not accept him" (John 1:11); "God so loved the world that He gave His only son . . . but men preferred darkness to the light" (John 3:16-19). The Johannine Christians also shared in this fate of rejection: "If the world hates you, bear in mind that it has hated me before you. If you belong to the world, the world would love its own; but the reason why the world hates you is that you do not belong to the world, for I chose you out of the world" (John 15:18-19). This sense of earthly alienation and yearning for a heavenly home pervades the Johannine ideology.

It would seem more than likely that this in-group solidarity and exclusivism, and the contemptuous oppositional tone of the relationships between the Johannine community and outside groups would have increased the likelihood of hostility, antagonism, and even persecution. The persecution was no doubt costly, and may have resulted in dislocation of the Johannine community from its original Palestinian roots to a place in the diaspora, such as Ephesus, where the Johannine church was situated by later church traditions.

Thus there is considerable evidence reinforcing the cultic dimensions of the Johannine movement. The hostility expressed in the Gospel toward other groups is directed not only against the synagogue and the Jewish leaders, but also involves a sense of estrangement and alienation even from other Christian groups (see table I). While the theme of

TABLE I
The Johannine Outgroups

Non-Christian		
I. The World	II. "The Jews"	III. Followers of John the Baptist
These preferred darkness to the light of Christ because they were evil. They are unbelievers, who are condemned by their choice and under the power of Satan. This reflects pagan persecution and antagonism against the cultic exclusivism of the Johannine community. Hatred of Christ and his disciples who were not of this world. The Johannines were strangers in the world, alienated. "World" broader than but included "the Jews."	Jews of the synagogues who rejected Christ and decided to expel from the synagogue all who thought him to be the messiah: particularly the Jewish authorities. Points of dispute: (a) claims about the oneness of Christ with the Father, making himself God's equal; (b) claims that the worship of Christ replaces the Jewish feasts and temple worship. Persecuted and executed Johannine Christians.	Some of John's followers joined the community, some did not. Claimed that John was greater than Jesus. Gospel insists that the Baptist decrease while Christ increased. John's adherents misunderstood rather than hated Christ; some hope for conversion.

Christian		
IV. Crypto-Christians	V. Jewish Christians	VI. Christians of Apostolic Churches
Christian Jews who remained in the synagogue, but could not admit their belief in Christ. Prefer the praise of men to the glory of God. Tried to maintain private faith in Christ with Jewish heritage. Choose Moses over Christ. Lumped with "the Jews," but way still open to confess faith publicly.	Converts who had left the synagogues but whose faith did not measure up to Johannine standards. May have represented followers of James at Jerusalem. Held low christology between IV and VI: Christ not divine, eucharist not Jesus' flesh and blood. For John, not true believers.	Mixed communities of Jews and Gentiles, separated from the synagogues, regarded themselves as followers of Peter and the Twelve. Moderately high christology: Christ was the messiah, born of Davidic descent, the Son of God, but without a clear notion of the pre-existence of the Word. Saw Christ as founder and institutor of the sacraments, and the church as the legitimate locus of apostolic teaching and pastoral mission. For John they did not understand Christ's true nature or the teaching function of the Paraclete, but they were the only other Christian group to whom the Johannine community could look for unity.

accusations against other Christian groups is not exclusive to the Johannine faction, in the Johannine documents the sense of exclusion of other groups from the Christian fellowship is more telling. Beyond these oppositional attitudes and the concurrent definition of the in-group of believers in opposition to various out-groups of nonbelievers, John's Gospel expresses a sense of alienation and superiority that sets the Johannine community apart. The Johannine Jesus is a stranger in the world, who is misunderstood and rejected even by those whom he came to save. It is the Johannine Christians who really understand Jesus, for they share with him the rejection and persecution of this world. They possess a unique grasp of the truth, and a more meaningful and more significant christology to which they have been guided by the illumination of the Spirit.

Despite the cultic and sectarian influences operating within the Johannine community, the major group of Johannine disciples were able to achieve some meaningful degree of rapprochement with other Christian groups. Presumably this reconciliation was made possible by the splitting within the Johannine community, siphoning off more radical and recalcitrant groups who followed the divisive path of sectarian development. The pessimistic outlook of the author of the Johannine epistles seems to have been in some degree prophetic ("the last hour" of 1 John 2:18). The splits between his own adherents and the secessionists had become definitive. As represented in the Johannine epistles, the community was torn by divisive schisms resulting in a collection of "house churches" rather than a well-knit community.

After the writing of these epistles, there is no further trace of a distinct Johannine community. The likelihood is that the contending groups were incorporated into the wider church on the one hand, and into the Gnostic movement on the other. As Perkins (1990b) suggests,

> . . . the schism between Johannine Christians resulted from divergent interpretations of the meaning of the inherited tradition. Some exegetes see this inner-directed schism as evidence that the Johannine community had played out the logic of its dualistic symbol system and become a sect. The schism may only intensify the process of rigid self-identification and isolation. The acknowledgment of Petrine authority in John 21 may have made it possible for some Johannine churches to amalgamate with Christians from other churches. But for others the Johannine symbol system could lead to the kind of "mythologizing ontology" provided by the 2nd-cent. gnostics (p. 946).

As the orthodox group merged with the church, it carried with it the high Johannine christology of the pre-existence of the Word, the basic theological ideology that they had so stoutly defended in the struggle with the secessionists. They had also preserved that christology from any tendencies toward docetism or monophysitism. In fact, the threat of heresy and the inability to protect against the threat of schism ultimately drove the orthodox faction to accept the authoritative structure which came into being in the church of the second century, in which the authoritative teaching figure was the presbyter-bishop. This structure had previously been quite foreign to the Johannine tradition.

The secessionists, on the other hand, freed from the moderating influence of the more orthodox perspective, drifted even further in the direction of an ultrahigh christology. If Jesus' earthly career had no real salvific impact, they now thought of it as having no reality at all. Thus the Johannine influence entered the currents of Docetism and Gnosticism, and created the basis for a new theology.

On the orthodox side, the church of the second century was at first wary of the Fourth Gospel and the Johannine tradition, since it had given rise to heresy and was being used so assiduously in the support of heresy. The addition of the epistles, however, offered a guide to a more correct interpretation that allowed the church to champion the Johannine view as orthodox over against its more extreme Gnostic interpretations. Ultimately writers like Irenaeus would use the Gospel in attacking Gnostic doctrines that were in fact derived from the teachings of the heterodox secessionists from the Johannine community. The contribution of the author of 1 John may thus have been to save the Fourth Gospel for the church.

The Cultic Process

The origins of Christianity thus reflect the workings of the cultic process in the roots of the Christian inspiration and in the early phases of its subsequent evolution. Our effort in the present study is to unearth the underlying psychological roots reflected in these more social and structural considerations. We can identify social forces contributing to more internal, subjective and psychological determinants, but the psychological factors themselves remain hidden. The limited data at hand point only generically to the sense of frustration, discontent, disillusionment, and rebellion that found its way into the early Christian movement. Jesus' mission was one of confrontation and conflict with the established religious authorities. The culmination was his own execution, setting the pattern and motif for the life of the early church. Persecution was the order of the day, and the early church set itself at first against the Jews, and later against the secular world of the Roman Empire. The sectarian and cultic origins of the Christian movement set the stage for conflict and persecution. In its relative separation, rejection of existing structures and exclusivism, the primitive Christian movement presented itself as a threat, not only to the religious authorities in Palestine and by extension to the synagogues of the diaspora, but also to the secular authorities of the Roman world.

The early church was thus heavily sectarian in character, emphasizing voluntary conversion based on a religious experience due to the influence of the Spirit. Its impulse in relation to the surrounding social structures was torn between a separatist and isolationist dynamic, on one hand, creating a pattern of rejection of the values and structures of the social environment and an attempt to replace them with the values and attitudes inherent in the cult, and on the other hand a need to open itself and engage with that hostile and rejecting environment in order to gain new converts and extend its own life course. The early church, then, arose in and maintained itself for a considerable period of time in a state of high tension with the social environment, a prime characteristic of cult movements. Rather than tending to support or reinforce the existing power structures of the prevailing social milieu, the earliest Christians emphasized their differences and antagonism to that milieu, and insisted on the individual needs for personal sanctification and salvation (Yinger 1957).

In addition to this cultic sense of isolation and in-group enhancement, there was also condemnation and rejection of the outsiders who did not embrace the ways of the cult and accept its beliefs and convictions. This fanatical adherence was linked to the role of the charismatic leader—such charismatic adherence and devotion was evident in the first disciples and became a predominant aspect of membership in the Christian movement. Charismatic attachment to the figure of Christ was reinforced by the powerful theology of the Word and the evolution of a high christology.

Cultic Variants

Rather than a unified and integrated social force, the early church was compounded out of a variety of local cults that only gradually evolved into a church organization. Segments of this protochurch evolved a variety of cult or sect forms, embracing all of the ideological subtypes suggested by Wilson (1959).[7] The early Jerusalem community, for example, was characteristically conversionist, basing its teaching on the new Gospel of Christ and on the pentecostal experience. They eagerly sought new converts who would accept Christ as their Savior, exclud-

---

[7] Wilson's (1959) typology is discussed in chapter 2 above.

ing none who would accept baptism. At the same time, the Jerusalem church tended to be dominated by conservative elements holding tenaciously to the traditional Jewish ways and resisting the mission to the Gentiles and its implied adaptations.

The early belief system of the church was messianic and adventist. The *parousia*, in which the present order would be overthrown and the last times realized, was expected imminently. Much of the early *kerygma* was apocalyptic, drawing many of its views from Jewish apocalyptic literature and possibly even from Qumran. Part of the erosion of the prophetic and charismatic influence in early church doctrine and preaching came with the realization that the anticipations of the final days had been premature, so that the idealized expectations of the rewards and glories of the second coming had to be abandoned in favor of a less illusory and more realistic perspective of the meaning of Christian life and purpose. The tradition of separation from the world and high moral purity had to give way to a coming to grips and an adaptation to the demands of living in the world.

The early church also had its introversionist qualities, turning its followers away from the world to a deeper and more spiritual sharing in the life of the community. This tendency is linked to illumination by the Spirit providing the sect and its members with a special sense of enlightenment and privilege. Echoes of these elements can be recognized in the Corinthian protognostics and in the more Gnostic segments of the Johannine community. These same groups reflect the Gnostic influence in their emphasis on a special *gnosis* or teaching that provided privileged status and an esoteric vehicle of salvation. Christ was for them a divine teacher, the exemplar of truth, rather than a Savior.

The success story of the emergence of the Christian movement out of this tangle of cultic variants toward greater degrees of unification, structure and organization is a byproduct of the further elaboration of the cultic process. The cultic process, as it increasingly defined and delineated cultic groups, clarified the lines of force binding the various segments of the Christian community together and simultaneously etched out the dimensions of acceptable orthodoxy over against unacceptable heterodoxy. Cultic heterodoxy became the touchstone of the progression towards church status. The lines of division were differently drawn in different contexts: the divisions regarding the eating of meat in Corinth were quite different from the issues of the role of the Judaic traditions in Antioch or the questions of cultic and Gnostic adherence to christological implications at Ephesus. But in each case, the cultic process worked out the patterns of differentiation that drove the group formation process in certain directions, forcing certain groups to the periphery and consolidating others in the position of orthodoxy.

Along with these shifts, as the orthodox communities became established, there grew with them a superstructure that preserved and sustained the central position of Christian orthodoxy and cohesion. By the end of the second century, all the pieces were in place, both doctrinal and structural, for a universal church.

Gnosticism

10

Pre-Christian Gnosticism

Origins

The story of the development and demise of the Gnostic movement extends the pattern of the cultic process well into the second and third centuries. The process of resolving tensions and splits within the Christian communities by gradual articulation of in-group boundaries and cohesion in opposition to the declaration of the boundaries and segregation of heterodox out-groups found expression in the emergence and evolution of Christian communities and the differentiation of the lines of orthodoxy and heterodoxy between themselves and Gnostic groups. Christianity was not the only sectarian cult to emerge from the rich brew of religious forces flourishing in Palestine and the Middle East at the turn of the millennium. Other religious movements reflected many of the same cultic and other influences that played a part in Christian origins.

One of the most revealing of these developments was the emergence of Gnosticism, a religious phenomenon that sprouted in the pre-Christian era, gestated during the early years of the new millennium, and finally came to full flower in the second century as an identifiable heterodox movement, both within and outside organized Christianity, only to shrivel as a definitive and separate movement and disappear in the late third and fourth centuries. It provides a dynamic template for the action of the cultic process as it operated at the beginning and early stages of development of the Christian church. As LaCarriere (1977) wrote, "Geographically speaking, primitive Gnosticism developed in the same places as dawning Christianity and the Judaic religions: Palestine, Syria, Samaria, and Anatolia. It was here, in these lands of apocalypse and revelation, in this crucible of all the Messianisms, in this cradle of arcane and mystical communities like the Essenes, that the first Gnostic thinkers appeared" (p. 43).

Gnosticism can be understood narrowly in terms set forth by the Christian Fathers as a heresy that split off from the main line of Christian thought, or more broadly as conceived by modern research, particularly the *religionsgeschichtliche* school, emphasizing parallels in ancient pre-Christian mythologies. The view emerged of a pre-Christian Gnosticism, forms of non-Christian gnosis, for example a pre-Christian Jewish or a Hellenistic pagan Gnosticism, possibly descendants of earlier Palestinian baptismal sects that influenced the origins of Christianity and can be found in both orthodox and heterodox Christian belief systems (Wilson 1958).

Scholarly opinion has been divided as to the origins of Gnostic views. As more information has become available, at least the beginnings of a tentative reconstruction have emerged. There is a more or less general consensus that Gnostic views probably derive from heterodox Jewish speculation coming out of the same background and close to the same time as the rise of Christianity. Documents from the Nag Hammadi library suggest that while many themes have a Christian dress (e.g., Christ as the revealer of gnosis), the content and form of speculations about the origin of the world and mankind are connected to heterodox Judaism. Many parallels can be found between Gnostic writings and New Testament writings, particularly in Paul and John.[1]

More recent research into the origins of Gnosticism have shifted the emphasis away from earlier oriental or mystery religion sources to a more consistent focus on pre-Christian heterodox Judaic sources. An early thesis of Friedländer (1898), recently resurrected after many years of disparagement, held that the roots of Gnosticism lay in the Jewish diaspora before the time of Jesus. It was a period during which Hellenistic influences had a powerful influence on Jewish religious thinking, particularly in the development of the allegorical method of scriptural interpretation. The allegorical interpretation of the Mosaic Law by such Hellenized Jews saw it as a form of divine philosophy preceding the Greek philosophers. The result was a division in diaspora Judaism between conservatives who followed the letter of the Law and philosophizers who adopted the allegorical approach. These forms of heretical gnosis would have reached Palestine at least by the first century and

---

[1] See chapter 11.

would have been extant in the time of Jesus. The polemics against these groups in the *Talmud* make it clear that forms of Jewish Gnosticism existed in Palestine from the first century, and that from the early second century, if not before, they posed a considerable threat to more orthodox Jewish groups.

The importance of Hellenistic influences on this development should not be underestimated, as is attested by the presence of Platonic elements in Gnostic mythology. Middle Platonism sought to join Plato and Aristotle with ancient oriental wisdom, turning to a symbolic and allegorical method to develop their views. Emphasis fell on the transcendence of the great and good God, the ultimate Good, and separated it from a creator god, the demiurge, of Plato. However, as the scholarly view of the origins of Gnosticism is being rewritten, the Greek and philosophic elements seem to be more peripheral, and the emphasis falls increasingly on the Jewish milieu as the locus of origin. Besides the influence of Middle Platonism does not come into prominence until the second century. Even the intellectual and philosophically eclectic aspects of Gnostic thinking may well represent the influence of Jewish wisdom circles of the Hellenistic period of Roman dominance just as well as any Greek circles—even with regard to the somewhat skeptical outlook of Gnostic teaching (Pearson 1990b). Pearson's (1990b) discussion reaches the following conclusion:

> Judaism, as a religion that takes history seriously, and that also has a marked tendency in the direction of messianism, provides ipso facto a context in which, given the critical circumstances of history, an attitude of revolt could easily develop. There is a strong case to be made for the view that ancient Gnosticism developed, in large part, from a disappointed messianism, or rather as a transmuted messianism. . . . Such a transmuted messianism, for the ancient period, is better understood as arising in the national homeland, that is, in Palestine itself, rather than in the Diaspora. But this is a very tentative judgment (p. 28).

Affinities have also been traced to the Egyptian magical papyri (Nock 1972), to the hermetic literature (Festugière 1949–1953, 1967), and even some of the writings reflecting the influence of the language of the mystery cults (Perkins 1980).

The problem of identifying sources is complicated by the complex interrelations among them. None of these sources operated in pure form without contamination from others. Gnostic systems in the second century were influenced by Christianity, but the argument for pre-Christian gnosis is more or less inferential. But early Christians were in constant dialogue with various Jewish sects, and the dissemination of sectarian views into Christianity could well have provided the basis for Gnostic views. Even early orthodox Christian views were syncretistic. Clearly the Gnostics participated richly in the syncretistic melange of Middle Eastern theological speculation. Gnostic speculative systems were compounded out of every imaginable conceptual ingredient—oriental mythologies, astrological systems, Iranian theologizing, traditional Jewish views, apocalyptic visions, rabbinical teachings, Christian eschatology, Platonic and neoplatonic elaborations (Jonas 1963).

Definition

The description of Gnosticism suffers from a lack of consensus as to exactly what is meant by the term and by a paucity of historical materials. Knowledge of Gnostic doctrines was originally limited to the adversarial accounts rendered by Christian apologists like Irenaeus, who attacked and criticized Gnostic teachings in an effort to refute them and defend the true faith. There is question how reliable and accurate such assessments might be. Knowledge of Gnostic systems has been enriched by the cache of manuscripts found at Nag Hammadi in Egypt in 1945–1946, but study of these Coptic materials reveals more substantive differences among various Gnostic schools and writers than had been suspected.

Some clarification of terms may help. By convention "gnosis" was taken to mean "knowledge of the divine mysteries reserved for the elite," not restricted to any specific religious movement. "Gnosticism" refers to the unique form of religious orientation developed in the second century, involving a coherent series of characteristics that included a prototypical form of dualism, and a series of sect movements that were vigorously attacked by heresiologists of the time. "Pre-gnosticism" applies to particular theological expressions that emerged from various ancient sources, but only came into a specifically Gnostic combination in the second century. Finally, the term "protognostic" is taken to describe more fully developed Gnostic systems that emerged prior to the second century (MacRae 1966).

In the confusing welter of doctrinal variations, there are certain core elements that seem consistent. Nock (1972) focuses on three predisposing characteristics: ". . . a preoccupation with the problem of evil, a sense of alienation and recoil from man's environment, and a desire for special and intimate knowledge of the secrets of the universe" (p. 940). "Gnosis" refers to a kind of knowledge that becomes a means of salvation or even is a form of salvation in itself. As Jonas (1963) commented, ". . . the claim to the possession of this knowledge in one's own articulate doctrine, are common features of the numerous sects in which the gnostic movement historically expressed itself" (p. 32). Gnosis was not merely knowledge of God so much as knowledge of the structure of the higher world and how to negotiate it to regain the heavenly abode, usually contained in myths in which key concepts are personified and allegorized (Dodd 1968).

Salvation came through the Heavenly Revealer who brought with him the gnosis that the powers and authorities of the lower world are contemptuous, arrogant, and evil. Ascetical practices and cultic rites, especially rejection of the body and its sexuality, were required to free the soul from the entrapment of matter. McGuire (1986) summarizes these common features as follows:

(1) a conception of the saving power of Gnosis, or revealed knowledge about the nature of existence in which the content of such Gnosis includes

(2) a radical disjunction between divinity and the powers that create and govern the cosmos,

(3) identification of the saved or salvageable element(s) of humanity with the divine, and

(4) a parallel identification of the remaining elements of humanity with the creating and ruling powers of the cosmos (p. 343).

There is another common note, shared with Jewish apocalyptic, namely that the world is so dominated by evil and ignorance that it cannot be redeemed. Only the divine spark imprisoned in certain men has the potential for salvation—and that only through revealed gnosis. The mystery, then, is how the supreme, transcendent, and all-good God could be responsible for such an evil world. The Gnostic answer was to postulate a series of intermediate beings, because of whose ignorance, sinfulness or dereliction, this evil world came to be (Grant 1961).

While the details of Gnostic cult organization, doctrine, ethical teaching, and ritual practice varied widely, they shared the conviction that salvation was a matter of acceptance of revealed knowledge bearing on the identity of part of the soul with the realms of heavenly light. This was the order of true divine existence: the *pleroma* was filled with the elaborate hierarchy of emanations from the true God that were entirely separate or divorced from the corrupt and inferior lower world of the material cosmos. This view of the universe set the Gnostics off from the pagans with their pantheon of gods, and from the Jewish and Christian vision of the cosmos as a divine creation. Gnosticism, even in its origins, seemed to represent a specific mind-set, a mentality, and an attitude toward the world that carried its own distinctive stamp.

Gnostic Themes

Dualism

All Gnostic systems involved a fundamental metaphysical dualism. There was a degree of hostility and antipathy to the created world—a place of violence, corruption, limitation, ignorance, passion, and relative chaos. The radical division between the divine world of light and the created world of darkness reflected a fundamental dualism characterizing most Gnostic systems.

The theme of "two powers in heaven" found its heretical expression in both rabbinic Judaism and Gnosticism, but reflected polemical processes at large in the ancient world (Segal 1987). The polemics between groups was translated into mythological themes—a kind of cosmic projection resulting in a radical dualism affecting all realms of being—God vs. world, spirit vs. matter, soul vs. body, light vs. darkness, good vs. evil, life vs. death. The misery and futility of human existence were connected with imprisonment in a material body, sharply contrasted with the spiritual realm, and were taken as the prime manifestation in human experience of the essential dualism of the universe (Dodd 1968).

This dualistic theology and accompanying hierarchy of heavenly beings found its way into Hellenistic religious thinking, probably through heterodox Judaic thought. The various mythological systems shared a common concern—how to explain the separation between God and the world, between man and the world, and between spirit and flesh. The Gnostic inspiration formed a radical departure from traditional modes of thought—particularly about the nature of the divine being and its relation to the world. Danielou (1973) summarized this aspect of Gnostic thinking:

> For a Jew, to say that God is transcendent is to say that he cannot be measured by any created thing, and is therefore incomprehensible to the creaturely mind; but at the same time it is to assert that his existence can be known. For the Platonist, to say that God is ineffable is to say that he surpasses any conception of him that the mind can form in terms of the sensible world; but it is also to affirm that, if only the mind can shake itself free from all conceptions of that kind, it will be able to grasp his essence. For the Gnostic, however, the matter goes far deeper. God is unknown absolutely, both in his essence and in his existence; he is the one of whom, in the strictest sense, nothing is known, and this situation can be overcome only through the Gnosis. It is, therefore, a question of radical dualism, distinguishing between the God of whom the world enables us to form some idea (who is merely the Demiurge) and the

God who has no connection whatever with the world, and who
can be known only by means of himself (pp. 335–36).

Some Gnostic cosmologies began with a pre-existent principle of
evil and darkness that has succeeded in trapping the divine light—a
characteristic view in Iranian Gnostic speculation, an adaptation of the
Zoroastrian dualism of opposed principles of Light and Darkness. Others postulated an original monistic heavenly world, out of which lower
orders of reality derived, usually by the fall of a being of light, often a
female wisdom figure, who was cast out of the realm of light and thus
became the god of the lower world, and whose offspring became a
demiurge, often identified with the God of the Old Testament. One
consequence of this fundamental and universal dualism was to drive an
unirradicable wedge between the divine and the world. Puech (1951)
described this unalterable division:

> One of the permanent and fundamental features of Gnostic thought
> is indeed an opposition between the world, or Creation, and God.
> The entire sensuous universe is experienced and judged as evil.
> God is not held responsible either for the evil that is in this world
> or for the world itself, which is evil. He absolutely transcends the
> world: he has no relation to it, for any relation would debase and
> enslave him; it would sully his inalterable purity and make him
> cease to be God in the supreme sense of the term. God did not pro-
> duce the world and he does not rule over it. He is not known by
> the world, by the intermediary of the world or in the world, which
> is not his work and the work of his government. If he intervenes in
> the world, it is to save men from the world, to encompass an es-
> cape out of the world, not to accomplish anything whatever through
> the world (p. 57).

Evil

Concern with the origin and significance of evil was a primary characteristic of the Gnostic mind—almost an obsession. The presence of
evil and the gross baseness of human existence were constant sources
of *angst* and concern. The Gnostic was beleaguered by the tyrannical
pressure of fate, cut off by the limitations of his own body, matter and
time, by all the temptations and humiliations of the flesh. He felt alien,
rejected and abandoned in this world—in revolt against the world,
which was evil, refusing to accept it or himself in his degraded and
fallen condition.

His constant effort had to be directed toward overcoming these limitations and constraints, and the evil in which he was submerged. He
had to strive for purity, for transcendence, for a return to the nostalgia

of his previous existence of infinite freedom and purity, the lost paradise that could be regained only through true gnosis. His fallen state did not eliminate but certainly obscured the innate superiority of the light within him. In Gnostic consciousness, side by side with the experience and dread of evil, there was the desire, the arrogant certainty beyond hope and faith, for the possession of absolute truth and omniscience that would vanquish and abolish all evil (Puech 1936).

The solution was sought in two conceptual phases of the revelation of the origins and destiny of man. The first phase involved the cosmic myth explaining man's origin not as the result of God willing evil, but rather, either that evil has always existed of itself in opposition to the good, or that evil comes into existence through the lessening of divine essence and presence through emanations or through the fall of some lesser transcendent being who became the creator of an imperfect and evil world. This first phase provided the framework for the second phase in which the revealing angel, wisdom figure or Christ brought the promise of salvific gnosis. The second phase proffered a soteriological myth in which, despite his fallen state of subjection to fate and sin, man had his source in the transcendent world and remained ultimately joined to the divine to which he could be recalled through redemption. The divine element within remained relatively unsullied by the accidental association with matter and evil, so that when the divine spark was awakened we could reclaim our destiny to return once again to the pristine, eternal, and enduring purity. This reclamation might require purifying rites in addition to the acquisition of gnosis. This system of salvific mythology was available primarily to the "pneumatic" or truly spiritual man who was capable of true gnosis; some systems apparently also extended the possibility of salvation to the "psychics" as well, but only under certain conditions (Puech 1936).

Jewish Gnosticism

Scholarly consensus holds that Gnosticism arose from heterodox cultic and sectarian divergences within Palestinian Judaism, from the ruins of Jewish apocalyptic eschatology: once the promises of the apocalyptic vision had proven illusory, one had the choice between settling for the dissatisfactions of reality or seeking escape from an alien world (Grant 1970). Gnosticism arose out of the same religious context, but the forces that drove it magnified the effects of the cultic process, and, in contrast to the evolving Christian church, resulted in a series of fragmented and rapidly multiplying sects that spawned a lush overgrowth of disparate religious systems retaining little mutual consistency or common doctrine, even though they shared the basic Gnostic elements. Consequently, there was no Gnostic church, and no recognizable Gnostic movement until the high point of Gnostic influence was reached in the second century. The syncretistic nature of Gnosticism suggests that many of its adherents originally belonged to and continued to identify with extant religious traditions—as a religious tradition Gnosticism stood in varying relations with other religious traditions, especially Judaism, Christianity and paganism. Even if it could be regarded as an independent religious movement, it appeared in some form of Jewish, Christian or pagan garb (McGuire 1986).

Gnostic views existed prior to the development of Christianity and had found a place among heterodox Jewish sects. The pharisaic party, dating from the second century B.C., was not well established as a religious movement in Palestine until after the destruction of the Temple when centers of tannaitic law began to exercise their influence. In the face of this relatively uncertain consolidation of Jewish belief, remnants of former pagan semitic and Hellenistic influences were preserved. There was during this intertestamental period no normative Judaism from which heretical views could diverge—there were only numerous competing groups of a religious tradition in flux centered on the Mosaic revelation (Neusner 1984).

Dualistic trends were already extant in Jewish heterodox thinking, under the influence no doubt of eastern religions and Hellenistic philosophical speculation. The apocalyptic literature produced by the Essenes at Qumran is especially noteworthy (Grant 1966). The existence of baptismal sects in Palestine even before the Christian era is suggestive of Gnostic influences. The Coptic materials discovered at Nag Hammadi reinforce the impression of connection with heterodox occultist Judaic thought, and it seems likely that there are linkages between Gnostic and kabbalistic thought (Jonas 1963). Even the "gnostic" views that Paul addressed in Corinth (1 Cor 1:10-17) were more likely Jewish than Greek in origin.

Jewish Apocalyptic

Gnostic ideas were expressed in Jewish apocalyptic and perhaps even in pharisaic teaching around the turn of the millennium. Many of these ideas found their way into the apocryphal literature of the period.[2] The prophets had put their faith in the intervention of God to

---

[2] The term "apocalypse" itself means "hidden" or "secret," referring to the esoteric doctrine concealed in these writings. The original connotation was probably that these teachings were not meant for common disposition, but were reserved for the learned or elite.

redeem his chosen people and renew the glories of the Davidic reign. The apocalyptic vision saw the world in more pessimistic terms and was even more strongly convinced of God's salvific intervention.

They expected God to destroy the world and build it anew. The book of Daniel gave approval to the struggle against Antiochus Epiphanes, and saw the success of the Maccabees as proof of God's saving hand. The failure of the Maccabean revolt transformed simple apocalyptic prediction of future times into a polemical advocacy of the holy war between the "sons of light" and the "sons of darkness" among the Essenes and later the Zealots.[3] This dynamic of visionary rebellion propelled a process that moved inexorably toward the cataclysm of A.D. 70 and beyond. Qumran was left in ashes and Jerusalem razed to the ground.

One sociological hypothesis that tries to provide a basis for the rise of apocalyptic visions is that the turning to apocalyptic promises and the general sense of a cosmic struggle between divine and demonic forces reflects the fundamental conflicts extant in the historical situation. Horsley (1989) explains:

> That is, "mythical fantasies" of a more humane future were almost certainly rooted in the experience of a concrete dualism, between the people's traditional way of life lived according to their sacred traditions, on the one hand, and political, economic, and/or cultural oppression that was breaking down or making impossible that traditional way of life, on the other. The dualism of God's agents versus Satan reflected the political-economic situation in which the people's lives were out of their own control and under hostile and/or alien control.
>
> Belief in demons or, more broadly, Jewish apocalyptic symbolization is thus yet another important aspect of the social conditions of and for certain (but not all) Jewish renewal or resistance movements. Besides simply reflecting the concrete situation, however, this belief in demon possession and a struggle between God's agents and demonic powers provided (at least some involved in) the Jesus movement and certain others (such as the Qumranites and apparently the popular prophetic movements) both with a way of understanding their oppressive situation and with a way of dealing with it (p. 98).

If we cannot claim a pervasive apocalypticism in ancient Palestine, it also seems clear that the literature of the Dead Sea community of Essenes contained many of the apocalyptic elements that would later emerge in

---

[3] See the discussion of the historical role of these sects in chapters 4 and 5.

Gnostic writings. Parallels abound between Jewish apocryphal litera-ture and Gnostic writings as is apparent in the Nag Hammadi findings. The many examples of Jewish traditions and the affinities of these Gnostic dialogues with Jewish apocalypses of the period point to the dependence of Gnostic views on pre-existing Jewish traditions (Perkins 1980; Segal 1987).[4]

Gnosticism and the Old Testament

The parallelism between the Wisdom myth as found in Judaism and in Gnosticism is of particular interest. The Sophia myth is found in both Gnostic writings and in the Wisdom literature of the Old Testa-ment, especially the books of Wisdom and Proverbs.[5] The parallels in-clude the idea that Sophia was personal and female, that she was joined in intimate union with God, that she was brought forth from or in the beginning (implying some form of pre-existence) and dwelt in the heavens, that she attended the throne of God or was herself enthroned, that she was identified with the Holy Spirit, that she played some role in the creation of the world, that she communicated wisdom and reve-lation to men, that she had descended into the world of men and reas-cended to her celestial home, that she it was who protected, delivered and strengthened Adam, that she was addressed as "sister," was asso-ciated with a seven-fold cosmic structure, was identified with life and called the "tree of life" (MacRae 1970). The Sophia figure was also asso-ciated with Eve, whose fall in the garden of Eden became the image for the fall of Sophia from the heavenly realm into the world of men.

The strength of these connections offers a basis for arguing that such Gnostic ideas were derived from a Jewish background, but not simply and not without ambivalence. MacRae (1970) summarized this complexity:

> But can the Jewish background explain the basic spirit of the Gnos-tic myth? The Jewish attitude was one of confidence in Wisdom,

[4] Perkins' work examines and analyzes the many resemblances between gnostic dialogues found at Nag Hammadi and apocalyptic Jewish sources—for example, apocalyptic cosmologies, exegeses of Genesis, and eschatological predictions. There are also formal characteristics that are common—the locale, names, activities, and mental dispositions correspond to introductions to resurrection accounts and to openings of Jewish apocalypses.

[5] These sections of Proverbs, especially chapters 8–9, are thought to be Canaanite in origin with parallels found in Ugaritic tablets and Phoenician inscriptions (Al-bright 1957).

resulting from the conviction that God made his Wisdom dwell in
Israel. How then explain the Gnostic hostility, or at least ambivalence, toward the personified Wisdom? Although in some accounts
Sophia is both the good revealer and the hapless originator of material creation, in others she is frankly despised as the source of all
that is evil. She falls, repents and is readmitted to the Pleroma in
some accounts, and in others her place is simply taken by error or
deception.

The answer to the question must lie in the realization that the
essence of the Gnostic attitude, as has often been stated, is one of
revolt, and it is a revolt against Judaism itself. Yet somehow it must
be conceived as a revolt *within* Judaism. The poignancy of the expression of it indicates this: the Wisdom of Yahweh has been a deception (pp. 97–98).

The dualism that was so prominent in Gnostic thinking was by no
means foreign to apocalyptic understanding. Many sectors of the Jewish community in various situations and periods developed conceptions of the deity that diverged from accepted rabbinical traditions
(Segal 1987). The prevailing alienation from political, social, and religious structures among apocalyptic thinkers led to a view of two ages
(the present evil, the future good) as well as a dualism of higher and
lower powers. The heretical idea of the "two powers in heaven" appears in rabbinical texts, but in confusing perspective that leaves it uncertain whether there is a common thread or not (Segal 1987). If the god
of the Jews were responsible for creation and the Law, then there must
have been a higher god who stood above the corruption and evil of the
world.

Gnosticism and Heterodox Judaism

Jewish apocalyptic continued to flourish until Hadrian's attempt to
build a Greek city on the ruins of Jerusalem and erect a new temple of
Jupiter Capitolinus. The result was the revolt of Bar Kochba ending in
the devastation of Jerusalem and the second destruction of the Temple
in A.D. 135. It was the end of Jewish apocalyptic and messianic hopes.
God had abandoned his people and many came to doubt his omnipotence and omniscience, and most of all his providence over his chosen
people (Grant 1966). The loss of any hope for justification, redemption,
and vindication by God in this world transformed the remnants of
apocalyptic into gnosis. Visions of a this-worldly series of apocalyptic
events were projected into the heavens. The dualism of apocalyptic
thought was magnified and the element of free choice driven into the
background. The world that had once been the arena for contending

forces of good and evil men and angels was transformed into the world of evil angels whose power could only be escaped through the power of gnosis. Old Testament prophecy gave way to dualistic gnosis.

Somewhere above the hostile heavens of the evil powers, there was a blessed abode to which men had to find a way to ascend in order to be saved. The spiritual part of man was called to this ascent into the highest heavens. The apocalyptic writers looked for the resurrection of the body; but for the Gnostics, there could be no such divine intervention—only ascent of the divine spirit in man could do it. The idea of the heavenly journey of the soul is quite ancient; it is found in Iranian and Mithraic sources. But it came to full flower in Jewish apocalyptic, especially the Testament of Levi, 2 Enoch and 2 Baruch, and in the Essene teachings from Qumran. It passed from these sources into Gnostic and Christian teaching (Grant 1966).

To the extent that Gnostic sects may have represented deviant forms of Jewish belief, they rebelled in a sense against traditional Jewish doctrines and rejected some of the most basic teachings of the Torah—the divinity of the creator, the obligation to observe the Law, and so on. Not that there was any consecrated orthodoxy to rebel against, but rather among the divergence of views that characterized Jewish religious thought of the period Gnostic leanings seemed to have occupied the fringes of consensus rather than any central position. In a sense, the eruption of apocalyptic visionary fanaticism in the catastrophe of A.D. 70 and again in the debacle of the messianic crusade of Bar Kochba buried the hopes of Jewish orthodoxy in a pile of rubble. As a result, the more deviant heterodox views found other places to strike their roots and flourish (Grant 1966).

Even in this antithetical mythological development, the use of biblical material and traditional Jewish forms of interpretation gave rise to a Gnostic synthesis that involved a hermeneutical principle. As Pearson (1990a) observes:

> This hermeneutical principle can be described as one of revolt. In the Gnostic reinterpretation the God of Israel, the God of history and creation, is demonized; the Creator and his creation are considered to be the product of a tragic fall within the divine realm; and humanity is seen to be a part of the transcendent God imprisoned by hostile powers in an alien environment. Inasmuch as the Gnostic synthesis reflects the use and reinterpretation of Jewish scripture and tradition, it is apparent that the Gnostic phenomenon itself originates in a Jewish environment as an expression of alienation from ("orthodox") Judaism. As a result a new religion, which can no longer be called "Jewish," is born (p. 38).

While this reconstruction of the history has its relevance, the question of a Jewish gnosis and the origins of later Christian Gnosticism from these Jewish roots is complicated. While there are plenty of indications of the origins of the Gnostic movement by way of revolution within Judaism, or as rebellion against Hellenized Jewish wisdom and apocalyptic circles (MacRae 1978), the demonstration of Gnostic elements in Jewish apocalyptic does not conclude to the existence of a Jewish Gnosticism as such. If Gnosticism and Christianity were both forms of Jewish heresy, the separation between Christianity and the synagogue took place only gradually over the course of much of the first century. The break did not become decisive until after the destruction of the Temple. Some of the antipathy to Judaism in Gnostic writings, as was also the case in the Johannine community if not beyond, may have been due to the expulsion of Jewish Christians from the synagogue as part of the Jewish reintegration under Jamnaic pharisaism toward the end of the first century. As Perkins (1980) observes:

> It seems probable that some of these heterodox Jews would find their way into Christian circles where Jewish tradition is both accepted and rejected. It is possible that this is the context in which what we know as characteristic Gnostic exegesis of the Old Testament arose. The esoteric and perhaps philosophizing interpretations of the Old Testament were turned against that tradition and its God (p. 18).

There is good evidence for the presence of such Gnostic influences in early Christianity. If we turn to the pastoral epistles of Paul, the letters to Timothy and Titus, the heretical teachings that Paul addresses were apparently forms of Jewish Gnosticism. The authenticity of the letters had been questioned on the grounds that the Gnostic material had to be from the second century. More recent scholarship has revised that opinion since the false teachings in question do not fit with the more developed Gnosticism of the second century and rather reflect a form of Jewish Gnosticism that is supported from other sources (Denzer 1968).

11

Gnosticism in Christianity

Introduction

The Gnostic vine found its way into the Christian vineyard and its fastgrowing branches intermingled and intertwined with those of Christianity. The Nag Hammadi documents give us reason to think that there are often striking parallels between Gnostic doctrines and Christian interpretations. They probably represent separate forms of religious development growing out of the same common soil dominated by sectarian Judaism (LaCarriere 1977; Perkins 1990a). They may both have been Jewish heresies (MacRae 1978) that were driven out of the synagogue and adopted a polemical stance against Judaism as their common enemy (Perkins 1980). The pattern of this development is poorly understood and much of the reconstruction is conjectural (Perkins 1990a), but, as Pearson (1990a) writes,

> One thing is clear, however: Gnosticism early in its development came to be attached in many areas to yet another religion that had been born out of Judaism, namely, Christianity. In "Christian" Gnostic circles the figure of Jesus Christ became the focal point for Gnostic revelation, and important apostolic figures from early Christianity became, in a developing Gnostic literature, interlocutors with Jesus for the dissemination of the Gnostic revelation (p. 38).

After the destruction of Jerusalem and the second Temple, survival of pharisaic Judaism required tightening of control over the synagogues and exclusion of any sectarians not adhering closely to monotheistic orthodoxy. The emerging Christian church and the rabbinical movement centered at Jamnia were the two main groups that arose from the ashes of pharisaism. All dualistic speculations, whether apocalyptic, philosophical or Christian, were condemned by the rabbis by the end of the first century. Segal (1987) hypothesizes, "that the radicalization of Gnosticism was partly a product of the battle between the rabbis, the Christians and various other 'two powers' sectarians who inhabited the outskirts of Judaism and Christianity" (p. 38).

The relations between the two traditions are difficult to disentangle in the face of uncertain chronology and the obscurity of cause and effect. The prevailing views are that either Gnosticism preceded Christianity and influenced its beginnings, or that Gnosticism arose as a Christian heresy or Jewish heterodoxy that only came into its own in the early second century, or lastly, that they both arose more or less simultaneously and mutually shaped the course of their subsequent development. This all took place in the thoroughly syncretistic milieu of the Middle East that had is effects even within orthodox Christianity (Jonas 1963).

The obvious debts of Gnostic teachings to Christianity say nothing about the character of so-called Gnostic doctrines that found their way into the writings of Paul or John, either influencing their teaching or serving as adversaries. Puech (1951) commented:

> If there have been Christian Gnosticisms, these were not properly speaking heresies immanent in Christianity but the results of an encounter and a fusion between the new religion and a Gnosticism which had existed before it, which was originally alien to it and in essence remained so. Here Gnosticism has assumed Christian forms, or forms which in the course of time became more and more profoundly Christianized, just as elsewhere it took on pagan forms, adapting itself to oriental mythologies, to mystery cult, to Greek philosophy, or to the occult arts and sciences (p. 55).

The emerging church owed much to Gnostic stimulus. Gnostic claims and attacks forced the church to develop credal formulas, to articulate a canon of Holy Scripture, and to develop and consolidate episcopal authority and ecclesial hierarchy. The Gnostic opposition also provoked a development of theological reflection and doctrine in the hands of men like Irenaeus, Clement of Alexandria, Origen, and others who took up the cause of the church in the face of the Gnostic onslaught. The Gnostic challenge kept the issues of freedom, grace and redemption in the theological frying pan longer than might otherwise have been the case.

Christian Gnosticism

The Gnostic quest for more esoteric knowledge of God and the antipathy to Jewish orientations found a more sympathetic hearing in Christian circles than in heterodox Judaism. The fact of a human Jesus who died on the cross was an obstacle that had to be overcome—one device was the idea that the heavenly revealer entered the man Jesus at his baptism and left again at the end so that what was left to crucify was no more than an empty shell. In general, Gnostic theologians sought to assimilate Christian ideas to contemporary thought, particularly Hellenistic thought patterns that dominated that culture (Wilson 1958). While many of the Christian Gnostics thought of themselves as belonging to the church, the effort to assimilate contemporary views brought with it the threat of so diluting or distorting the Christian message that the essence was lost. While these Christian Gnostics clearly had found a place within the body of the church, they also claimed a higher knowledge, a more spiritual interpretation of the Christian message (Perkins 1980). When the great bishop Ignatius was arrested and sent to Rome, his letters reflected concern over the unity of the church in Antioch, probably due in part to the activity of Gnostic teachers (Grant 1970).

The redeemer figure played a central role in Gnostic belief since through him the salvific *gnosis* was revealed to men. The idea cannot be demonstrated to belong to pre-Christian sources and probably reflects a syncretistic acquisition from Christianity (Wilson 1958; Grant 1961). In pagan lore, there were gods who died and rose, but they provided no saving knowledge. The Gnostic need for salvation was driven by a sense of alienation and not belonging to the world of ignorance and evil, along with a nostalgia for return to that prior state of perfection lost when he was imprisoned in matter. If man's spirit is trapped in an alien body, only through salvific *gnosis* could he be saved. Gnostic interpretation could not allow salvation through a man who was crucified. Salvation had to come from the supermundane realm of pure spirit. The spiritual Christ came from above, and only a corporeal Christ could be crucified.

Salvation was due to *gnosis* rather than to any savior whatever his guise. The meaning of *gnosis* encompassed immediate redemption, the revelation of the secrets of salvation. The crucifixion had no role in this. When the crucifixion was admitted, it was reduced to the status of an occasion for Christ's spiritual teaching, not as a salvific sacrifice in itself.

But in nearly every case, the Gnostic redeemer was identified with Christ or modeled after him (Grant 1966). Gnostic speculations about Wisdom drew a picture that found reverberations in the higher christology in which Jesus was identified with the divine *Logos*—a theologized view of Christ that found its way into the teaching of Paul, John, and some Gnostic teachers. This view may have been at variance with the emphasis on realized eschatology that put the stress on the imminent end of the world.

The disappointment of apocalyptic hopes led to a Christian vision of the Messiah radically different from Jewish notions—a view that became "to the Jews a stumbling-block, to the Greeks foolishness" (1 Cor 1:24). Salvation for the Gnostic was from his alienation and entrapment in an alien body and world; for the Jew and Christian, salvation from sin was achieved through faith, penance and obedience to God's will. The Gnostics in general preferred to associate their teaching with the risen Lord—the revealer of a higher spiritual truth—rather than the earthly Lord.

Gnostic ethical views and practices were fraught with ambiguity: if some were given over to an almost compulsive promiscuity, others espoused a radical and rigid asceticism. While they rejected conventional laws or mores, especially those based on the Old Testament, the methods for freeing themselves from enslaving rules imposed by the hateful world-creating demons differed radically. Some claimed that violation of these constraints was necessary in order to receive *gnosis,* a view that led to sexual license and perversion—the sense that sin was liberating. For them sin was the price to be paid for ultimate freedom. It became a positive prescription of immorality and sin as a way to salvation—a Faustian archetype that would return in medieval guise in Sabbatianism and subsequent messianic aberrations (Scholem 1973; Meissner 1995). Others viewed sex and marriage as an invention of Satan, and therefore prescribed complete sexual abstinence, and some even forbade the eating of meat. Libertinism and asceticism were opposite sides of the same psychic coin, both expressing the Gnostic rejection of and revolt against nature (Jonas 1963). As might be expected, the elevation of these beliefs to an ideology became the basis for polemics and contention between and among Gnostic groups (Perkins 1980).

Gnosticism in the New Testament

Paul

Gnostic influences can be traced in some New Testament writers—Paul's early letters have an apocalyptic emphasis, for example his effort to correct the idea that the day of the Lord had already dawned

(2 Thess 2:2). The apocalyptic emphasis seems to give way to protognostic thinking (Grant 1966). Gnostic or pregnostic ideas were probably present in the Corinthian community. One of the criteria for protognostic teaching has been the emphasis on a realized eschatology, but the converse inference from realized eschatology to Gnostic influences is at best precarious. The tension between an eschatological view realized in the present and the postponement of eschatological hopes to some future point existed in both Christian and Gnostic views. In some Gnostic texts the immediate realization of eschatological expectations was viewed within a broader context of a futuristic gathering of all the sparks of light into the heavenly realm of Light (Peel 1970).

The public and professional involvements of higher class Christians were associated with a greater degree of integration into the surrounding pagan society. One of the characteristics of these church members from higher social strata was the place of *gnosis* in their approach to religion. Their special knowledge or understanding allowed them to transcend the obsolete religious restrictions that seem to have been matters of conflicted conscience for the less privileged. As Theissen (1982) suggests regarding the eating of meat sacrificed to idols, the only comparable position among Christians on this issue came from more explicitly Gnostic groups of a later date. Eating of meat sacrificed to idols was certainly not a common characteristic of the Gnostic movement, but it was one typical behavior among others. The prohibition against eating such consecrated meat was more uniform in orthodox Christianity. They also sought the gifts of the Holy Spirit *(charismata)*—the power to heal, perform miracles, prophesy, glossolalia, interpretation of tongues, and so on (1 Cor 12:4ff). Possession of the Spirit would free them from all constraints (1 Cor 6:12), even sexual (1 Cor 6:15-16).

The connections between such Corinthian *"gnosis"* and later Christian Gnosticism are both controversial and scarcely direct. But the analogies persist. In both instances, we can see a reshaping of the Christian faith resulting from inclusion of higher social classes. Along with higher levels of social stratification, certain other characteristics emerged, including a higher intellectual level, an emphasis on knowledge, a form of elite self-consciousness, and a greater openness to interchange with the surrounding social environment. The Gnostic system of thought emphasized special knowledge and a high degree of intellectual capacity. Emphasis on knowledge and the power of understanding, particularly its role in the discernment of salvation, is also an upper class characteristic. Salvation took place less through the power of a deity than through the inner possession of understanding.

For the Corinthian "Gnostics," true knowledge took the form of acknowledging that idols do not really exist—a form of demythologization. Such knowledge was liberating and tended to be associated with a somewhat superior attitude, looking down on and devaluing those who do not possess it. Gnostic writings tended to reflect an acutely elitist consciousness which drove a wedge of separation between those possessing true knowledge and understanding as opposed to those who believed only by faith. Normal Christians in this perspective were second-class citizens. This reflected the degree of internal stratification in Hellenized Christian communities, as in Rome and Corinth, where upper class Christians self-consciously set themselves apart from the everyday Christian community. The distinction between the "strong" and the "weak" at Corinth, or references to the spiritualists and the worldly seem also to be based on the possession of special wisdom. In addition Gnostics tended to be much more open to and involved in the culture of pagan antiquity. They tended to take part in the delights of the day, banquets and theatrical performances, engaged in the social life of the city, and were no more strict about sexual morality than the rest of the community. This liberality obviously also included a lack of scruples about eating meat offered to idols.

Christian Gnosticism of the second century was in large degree a theology of the upper classes. The same characteristics found in later Gnosticism also played a role in the Corinthian community. As Theissen (1982) comments:

> In the case of the Corinthian gnostics we also find a certain level of education, the significance of knowledge and wisdom for ethics and salvation, and an elitist self-consciousness within the community which goes hand in hand with a considerable liberalism about associating with the pagan world. In both instances these characteristics taken together point to an elevated social status (p. 136).

The split and the tension of powerful ideologies within the Corinthian community seemed inevitable. On the one hand, more Hellenistically inclined upperclass Gentile converts were strongly influenced by Gnostic ideology and social attitudes. But at the same time, there persisted a powerful and pervasive influence of older traditions, derived from both pagan and Jewish sources, on the more numerous, if less influential and prominent, members of the lower classes. The evolving life of the nascent church was caught between these powerful ideological forces representing derivatives of an earlier, possibly obsolete protest movement on one hand, and the more sophisticated, enlightened, adaptive and upper-class influence stemming from the increasing surge of Hellenistic converts.

Paul's letter to the Corinthians displays the problems inherent in Judeo-Christian eschatological preaching as well as the tensions resulting from the presence of both Jews and Gentiles and differential class status in the church. He addresses those who have turned against Judaism, but held exalted opinions of their own status, possessing special wisdom and *gnosis*. Some even claimed a somewhat idealized view of themselves, based on the Cynic-Stoic image of the "wise man,"—powerful, well-born, rich and royal (1 Cor 1:26; 4:8).[1] They regarded themselves as spiritual men ("pneumatics"), superior to others who were no better than "psychic." Dupont (1949) identifies these possessors of special *gnosis* with the Christ party who boasted of a special relation to the Savior not shared with other Christians. He comments: ". . . the importance attached to *gnosis* in the list of the charisms is due to the influence at Corinth of Jewish preachers who would seem to have been at the bottom of the factions in the community, and to be more precise, would be the promoters of 'the Christ party'" (p. 261).[2] Paul acknowledges the gifts of those who prided themselves as spiritually superior, but his point is that faith, hope, and love are more important than *gnosis* and ecstasy—a fundamental Christian teaching (Nock 1972). For Paul, Christ's revelation is indeed a mystery, a form of *gnosis*, but, far from being any sort of esoteric or secret doctrine, it was to be preached from the housetops (Rahner 1963).

These views might have reflected both the experience of "spiritual" activity in the community and a view of a realized eschatology—the kingdom had already come and they were filled with spiritual wisdom. From the perspective of Gnostic eschatology, the end times were already realized and expectations of any future renewal were minimal. The delay in the arrival of the promised parousia may have intensified pressures to realize eschatological rewards in the present. The guarantee of these rewards for the Gnostic was his possession of an immortal pneuma or heavenly light (Peel 1970). These sectarians had replaced an eschatology in process by one that was fully realized. They also placed special emphasis on the notion of Jesus as the wisdom of God (1 Cor 1:18–2:5). Themes of rejection of sexuality (1 Cor 6:12-20), distinctions between classes of men—psychic vs. pneumatic (1 Cor 2:14-16)—and denial of the resurrection (1 Cor 15:29-32; 2 Cor 5:1-5) seem to draw closer to Gnostic positions, but the framework of thought and the identity of these groups remain obscure.[3]

---

[1] See the discussion of the socio-economic aspects of the status of this elite and the stratifications in the Corinthian community in chapter 8.

[2] Cited in Kugelman (1968).

[3] Grant (1970) noted that the Corinthian Gnostics were not gnostic in the more developed sense of the second century, but that their position was quite similar to that espoused by the second-century Gnostic Prodicus and his followers.

Paul challenged the Colossians' speculative angelology by confrontation with his own realized eschatology. This teaching held that angelic beings (elements) had control over all creation and human affairs, and that "knowledge" of these higher beings was necessary to propitiate them. They were regarded as mediators between God and the world, of which Christ was one. These ideas contained a theosophic mysticism that would later develop into explicit Gnosticism, laying claim to exclusive knowledge of celestial beings. Jewish influences were prominent in this teaching—at Qumran great emphasis was placed on these angelic beings and their influence in the world (Grassi 1968). Worship of such principalities and powers was probably pregnostic, but does not fit with the Gnostic repudiation of the evil powers of the demiurge.

The development of Paul's thought from the period of Thessalonians laid increasing emphasis on a realized eschatology with less emphasis on the future coming of the Lord. The Colossians may not have advocated Gnostic ideas, but the Gnostic flavor in Paul himself seems to have grown. The dualism of spirit and flesh, convictions about the existence of the principalities and powers, his references to the "god of this world," and his own claim to special and privileged revelation (2 Cor 12:4), all have a Gnostic ring to them (Nock 1972). Exegetical opinion varies, but the hymn in Col 1:15-20 may represent an adaptation of a pre-Christian Gnostic hymn based on the Gnostic concept of the *Urmensch* ("archetypal man"), the image of God who served as a mediator in both creation and redemption, as well as embracing references to Christ as the Wisdom of God (Grassi 1968).

By the time of the letter to the Ephesians, the Gnostic flavor is even stronger. The date is possibly after the destruction of the Temple, but in any case the Gnostic impression is inescapable. The church and Christians have ascended to the heavenly realms to reveal the wisdom of God to the principalities and powers. Paul announces a spiritual war against the powers of darkness:

> Finally, grow strong in the Lord, with the strength of his power. Put God's armor on so as to be able to resist the devil's tactics. For it is not against human enemies that we have to struggle, but against the Sovereignties and the Powers who originate the darkness in this world, the spiritual army of evil in the heavens. That is why you must rely on God's armor, or you will not be able to put up any resistance when the worst happens, or have enough resources to hold your ground (Eph 6:10-13).

If the words are not Gnostic here, the music is. The apocalyptic expectations of earlier epistles are here transformed into cosmology. Here again, the conclusion is not forced on us that Paul was influenced by Gnostic teachings, since most of these doctrines were extant in current Jewish apocalyptic literature and thought with which Paul was quite familiar. As Cerfaux (1959) commented: "When his thought is not independent, Paul thinks in terms of what was current in Judaism, whether sapiential or apocalyptic, but he would remain acceptable in Hellenistic circles. Gnosticism had roots in this same Hellenistic milieu, and its oriental colouring need not lead us to conclude, before all other hypotheses are tried, that we have to look very far afield in assessing possible influences on Paul's theology" (p. 372).

Later Gnostics would lose no opportunity to read Paul as supporting their systems, as the author of 2 Peter would later complain (3:15-16). The pastoral epistles would attack "myths and genealogies" (1 Tim 1:4) and "Jewish myths" (Tit 1:14) that probably reflect Gnostic cosmologies, derived from forms of Jewish Gnosticism.[4] 1 Tim (6:20-21) warns against Gnostic false doctrines. These false teachings were erroneous and highly divisive, leading to strife and contention that threatened the harmony and unity of the Christian community at both Ephesus and Crete where Timothy and Titus exercised their apostolate (2 Tim 2:23). Were the Church Fathers right in thinking that this attack was directed against Gnostic systems of the late first and early second centuries (Grant 1966), or at least against Gnosticism in some embryonic form (Wilson 1958)? Around these doctrinal polarizations, the tensions and conflicts of emerging Christian communities and parties came to sort themselves out. The doctrinal struggles reflect the underlying forces of the cultic process as it shaped the patterns of orthodoxy and belief at the very roots of early Christianity.

John

The question of Gnostic influences in the Gospel of John is problematic: Bultmann (1941) even suggested that the original evangelist might have been a Jewish Gnostic convert to Christianity who drew on Gnostic source material. Later redactors would have tried to harmonize John with the synoptic tradition and with church teaching. The result would have been a demythologization of the Gnostic redeemer myth by attaching it to the person of Jesus and the transformation of Gnostic dualism from a metaphysical to an ethical dualism (Kselman 1968).[5]

---

[4] See chapter 10 on Jewish gnosticism—the apocryphal *Book of Jubilees* is typical.

[5] Segal (1987) comments that the Johannine community fits the description provided by Douglas (1970) for communities characterized by dualistic beliefs. See chapter 9.

There are certainly similarities between John and Gnostic literature. John's dualism encompasses two orders of being, one above and the other below, with implications similar to Gnostic teachings. The contrasts are sharply drawn: true vs. false, light vs. darkness, spirit vs. flesh—to belong to one is to be excluded from the other. But at the same time the orders are not totally divorced—the light shines in the darkness but the darkness does not completely overcome it (John 1:5).

References to "the Ruler of the World" (John 12:31, 14:30, 16:11), who may be equivalent to Paul's "God of this World" (2 Cor 4:4), describe his demonic power and may reflect the Christian reaction to exclusion from the synagogue—the "Jews" are governed by this demonic power and can expect divine judgment because they are of this world. The Ruler of the World is evil because his world is evil, as are the Jews who represent the world in opposition to Christianity. The Johannine community felt excluded from the Jewish community in ways the Synoptics did not. The Jews became the projective object of latent hostilities that translated into the language of persecution.[6]

It is not clear whether the relation between Christ and the Father reflect Gnostic descriptions of a heavenly revealer—the "I am" form of discourse that occurs so frequently in John[7] was common enough in Gnostic writings referring to the revealer, but parallels may have been due to both Gnostic and Johannine communities simply having drawn on a common fund of religious symbols and formulations extant in the religious milieu (Perkins 1990b). The same could be true of references to the Paraclete or the Spirit of Truth, the angel protector of the church, whom Jesus promised to send once he had departed this world. The antagonism between the Spirit of Truth and the Ruler of the World closely paralleled the theology of Qumran—the angel who led the forces of light against the forces of darkness was called the Spirit of Truth (Segal 1987).

For all of these usages, John remains protognostic; it had not yet reached the doctrinal extremes achieved by the second-century Gnostics. The Ruler of the World fell short of becoming a demiurge since he did not create; he was at best the lord of the demons, a role he filled in apocalyptic Jewish systems. And if they regarded the Jews as children of Satan, the Johannine community did not want to reject the Old Testament or the creator God of the Jews. Their claim was that they alone remained loyal to the prophets (Segal 1987). Parallels with the Dead

---

[6] See chapter 9.

[7] "I am . . . the bread (John 6:35, 41, 48, 51), . . . the light (John 8:12), . . . the door (John 10:7, 9), . . . the resurrection (John 11:25), . . . the way (John 14:6), . . . the vine (John 15:1, 5)."

Sea Scrolls in John suggest that he may have been trying to cast the mission of Jesus in terms closer to Qumran views—the contrast of light and darkness, truth vs. falsehood, the sons of light under the banner of God and the sons of darkness under the devil, the idea of salvation by overcoming the world, and the notion of an eschatological community living in the world, may all reflect this connection (Grant 1966).[8]

The whole prologue has a Gnostic ring except for the critical phrase, "The Word was made flesh, he lived among us . . ." (John 1:14). For Gnostic understanding, it was essential that the divine Christ could not be regarded as human or that the spiritual Christ be separate from the human Christ. Nonetheless the portrait of Christ in John was spiritualized and theologized in a way that would have had greater appeal to Gnostics. Certainly they were not slow to make use of John—Valentinus did little more than transpose the Gospel into a Gnostic mode (Wilson 1958). Quotations from John or echoes of it abounded, especially in the teachings of Basilides and Valentinus. Early Gnostic exegeses of the Gospel, among the earliest we know about, found Gnostic themes and doctrines in John's text—whether they were authentically Johannine or not is another question. As Dodd (1968) commented, "If there is an affinity, it would seem to be due to some degree of common background behind the thought of orthodox and heretical teachers" (p. 102).

The *logos* doctrine in John was especially tempting meat for Gnostic mastication. The divine *logos* descended from the higher unknown God, defeated the forces of darkness by his triumph over the cross and death, and returned once more to his heavenly home, thus opening the way for his followers to regain their heavenly abode. John's *Logos* was the mediator between the upper and lower spheres: He revealed the supreme God to men and opened the way to heavenly ascent (Dodd 1968). If the story was Gnostic in form, the content was not—the dualism was always limited, the incarnate Word was a real human being who suffered and died. John probably assumed a place somewhere between Judaism and Jewish Christianity on one side and Gnosticism on the other (Grant 1966). The discovery of the Gnostic library at Nag Hammadi in 1946 has made it clear how much John reflects a different world of thought from its Gnostic contemporaries. Many of the Gnostic usages probably reflect protognostic influences from Palestinian Judaism rather than later Gnostic affiliations as such (Vawter 1968).

The first epistle of John directly attacked Gnostic-like ideas, particularly those that would try to divorce moral conduct from intellectual convictions. The polemic was directed against a sort of faith-without-

---

[8] See the discussion of the Qumran community and its influence on the origins of Christianity in chapter 5.

works approach associated with Gnostic views of salvation through *gnosis* alone. By the same token, some form of early Gnostic laxity was probably the target of the denunciations in the book of Revelation (2:6, 14-16, 20-24). Presumably the Gnostic stress on liberty influenced some more heterodox groups to partake more fully in the pagan and syncretistic world around them. The Nicholaitans are mentioned (2:6, 15) who practiced promiscuous sexuality and eating of meat sacrificed to idols (Grant 1961). Also the attacks in Jude (8:8, 16, 18) were probably aimed at a similar Gnostic aberration,[9] probably some embryonic form of antinomian Christian Gnosticism (Leahy 1968).

John's Gospel, coming on the scene in a more evolved context of Gnostic influences (its *Sitz-im-Leben* as it were), carried a greater weight of Gnostic-like themes resonating sympathetically with the theological modality, elevated symbolic discourse, and higher christology that characterize it. If the Fourth Gospel came closer to the world of Gnostic ideas, it maintained its own separate and distinctly Christian flavor. The centerpiece remained Jesus Christ, the Son of God, who stood above his revelatory mission and assumed his place in the highest heavens, equal to the Father in power and divinity. The relatively Gnostic quality of the gospel may reflect the disjunction of the Johannine community from other Christian communities, as well as its position as mediating between evolving Christian theology and Gnostic speculation. It therefore marked a critical juncture in the evolution of the cultic process as the historical and doctrinal dialectic among the communities of the nascent Christian church underwent their uncertain development and advanced into the second century.

Christianity versus Gnosticism

The challenge posed by Gnostic systems to Christian orthodoxy was taken up in the second century by Christian apologists—the most important of whom were Clement of Alexandria and his pupil, the great Origen. They lived and taught in the teeming intellectual ferment of Egyptian Alexandria, where contemporary currents of religious and philosophical thought were melded in a syncretistic batch of intellectual influences. They met the challenge of contemporary Gnostic speculation by elaborating a powerful array of theological conceptions. While they set themselves against the Gnostic deviations that they saw as antithetical to Christian truth, they could not escape Gnostic influences that colored their views and influenced their vision of God and His creation.

[9] See 2 Pet 2:1-22.

Clement of Alexandria

Along with the philosophical influences of Middle Platonism so dominant at Alexandria, there were influences from Judaic apocalyptic traditions, centered on expectation of a final eschatological event that would overturn the present order. Danielou (1973) summarized the position of the Alexandrian apologists as follows:

> In Clement there is a direct importation of Judaeo-Christian *gnosis* . . . expressed chiefly in his speculations on angelology. In addition there is a reaction against heterodox *gnosis,* and a first attempt to construct a *gnosis* that is Hellenistic and orthodox. Origen takes over this enterprise with that genius for systematization which marks all his work, and at the same time with a still more outspoken hostility toward the dualism of the heterodox. With this in mind he constructs a *gnosis* based on variations in the use of freedom to set against the dualist *gnosis* based on ontological differences of nature (p. 446).

Clement's purpose was to preserve from oblivion the Gnostic tradition he received from his own teachers, representing the essence of Jewish apocalyptic. The notion of *gnosis* was central to his thinking—referring first to any kind of knowledge, but then especially denoting a special and privileged knowledge reserved to the elite. Such *gnosis* derived from revelation rather than reason, and involved knowledge of God and the whole universe. This *gnosis* was the wisdom Christ brought with him and taught to the apostles, a knowledge of past, present, and future that was secure because revealed by the Son of God. This *gnosis* had been handed down in succession from the apostles, but in an unwritten form and only to a select few. It was transmitted orally to the apostles and could not be regarded as synonymous with the apostolic tradition which was both written and oral. The wise man seeks the knowledge of divine things by contemplation and study, but he does not attain true *gnosis* until he is illumined by the Spirit.

Origen

Origen's view of *gnosis* differed somewhat—he saw it as esoteric knowledge, but derived completely from Scripture. The Scriptures contained mystical teachings coinciding with apocalyptic understandings of the mysteries of the beginning and the end of the universe. Origen discerned the apocalyptic elements in the scriptural writings, teachings intended only for the elect. This deeper knowledge of the Scriptures, both Old and New Testaments, could only be achieved by those possessing the key taught by Jesus, and then only to a select and privileged few.

Clearly, Origen and his teacher Clement shared the same store of ideas found in Gnostic dualism and rabbinical *kabbalah*. The common source was Jewish and Judaeo-Christian apocalyptic, whose ideas were incorporated into the mainstream of Christian theology. Both thinkers were caught up in the intellectual currents of their world, and in the maelstrom of ideas and ideologies of the syncretistic culture of Alexandria. They could hardly escape the influence of Gnostic views, especially since they were so closely allied with the common Judaic sources of their religious inspiration. It took several centuries of theological discourse and the hardening of orthodox and heterodox Christian views to delineate the line of differentiation between these Christian theologians and their Gnostic adversaries.

One of the fundamental issues separating these traditions at their ideological roots was the distinction between the fundamental teachings open to all believers and those more advanced or sophisticated truths reserved to a select few. Little of Clement's Gnostic speculation added anything of substance to the basic catechesis. His effort was directed at providing more complete and intellectually satisfying answers to questions arising within the deposit of faith. Here the Gnostic systems and Christian *gnosis* parted company. In the Gnostic systems, the truth given to the "spirituals" or "pneumatics" was not meant to explain more popular myths and stories, but proffered a quite radically different understanding of the nature of the cosmos of a different order that was closed to most of the faithful. The simple doctrine offered more generally to the faithful was in this perspective not the true faith, but a deception to keep the secret mysteries hidden from unworthy eyes. This was a line that even Origen did not cross. The emerging church, in its struggle to find its own truth and identity, had to resist the temptation offered by the Gnostic seduction and to keep clearly before its collective mind the sense that any doctrine that was not open to the understanding and belief of all the faithful could not be the true faith of Jesus Christ (Baker 1973).

Conflict Between Gnosticism and Christianity

Gnosticism seems to have drawn on much the same audience as Christianity so that the gradual emergence of an acrimonious conflict between the two movements seems all but inevitable. Grant (1970) commented on the Gnostic threat to orthodox Christianity:

> The Gnostic movement presented a threat to ordinary Christianity because its leaders could provide highly subtle exegesis of the mysterious sayings of Jesus and isolated texts from the Pauline

letters; in addition, they used books purporting to contain the authentic sayings of Jesus, known only to a select group of disciples. Their spirituality appealed to men and women alienated from Graeco-Roman society and from conventional education and morality. The sheer novelty of the doctrines doubtless attracted some adherents. We may suppose that in some measure Gnosticism was a parody of Christianity, but in its time it evidently looked like an alternative (p. 121).

Only gradually did the two movements define themselves as oppositional, both to the extent that Christian doctrinal positions received increasing clarification and refinement and in the measure that Gnostic speculation, driven by forces of syncretistic inclusion and cultic deviation, developed increasingly esoteric and unrestrained themes of speculation. In this contest for the minds of men, Gnosticism was the aggressor, an embattled cause that challenged the nascent church at its roots (Jonas 1963).

While the forces operating within the Christian ranks were propelling the nascent church towards increasing consolidation and unity, the counterforces in the Gnostic ranks pulled in the opposite direction—toward increasing diversity and fragmentation. Gnostic doctrines proliferated, each teacher taking himself as the revealer of truth and each adopting his own idiosyncratic position. Irenaeus wrote:

> And each of them says that this wisdom is the one which he has discovered for himself, that is, the product of his own imagination, so that according to them it is fitting for truth to be at one time in Valentinus, at another in Marcion, at another in Cerinthus. . . . For each of them is so completely perverted that he is not ashamed to preach himself, distorting the rule of truth.[10]

The Fathers of the early church responded with vigorous denunciation and a detailed exploration of the origins of Gnosticism to expose its errors, particularly its roots in Hellenistic philosophy so antithetical to Christian truth. Against Greek notions of the relation between the divine and the world, they opposed the biblical doctrine of creation and of divine governance of the world—a clear opposition to the Gnostic view of the antithesis of God and the world. The Gnostic notion of the two divinities, one supreme and unreachable, the other the deceitful and evil creator of a troubled and alienated world, was fundamentally opposed to the Christian conception of the relationship between God and his creation.

---

[10] *Adversus haereses* III, 2, 1, cited in Danielou (1973), p. 149.

The Gnostic mind was obsessed by its sense of evil, its origins and its reasons. As Puech (1951) observed,

> It is indeed more than likely that the enigma of the scandalous presence of evil in the world, the intolerable feeling of the precariousness, evil, or ignominy of the human lot, the difficulty of imputing a meaning to this existence of evil, of attributing it to God and of justifying God at the same time—that these are the source of the religious experience which gave rise to the Gnostic conception of Salvation (p. 64).

The Gnostic was crushed by the weight of adversity and the servitude of matter. He could only explain this burdensome degradation by a fall from a higher state—something better than the reviled and hated prison and exile he experienced in this world. The result was a movement of revolt and rejection of his present state and a refusal to accept the world or himself as he was, and a revulsion against time with a passionate desire to negate time, especially that time that was conceived as strange, servile, evil, that strangled man in a life of misery, strife, care, dividedness, debasement, exile, servitude, and oblivion. He was left with a yearning for his former existence that could be restored only by rejection of the body and the material world.

One difficult bone of contention was the issue of a realized eschatology—as was evident in the arguments between Paul and the Corinthians. The recently discovered Coptic texts lend support to traditional views of Gnostic eschatology, making a close connection between baptism and the realization of eschatological hopes—baptism meant freedom from death and a calling to divine consubstantiality. In some texts the reception of *gnosis* implies full realization of one's divine nature and salvation in the present. There was conviction that the spiritual man, illumined by *gnosis*, had already been transferred to the realm of Light. For the Gnostic, the day of eschatological fulfillment had already arrived in the present (Peel 1970). All of this was ultimately antithetical to Christian views of a future eschatological fulfillment, but the issues were often murky because of lingering expectations of the parousia. As these expectations faded, the positions hardened. The ambiguities are found not only in Christian sources, but in Gnostic sources as well, some even looked forward to a future eschatological realization, some even went so far as to believe in a form of resurrection (Peel 1970).

The crisis of faith and doctrine reached its apogee in the mid-second century. The reaction within the church took the form of increased assertion of episcopal authority, the bonds of church membership were drawn more tightly, the Roman church assumed a position of leadership among its sister churches, the disciplines of initiation and baptism were consolidated, the liturgy was constrained within official and obligatory formularies, and church laws were codified. Many remained within the communion of the church, but came to grief over controversies dealing with the christological and trinitarian beliefs (Lebreton and Zeiller 1962).

Polemics

Much of the Gnostic campaign was carried on in a strongly polemical tone. In the Thomas tradition, opponents were attacked as apostates whose doctrine led the minds of men astray. The Christians had revelation but no knowledge, and they lacked ascetical praxis. Gnostics should have nothing to do with Christians. The ascetical practice of the sect was defended as an essential aspect of the revelation of the Savior. In the Petrine apocrypha, Peter emerged as a central symbol of orthodox opposition to Gnostic Christianity, particularly associated with the emergence of hierarchical authority in orthodox communities.

The effort was made to claim Peter's authority for Gnostic Christianity. The polemic (Perkins 1980) took the following form:

(1) The Old Testament is rejected and its heroes mocked because they reflect the folly of the archon who inspired it.

(2) Christ is identified with the Father or the highest divine triad; he is greater than Sophia or any of the powers and aeons.

(3) The christology is docetic, ensuring that Christ could not be defiled by possessing a body. The archons could not harm him: they only crucified an image while the spiritual Christ laughed.

(4) Christ's death was not redemptive or salvific.

(5) The orthodox persecute the Gnostics out of hatred. It is they who cause division and disharmony in the church.

These themes reappear in various Gnostic texts and seem to reflect a standard form of Gnostic anti-Christian polemic. This polemic seems to have been the result of the pressure exerted by orthodox authorities in the church against Gnostic teachers.

Christology became a critical focus of debate. They accused the orthodox of preaching salvation through appeal to the name of a dead man, referring to the death of Christ. Those who adhered to the crucifixion were still trapped in bondage to the powers of the world. Arguments were advanced to show that Christ did not suffer crucifixion: if the Savior was crucified in his bodily form, the spiritual part could not have suffered and separated from the body before any suffering was inflicted in order to return to the Father.

Gnostic doctrines, in the face of orthodox rejection and persecution, were propounded as teachings of the postresurrection Jesus to his disciples. Orthodox authorities were equated with hostile cosmic archons, but despite their opposition, the Gnostics were resolved to carry on the mission given them by the Lord in the beginning and spread the true enlightenment throughout the world. The intensity and quality of polemical opposition differed from case to case and community to community (Perkins 1980). Gnostic antipathy toward the ecclesiastical hierarchy that began to emerge in the second and third centuries was also marked. The Valentinians particularly took the demiurge and his archons as cryptic symbols for orthodox bishops (Pagels 1976).

Decline

By the time the third century rolled around, the heyday of Gnosticism was over. Clement of Alexandria and Origen had produced volumes of anti-gnostic works effectively refuting the Gnostic challenge. Hippolytus carried on the counterattack at Rome. By the beginning of the third century, the Church had taken a firm stand against Gnostic syncretism as well as the montanist apocalyptic revival (Grant 1970). The diversity of Gnostic teaching and their consistent lack of organization made it almost impossible to maintain any solid position in the face of the increasing solidity of church structure and clarification of doctrine.

Gnostic thinking also failed to keep pace with cultural shifts in the third century, especially in the emerging priority of a written canon over oral expression—an aspect of increasing literacy and emphasis on communication through the written word. The Christian canon filled this need and the Gnostic movement had no sufficient organizational basis to accomplish this task. The increasing resource of philosophical analysis gradually imposed different standards of intelligibility and analysis (Perkins 1980). Gnostic adherence to more amorphous standards of oral interpretation that had prevailed in the second century prevented their progressive development of doctrine. Christian writers toward the end of the century seem to have forgotten Gnosticism or knew next to nothing about it. Eusebius' *Ecclesiastical History* hardly mentions them.

If Gnosticism no longer existed as a religious movement, the concept of *gnosis* as esoteric divine knowledge lived on. The Iranian prophet Mani and his Manichean followers raised a new challenge to

Christianity in the third century. Mani's system became a powerful religious force that generated one of the major religious traditions in history—"the last powerful manifestation of Gnostic spirituality in the ancient world" (Perkins 1980, p. 3). Even the great Augustine was a Manichean adherent for nine years because he thought that it embraced the true philosophy.

Until the beginning of the sixth century, radical Gnostic movements continued to proliferate in Persian dominated Mesopotamia, occasionally extending into the empire (Brown 1969). A later revival of Gnostic ideas came in the seventh and eighth centuries with the rise of the Mandeans, a small baptist sect still surviving in Iraq and Iran that preserved Gnostic materials and ideas—a form of non-Christian, possibly pre-Christian, and certainly anti-Christian Gnosticism. A few centuries later the Bogomils, the "friends of God," a Gnostic-like sect that revived Manichean ideas surfaced in Bulgaria. Splinters of this movement persisted for centuries in parts of Yugoslavia. The Catharists and Albigensians of the Middle Ages may be counted here. As LaCarriere (1977) wrote:

> Gnosticism enters history, implants itself in the bosom of national communities, founds its own churches with priests and deacons and becomes a veritable temporal power in itself. . . . as a hotbed of revolt against all the temporal powers, Gnosticism inevitably found itself confronted with the movement of history, and the repressive measures to which it was subjected compelled it to forge a social and political body, an autonomy, a destiny all its own. Wherever it sets foot, wherever the word is spread, it creates pockets of rebellion—religious or political—against the official Church and the secular authority which is its expression. . . . Moreover, the peasants will be more sensitive to its political and social implications than its religious ones. But, through this bias, the Gnostic groups become virtually communities of insurgents, gathering together thousands of peasants and artisans, and obliged henceforth to establish their own laws, their own organization, and even their own army. Clearly there is something paradoxical about this destiny. Born out of a radical rejection of history and society, Gnosticism by its very success gives birth in turn to a history and to societies, ephemeral no doubt but whose very existence and tragic fate will nevertheless long remain exemplary (p. 113–14).

The same spirit may have pervaded Gnosticism in its heyday of earlier centuries.

12

The Gnostic Phenomenon
and the Cultic Process

The Cultic Process

The study of the Gnostic phenomenon, from its earliest protognostic stirrings through its gradual emergence as a distinctive pattern of religious thought to its effulgence as a full-blown religious movement, provides a unique demonstration of the cultic process at work. The cultic process, as is evident in the above detail, operates in the formation and diversification of religious groups. The lack of unity, diffusion, diversification, differentiation, and almost unrestrained and wild proliferation of divergent sects and cultic formations within the Gnostic movement can be seen as reflecting the dynamic diversification of the cultic process. Gnostic sects, even in their nascent form as divergent doctrinal emphases within the loose body of religious thought constituting Judaic rabbinism of the first century B.C., were in process of dissociating and separating from the main body of religious tradition in Palestine. They were born in the maelstrom of heterodox sectarian movements that populated the periphery of the Jewish religion. Irenaeus' descriptions of their pressure towards diversity were much to the point:

> Let us now look at their unstable opinion—how, when there are two or three of them, they do not say the same things about these matters but express opposite opinions as to contents and names.

> Every day each one of them, in so far as he is able, produces some novelty. For no one is "perfect" among them who is not productive of great lies. Since they disagree with one another in teaching and in tradition, and the more recent converts pretend to find something new every day and to produce what no one ever thought of, it is difficult to describe the opinions of each.[1]

The direction of Gnostic thought and group structure was continually toward division and diversity rather than unity. The development of official rabbinical Judaism and Christianity followed the opposite path of increasing unity and consistency as their respective religious traditions moved along the path of history. The Gnostic pattern was much more one of the continuing formation and deterioration of groups, each seeming to split in the direction of its own idiosyncratic doctrinal emphasis or character. The half-life of these groups was severely limited insofar as they continued to embody the negative dynamics of the cultic process. Only those movements succeeding in establishing a more consistent church structure, e.g., the Valentinians and the Marcionites, and later the followers of Mani, were able to enjoy more than ephemeral life spans on the tabloid of history.

The pattern of these groupings was fairly typical—a splinter group would dissociate from a larger religious movement under the inspiration of a prophetic leader who set forth the claim that he possessed the true knowledge revealing the secrets of the universe and serving as an infallible guide to salvation. These doctrinal and structural divergences thus followed patterns dictated by the cultic process. The original inspiration that seeded the fragmentation of any group was doctrinal—based on the inspiration, intuition, and claimed revelation of the leader, who then communicated his unique religious vision to his followers. When the consolidation of these variant views had reached a certain point of articulation, and when the independent strength of the group of followers had reached a point of sufficient social power, the freshly minted heresy arrived at a juncture at which there was little choice left but to separate from the parent group or become resubmerged within the main body of belief and believers.

Cult Organization

The revolt against the powers and evil of this world reflected a sectarian mentality that was essentially "parasitic" (Perkins 1990a), that is, dependent on a larger religious culture and organization against which

---

[1] Cited in Grant (1966), p. 11.

it could rebel and whose doctrine served as a likely target for rejection and attack. Gnosticism lived off the substratum of ideas and orientations inherent in the cultural sources from which it drew its life and strength. Gnostic mythology is hardly imaginable without reference to biblical themes and to Greco-Roman philosophical and religious traditions. It may have been that the primary audience for Gnostic doctrine was the emerging class of bureaucrats and the more literate classes found in the urban centers of the Roman Empire. They did not constitute an aristocratic elite, but were intellectually alienated from their ancestral religious roots. In the Gnostic vision, they became the true elite.

The ultimate rejection of all systems of thought and the view of the world as evil and corrupt left little room for them except at the fringes of extant social structures. They refused conventional social life—refused to compromise with false and corrupt social institutions: they condemned procreation, marriage, family, and refused to obey any and all temporal powers whether pagan or Christian. As LaCarriere (1977) expressed it:

> To sum up the essential position of the Gnostics in still simpler terms, let us say that in their eyes the evil which taints the whole of creation and alienates man in body, mind, and soul, deprives him of the awareness necessary for his own salvation. Man, the shadow of man, possesses only a shadow of consciousness. And it is to this one task that the Gnostics of the first centuries A.D. deliberately devoted themselves, choosing paths which were not only unorthodox but which, moreover, greatly scandalized their contemporaries: to create in man a true consciousness, which would permit him to impart to his thoughts and deeds the permanence and the rigour necessary to cast off the shackles of this world (p. 11).

Knowledge of the social structure and organization of Gnostic sects is sparse at best. They criticized the hierarchical organization of orthodox communities for claims on divine authority and for the fact that they ruled over and persecuted the Gnostic elect. Many Gnostic groupings seem to have arisen as adherents to private teachers claiming a higher wisdom—e.g., Justin Martyr, Marcion, Valentinus, and Ptolemy in Rome. They gathered disciples around them and taught their own idiosyncratic brand of Gnostic wisdom. Similar relations between teachers and disciples seem to have been the case in Alexandria as well, especially around Basilides and Isidore among the heretical sects, and Clement and Origen among Christians. Not uncharacteristically, these teachers claimed the derivation of their teaching from some source of revelation, tracing their views to one of the apostles or early disciples or other sources. Often enough the links were anonymous or presumed to reflect some special and hidden source of knowledge—at least in some cases a special divine revelation. The groups came to form schools in which the teaching was systematically transmitted and kept secret. In some groups the meetings were also for liturgical and sacramental purposes.

Writing of the *Gospel of Truth,* McGuire (1986) concludes that Gnosticism as a cultic movement was in no way superficial in its approach to psychological needs; rather it developed a distinctive theology that generated corresponding patterns of social and ethical life. She comments:

> The Gospel of Truth vividly illustrates the social meaning and power of a gnostic vision of the gospel. Through its creation of a symbolic world, the Gospel of Truth has the power to sustain a community of believers and provide theological justification for preaching its message and extending its boundaries. The "Gnostikoi" who read this text understood themselves as an inner circle of awakened ones, members of the Entirety returned to their source (p. 355).

The attitude toward outsiders is characteristic. The elite were called to open the eyes of the blind and thus complete the work of cosmic conversion willed by the Father. However, it is more characteristic of Gnostic texts to divide mankind into Gnostics and nongnostics, and imply that the latter are in some sense ontologically inferior (Perkins 1980).

We can note here that these sects fulfilled the characteristics of Gnostic sects (Wilson 1959).[2] These groups or communities centered themselves on a body of esoteric doctrine based on a special revelation exclusive to the members of the sect and essentially secret. This special gnosis held a dominant position in the sect, setting the members apart from nonmembers and ensuring them a privileged and superior religious status. This special gnosis took precedence over all other sources of religious learning—the Bible, authoritative teaching by religious guides other than the cult leader, etc. Among Christian Gnostics, Christ was regarded more as a revealer and a guide to gnosis and salvation than a Savior—that is, salvation came through the gnosis he brought rather than through his own salvific acts. Conversion took the form of offering truth and knowledge to the outsider in the hope of drawing him along the path toward deepening understanding and enlightenment. Other religious groups were regarded as ignorant or misguided and religiously inferior.

---

[2] See chapter 2.

Sectarianism

The sectarian quality of Gnostic groups reflects another aspect of the operation of the cultic process in the emergence and structuralization of these religious movements. These religious groups reveal an antipathy to social structures, a state of liminal undifferentiation (Gilhus 1984) as a transition to new and more stable social structures. They present the picture of an undifferentiated community of equals under the authority of elders or spiritual guides. Family ties and obligations are minimized, personal property is eliminated and sexual ties are determined as insignificant. Such a cultic group always confronts established social structure, whether in a liminal phase moving toward full religious establishment or in opposition to institutional positions within other religious structures. It takes a position both hostile to existing religious structures and supportive of the structure within which it functions. As Gilhus (1984) comments: "Both directions are clearly present in the gnostic religion. The anti-structure of gnostic communitas is revealed in its antinomian character, be it as freedom from or as rebellion against the Law; in the violating of family ties, either in the form of absolute asceticism or as promiscuity; and in the abolishment of status-distinctions" (p. 319).

Moreover there was nothing in the Gnostic symbol systems that could serve as a force for more general social cohesion and unification. Metaphors pertaining to unity served the needs of ingroup harmony, but only in their application to small groups. While Gnostic symbols and myths mirrored social disruption and conflictual upheaval, they offered little resource for reconstructing the social order in any meaningful terms. Doctrinal exigencies forced them into a position of unremitting marginality on the fringes of the social order and established social institutions. Their preaching proclaimed a doctrine of refusal and rejection—refusal to participate or compromise with false and corrupt institutions, refusal to marry, live in families and bring children into the world, rejection of and refusal to obey temporal powers, whether pagan or Christian, and a rejection of all other religious authorities.

There is an element of pervasive, if often implicit, alienation permeating Gnostic thinking and writing. In the Gnostic view of the human condition, man is condemned to live in the darkest circle, a prisoner of alienating matter, shipwrecked survivors sentenced to unending solitude. As Armstrong (1967) wrote:

> A man should not be called a "Gnostic" unless he believes in an esoteric revelation or has the distinctively Gnostic attitude of mind. . . . A Gnostic in the second sense is a person who feels himself deeply alienated from this world in which we find our-

selves and in revolt against the powers which govern it. He reverses the values which are implied for a Greek philosopher in the very word Cosmos, and utterly rejects that esteem for God's good world and therefore for its maker which is central in the great public revelations of Judaism, Christianity [Cited in Perkins (1991), pp. 16–17].

Cain held a unique position in Gnostic lore as the prototype of the outcast condemned by God to wander the face of the earth as a fugitive, alienated and alone.

Man's inherent separateness from the world and his alienated position within it are persistent and characteristic Gnostic themes. As Jonas (1963) expressed it:

Gnosticism . . . removes man, in virtue of his essential belonging to another realm, from all sameness with the world, which now is nothing but bare "world," and confronts him with its totality as the absolutely different. . . . to such a one, all the world is indifferently alien (p. 263).

Disgust for the material world and all that it represented translated into disgust for their own bodies and a disinclination to have any dealings with the external world, let alone have any investment in improving it (Brown 1972). Yet references to separation from the body seem to have more to do with concerns about the effects of troublesome emotions—envy, anger, jealousy, lust—more a reflection on inner psychic conflicts than a purely ideological stance regarding matter (Perkins 1991). As Puech (1951) commented:

Disgust or hatred, terror, anguish and despair, and piercing nostalgia are the sentiments he experiences in his servitude to time. Marcion, for example, denounces in the most brutal terms the ignominy of the existence led by man, engendered in obscenity, born amid the unclean, excruciating, and grotesque convulsions of labor, into a body that is a "sack of excrement," until death turns him into carrion, a nameless corpse (p. 68).

These aspects of the Gnostic belief systems bring us closer to the dynamic undergirding of the cultic process in the paranoid process. The expressions of alienation, isolation, and hatred of the world are not unlike attitudes found in paranoid psychopathology.

Antinomianism and Persecution

Consistent with the theme of alienation and the motif of the existence of the outcast, we would have to include the often striking antinomian quality of Gnostic attitudes. As Jonas (1963) has commented:

> This opting for the "other" side, for the traditionally infamous, is a heretical method, and much more serious than a merely sentimental siding with the underdog, let alone mere indulgence in speculative freedom. It is obvious that allegory, normally so respectable a means of harmonizing, is here made to carry the bravado of nonconformity. Perhaps we should speak in such cases, not of allegory at all, but of a form of polemics, that is, not an exegesis of the original text, but of its tendentious rewriting (p. 95).

Even the libertinism, sexual promiscuity, and provocativeness espoused by many Gnostics carried with it an antinomian cast. Again Jonas (1963):

> To scandalize has always been the pride of rebels, but much of it may satisfy itself in provocativeness of doctrine rather than of deeds. Yet we must not underrate the extremes to which revolutionary defiance and the vertigo of freedom could go in the value-vacuum created by the spiritual crisis. The very discovery of a new vista invalidating all former norms constituted an anarchical condition, and excess in thought and life was the first response to the import and dimensions of that vista (p. 274).

We can add that the antipathy to the God of the Jews and the Old Testament and his spiritual demotion to the status of demiurge carried in it the seeds of antinomian animus. The humiliation of the demiurge was an expression of the cosmic reverberations of the revolutionary aspect of Gnostic thought translated into antinomian revolt against all manifestations of the work of the demiurge in this world. The demiurge was not responsible only for creation of the world, but for his law that was meant to enslave man and subject him to an inexorable cosmic fate (Jonas 1963).

A striking example of this antinomian quality were the Euchites, who, in addition to their practices of ecstatic prayer and their obsessions with struggling against the devil, refused to involve themselves in the contingencies of daily life. They rejected all forms of work, manual or intellectual, supporting themselves by begging, living in itinerant groups wandering the roads at random and sleeping in the open air. They rejected any authority, civil or ecclesiastical, and refused to obey or submit to any legitimate power. They became, in addition to being vagabonds and beggars, outlaws as well. Their intransigence was bolstered by their attitude that, once they had driven the demon out, they had achieved perfection and were no longer subject to any defilement by this world and were invulnerable to the compromises imposed by this demonic realm (LaCarriere 1977).

In certain Gnostic treatises the antagonism between the God of the Jews and Christ was starkly drawn, parallel to the antithesis between orthodox and Gnostic versions of Christian belief—the God of the Jews brought sin and blindness into the world, Christ forgave sin and healed the blind (Koschorke 1978). We do not know whether the rabbis ever persecuted the Gnostics, as the Christians did, but both rabbis and bishops would have regarded Gnosticism as a dualistic heresy (Segal 1987).

It is not unreasonable to assume that the social antipathy of Gnostic positions was motivated in part by social conditions. When Christianity reached a point in its development in which it was no longer the target of virulent persecution, it turned its newfound power to repressive uses, to making martyrs rather than suffering martyrdom—another variant in the expression of the cultic and paranoid processes. The former victims of persecution in their turn become the persecutors. This would hardly do much to alleviate the Gnostic conviction that all power is corrupt and alienating. Gnostic preachers continued to attack all established powers, whether Christian or pagan, since there was not much to choose between them. The social structures and vested interests of the society in which they lived did little to disabuse them of their conviction that "they were totally alienated creatures, right down to their very encephalic cells, and condemned to lifelong enslavement, from which only a full awareness of man's inert and slumbering condition could save them" (LaCarriere 1977, p. 29).

Even in the earlier strata of the development of the Gnostic movement, expulsive mechanisms were at work to expunge the more radical Gnostic groups from the bastion of traditional rabbinical belief. The label of the "two powers" heresy was applied to different groups—Christians, Gnostics and other heterodox Jews. The rabbinical strategy of lumping several sectarian groups under a single heading sharing a common heretical belief was an effective method of dealing with this opposition. The label was inaccurate for the Christians who did not believe in two deities and regarded themselves as thoroughgoing monotheists. The label was certainly apt for radical dualistic Gnostics (Segal 1987).

Much of the debate hinged on the conception of mediation. Christians, as in the Johannine group, made Christ the only mediator between God and man; for the rabbinical community any notion of mediation that introduced division into the godhead was prohibited. We are left with three main groupings—rabbinical, orthodox Christian, and heterodox Jewish or Christian communities. The heterodox Gnostics spawned a series of multiple intermediaries crowding the cosmological levels between the highest heaven and the world with layers of hypothetical entities and powers. The dividing lines between the in-group and the out-groups were differently drawn. The rabbis drew the line between believers in the one true and undivided God and those who believed in more than one god. The Johannine group drew the line between the Jews and the believers in the mission of Jesus.[3]

It is difficult to know the degree to which the barrages and counter-barrages of polemical discourse reflect the ravages of outright persecution. The temper of the times and the impassioned fervor of theological debate, and the extent to which religious and political issues tended to intertwine so that any boundaries between them were often indiscernible if not absent, make it hard to believe that there were not harsh consequences following the espousal of deviant views on the part of these many sectarians. The Jewish persecution took the form of exclusion from the synagogue—excluding suspect individuals from the synagogue services, or issuing curses against the sectarian equivalently barring him for life (Segal 1987). The word "persecution" creeps into the discussion almost hesitantly and uncertainly. To the extent that Gnostic groups were affiliated with the Christian Church, they were subject to persecution along with their Christian brethren, regardless of the doctrinal differences that separated them—doctrinal differences that might not have impressed their pagan and Roman persecutors. There were also apparently times when some of the Gnostic groups went underground, times when their meetings were prohibited and books burned. This was certainly more often the case in the fourth century when Christianity came into power and the Gnostic movement had been branded and refuted as outright heresy. It has been suggested that one force driving Gnostics into the nascent monastic movement in Egypt was that it provided a way of escaping from the pressures of persecution in the villages (Robinson 1977; Wisse 1978).

Ideologies in Conflict

Gnostics tended to connect their teaching with the appearances of the risen Christ rather than the gospel teaching of the earthly Christ. But this emphasis accented the hidden and secret character of the true revelation of the Savior. Often this emphasis on the hidden character of the revelation is mentioned in conjunction with some mention of persecution against the Gnostics. In other words, preaching of the true revelation, the secret gnosis, invited persecution—presumably more than dialectical opposition. Persecution was linked to rejection of Gnostic doctrines, particularly by orthodox authorities who were often equated

[3] See chapter 9.

in Gnostic accounts with hostile cosmic archons. The disciples were often told that persecution lay before them, because the archons, both heavenly and by inference this worldly, were hostile to them. Allusions to exclusion of Gnostics from the Christian community or to some disciplinary action against them are more frequent where the orthodox position had consolidated to the point of viewing the Gnostic movement as decisively heretical (Perkins 1980).

Segal (1987) has suggested that Gnosticism was driven into a more radical posture by the battle between the rabbis, the Christians and various other "two powers" sectarians on the outskirts of Judaism and Christianity. Rabbinical polemics were motivated by the desire to oppose any dilution of the strict monotheism so central to their tradition and religious system. Efforts to establish a normative Judaism led to the exclusion and radicalization of marginal sectarian communities, a process that may shed some light on phenomenological similarities among various protognostic groups and their antithetical bias toward Judaism and Judaic beliefs about the nature of God.

At issue here are the dynamics of ideological groupings in conflict. A key question concerns the linkage between a group's social position and structure and its symbol system (Douglas 1970). The argument is that we can expect groups undergoing profound social conflict to express those conflicts in displaced fashion in their ideology and views of the divine economy. Douglas argued that dualism was a characteristic form of belief in small, competitive communities—"Small competitive communities tend to believe themselves in a dangerous universe, threatened by sinister powers operated by fellow human beings" (p. 137). Groups viewing the world in such negative, hostile and paranoid terms tend to live in small, closed communities with a high degree of internal social pressure. They tend to see themselves as objects of persecution—whatever the reality (the paranoid "kernal of truth"), these feelings tend to be magnified and expressed in terms of the hostility of cosmic powers. Rationalization on this basis may serve as the basis for splitting and separation in the community and expulsion of deviant subgroups.[4]

In the turmoil of contention among these competing sects, theological differences became the basis for cult groupings. The divinity or nondivinity of God's mediating agent was a central defining issue. Opposition to the "Jews" among the Johannine group facilitated group definition within the group and the clarification of group identity; the mythology thus was brought into the service of social and psychological

---

[4] This analysis has also been applied to the Qumran community (Isenberg 1975) and to the Johannine community (Charlesworth 1968–69).

needs. The same needs and conditions were at work in various Gnostic groups as well, but, whereas the radicalization of the Jewish concept of God became the target for Jewish persecution of Johannine Christians, radicalization of the Jewish demiurge came to reflect persecution of Gnostics by Christians using Hebrew Scriptures to attack Gnostic heresies. Both Johannine Christianity and Gnosticism evolved within a common situation in which they were forced to define themselves in basically oppositional and polemical terms. As Segal (1987) comments:

> I wish to point out only that similar social conflicts have a similar effect on theology and hence in normative group definition. In this case there is a sequence of perceived social conflicts between many competing groups of Jews and Christians, all of which tended to make each group's central definition stronger. The gospel of John was important to Christian gnostics as it was to all varieties of Christians. Some of the themes in it were radicalized by extreme gnostics under analogous circumstances of perceived opposition. One of the results of social conflict is almost always the sharpening of any sect's understanding of its central principles in contradistinction to its feared and hated enemies (p. 73).

Gnostic Mythology

Variations in myth and cult reflect different conceptions of the self entertained by various Gnostic groups. Gnostic style included a marked penchant for translating abstractions into personifications. The rhetoric was cast in polemical terms of dramatic polarizations between what was "for us" and what was "against us." The dynamics of in-group identification as separate from and antithetical to the out-group were prominent, especially where Gnostic groups found it necessary to define themselves over against more general philosophical or religious contexts (Perkins 1991). These dynamics are familiar aspects of the cultic process.[5]

Religious preoccupations tend to reflect tensions in the social order. The strains and stresses in the social order were displayed at large in the vast tapestry of Gnostic cosmogony. The lower powers refused to acknowledge their origins and pay obedience and reverence to higher powers, and so became envious, quarrelsome, and contentious. Perkins (1991) cites a passage from the *Tripartite Tractate*, one of the Coptic codices from Nag Hammadi:

> They thought that they themselves were like those who exist of themselves and were without source since they did not see any-

---

[5] See the discussion in chapters 13 and 14.

thing existing before them. Therefore they live in disobedience and rebellion; not humbling themselves before the one because of whom they came into existence.

They wanted to command each other; outdoing one another in vain ambition—the glory they have has within it the cause of the structure that will come into being. They were likenesses of the exalted ones, who are borne up. They loved laying commands on each other according to the glory of the name of which they are shadows; each imagining himself to be superior to the rest (p. 14).

Perkins adds this comment:

Thus, the whole section describes the causes and the perils of social disorder once individuals seek to exalt themselves above their birth or station—much as Homer enforces the social code by showing the negative results when it is violated. Reading this story, the Gnostic may well learn that the haughtiness and ostentation of the rich is one of the main causes of social disharmony. Something that would hardly surprise him given the violent and illegal seizure tactics that were often used to add to one's land or to collect taxes (pp. 14–15).

The Gnostic mind was able to transform the opposition between groups into a cosmic mythology. They developed a polemical displacement of this worldly opposition into a cosmic opposition centered on the evil archons and especially the demiurge. The connection between aeons or archons and humans made the identification between the orthodox persecutors of the sect and the evil archons rather easy. Descriptions of orthodox bishops paralleled descriptions of the evil archons (Pagels 1976). These cosmic tyrants were envious and hostile to man and sought to deprive him of any good. People were familiar enough with the abuse of superior position and power to brutalize and take advantage of those who were too weak to resist. The God of the Old Testament was regarded as one of these evil archons.

Psychodynamic Aspects

The Gnostic movement played out the dynamics of the cultic process in dramatic fashion. From its inception, hidden in the murky currents of apocalyptic Judaic heterodoxy, the forces were set in motion splintering religious affiliations and groupings and setting the wheels of group fragmentation and segregation to turning. The high point in this process of polemical demarcation was reached in the proliferation of heretical Gnostic sects that achieved their pinnacle of differentiation and oppositional tension in the second century.

The most noteworthy characteristic of these cultic divergences is their highly oppositional, exclusionary and polemical quality. Each grouping seems to have sought and found its own sense of cohesion and identity by defining itself in opposition to other groups. Adherence to a set of beliefs, no matter the degree to which such beliefs might be uniquely distinctive or differentiated from the belief system of surrounding groups, seems to have been inadequate to satisfy the need felt by these sectarians for consolidation of their own religious commitment and self-definition. Opposition and polemical antagonism to outside groups was an added ingredient that seemed necessary to meet inner psychic needs. I will argue that it is more than a mere fact of life that such in-group structures have enemies forcing them to defend their ideology and their territory—whether psychic or physical— rather the presence of enemies fulfills a necessary psychic function. The role and function of the enemy fills an important need at the root of the formation and sustenance of many, if not all, social groupings—religious no less than political.

As we have seen, a number of authors—relying on the conceptualizations of Douglas (1970)—have concluded that some significant part of the Gnostic mythologies resulted from a displacement of conflicts and tensions in the social order to the realm of heavenly mythology. In these terms, we can read the descriptions of the dramatic actions of archons and aeons, and the other powers that inhabit the heavenly realms, as reflections of the polemics, struggles, persecutions, oppositional and antithetical conflicts constituting the hostile environment of Gnostic group life. However, I would like to carry the discussion a step further to argue that projective mechanisms of a more a basic sort were at work in generating these phenomena.

Brown (1968) has offered some caveats regarding use of psychoanalytic assessments of ancient religious movements, particularly directed at the use of such ideas by Dodds (1965). He warns us that the psychoanalytic perspective may well take away with one hand what it offers with the other. It may help us to understand the dreams—whether private or collective—of religious systems or ideologies, but its diagnostic emphasis tends to interpret these phenomena only in terms of their neurotic elements. The risk is an unduly static view of cultural and religious change, one that has little to say about how the religious crisis came about or what is to follow. It should be abundantly clear, from the course of the discussion thus far, that the analysis here in terms of the cultic and paranoid processes is not focused on pathology, but envisions these processes as endemic to the human psychic condition and therefore open to the vicissitudes of both constructive and adaptive elaboration as well as to the potential for pathological distortion. With this caveat in mind, the first consideration in developing these psycho-analytic hypotheses falls on the projective elements embedded in the Gnostic mythologies. Emphasis falls here on the elements of narcissism and aggression that color the whole of the Gnostic enterprise.

Aggression

Aggressive derivatives are writ large in the Gnostic scripts.[6] Hostility and destructiveness abound. The vast expanse of the universe is thronged with evil, deceitful, hurtful, punitive, destructive agencies responsible for the creation of this evil and corrupt world. They continue to work their evil wiles to destroy and demean human beings and keep them enslaved and entrapped in their place of torment and pain. The Gnostic mythology of intermediary beings—the archons, angels and aeons—filling the space between the supreme and highest God and the lowest and meanest level of existence, elaborated a vast panorama of evil destructiveness that not only served to explain the anomaly of an evil and corrupt world and human existence, but had the primary purpose of ensuring the enslavement and entrapment of man in his dark circle of fire. The Freudian devices of splitting and projection operate here at full blast—as Dodds (1965) wrote, "And, finally, the splitting of God into two persons, on the one hand a remote but merciful Father, on the other a stupid and cruel Creator, seems to reflect a splitting of the individual father-image into its corresponding emotional components: the conflict of love and hate in the unconscious mind is thus symbolically resolved, and the gnawing sense of guilt is appeased" (p. 20)—echoes of Schreber and his Gods.[7]

In psychoanalytic perspective, the Gnostic world appears like a gigantic apparition of a kleinian fantasy panorama of the paranoid-schizoid position magnified to world-, even cosmos-encompassing scope. It is a vision of the death instinct elevated to a cosmogonic principle of cosmic force and determination. The essence of Gnostic systems

---

[6] An appeal to aggression in psychoanalytic terms is itself controversial. Aggression, in itself, is not destructive. In the classic Freudian drive psychology, it is defined as such. More recent thinking has tended to revise our view of aggression to define it in broader terms allowing for both constructive and adaptive uses of aggression, along with the potential involvement of aggression in hostility and destructiveness. Further discussion of this issue can be found in Buie et al. (1983), Meissner et al. (1987), Meissner (1991a), Rizzuto et al. (1993), and Buie et al. (1996). In this perspective, hostility and destructiveness are motivational states that may involve aggression but are not caused by aggression.

[7] See the discussion of the Schreber case and its relevance for the paranoid process and application to the cultic process in chapter 1 above.

shares a common emphasis on the victimized and vulnerable position of man cast adrift in a hostile, persecutory, and alienating world. The position is essentially paranoid, if not clinically at least in a broader sense of the human actor cast out in a perceptibly hostile and paranoid context. If the average Gnostic believer was not paranoid, we have reason to think that certain key figures in the history of the Gnostic saga were in fact subject to paranoid delusional symptoms. The delusions of grandeur of Simon Magus (Acts 8:9-25) or Valentinus' conviction that the *Logos* had appeared to him smack of the delusional and hallucinatory. We might also readily speculate that many of the ecstatic experiences of revelatory inspiration and illumination on which Gnostic teachers placed so much emphasis may have been delusional episodes cast in religious and revelational terms as mystical illuminations.[8]

The projective hypothesis would maintain that the source of these aggressive derivatives lies within the human breast, that these powerful and destructive powers are no more than projections and imaginative elaborations of the aggressive destructiveness stirring within the human mind and heart. The same projective mechanisms were at work in polemical diatribes against agents of opposition and persecution inhabiting the more mundane habitats of this world. In their struggles against the forces of orthodoxy, part of the persecutory *animus* directed against orthodox preachers and bishops opposing the Gnostic cause derived from the projection of hostile and destructive impulses stirring within the Gnostic polemicists themselves.

These aggressive derivatives found their way into the outside sphere and came to life in both persecutory humans standing in their way and in the even greater evil archons obstructing the Gnostic yearning to return to the heavenly abode. Thus the linkage between tensions and conflicts in the social order and the archetypal hostility and destructiveness written into Gnostic mythology is underwritten by the deeper projective processes displacing conflictual destructive impulses to the external sphere (Meissner 1978b). We can note for further reference that not only were projective devices in play here, but that they were elaborated and systematized into a conceptual and religious schema providing a context of meaning and conceptual coherence. An elaborate theological theory was evolved to support these aggressive derivatives and provide an account for their existence—the "paranoid construction" (Meissner 1978b, 1986b).[9]

---

[8] The experiences attributed to Marcion and Mani, among others, would be cases in point.

[9] See the discussion of the mechanisms of the paranoid process in chapter 1 above.

Aggressive derivatives were not merely projected at large on the gigantic stage of cosmic forces, but they were turned inward to be internalized and become a powerful force for self-degradation and self-hatred. The consequence was the creation of a powerful superego dynamic placing the believer under an edict of self-condemnation and introjection of the sense of evil and corruption. The ideological disgust with the evil of the world was thus internalized as disgust for their own physical bodies, glorying in heaping abuse on their bodies—"a filthy bag of excrement and urine." Hatred of the world and themselves was transformed into severe ascetical practices, translating hatred into self-torment. The same hatred found its way through projective channels into massive hostility to the religious outsider and his out-group, or was transformed into a sense of guilt calling for repair and redemption of the damaged and fallen (Dodds 1965). This contempt of the world and of man's physical existence was not the exclusive preserve of the Gnostics, as Dodds (1965) has pointed out; it was endemic to the culture of the period, manifested more dramatically among Gnostics and Christians, if somewhat more mildly among Hellenistic pagans.

Narcissism

The narcissistic components also play themselves out in grand style in the Gnostic cosmology and anthropology. The concept of a special elite, called before the rest of mankind to gnosis and salvation, is redolent with overtones of narcissistic superiority—a kind of religiously embedded grandiosity. This powerful sense of in-group superiority was accompanied by devaluation and contempt for all other religious groups—the antipathy and contemptuous superiority was directed primarily against the Jews and their hated God, but also against the Christians and the emerging church. Thus the seeds of conflict and persecution were sown.

Narcissistic derivatives were woven into the tapestry of the Gnostic universal mythology. While destructive derivatives were embodied in the forces of darkness, narcissistic elements found their grandest illumination in the mythology of Light and the ultimate salvific power attributed to it. The favored elect identified themselves with the forces of light, postulating that they were the privileged few in whom the balance of light over darkness assured their salvation. The very concept of the Light and the considerations of its role in the destiny of men can be regarded as the product of a massive and group reinforced projection of narcissistic derivatives onto the cosmic scope of universal implication and belief. The investment of the belief in such salvific forces and powers served to defend these relatively impotent and alienated victims from the destructive wrath of their own aggression displayed on the scale of cosmic consequence. The greater the power of these aggressive and destructive forces bent on the annihilation and degradation of the human race, the more lofty, inspiring, powerful and convincing had the strength and magnitude of the forces of Light to be.

The flagrant narcissism and grandiosity inherent in the stance of the Gnostic prophets, who were privileged to receive a special revelation setting them apart from and above their fellow men, is unmistakable and reminiscent of Schreber.[10] This phenomenon, so regularly repeated in the Gnostic movement, calls attention to the psychodynamics of the individual Gnostic leader and teacher, each of whom propounded a unique and exclusively salvific gnosis. If we assume for the sake of argument that the leader's position and illumination is dictated psychically by profound narcissistic needs, the momentum of the argument carries us on to a consideration of those dynamic forces that drew adherents to the Gnostic prophet, such that large numbers came to accept and believe in his revelation as the ultimate religious truth.

The role of narcissism in redressing the balance of forces dragging the Gnostic into the pit of despair and hopelessness is clearly etched in nearly every Gnostic utterance. The dynamic equation demanded that the depressive and paranoid view of the world and human life pervading all Gnostic reflection had to be restored by narcissistic mechanisms. If man was sunk in the abysmal swamp of existence, ignorance, impotence and evil, his belief had to provide a counterpoise of enlightenment, power, and self-enhancement. As Puech (1951) commented:

> Side by side with the horror of evil there is, in the consciousness of the Gnostic, a desire—transformed into an overweening certainty, a certainty that is more than hope and faith—of possessing an absolute Truth, a total Knowledge, in which all the riddles raised by the existence of evil are solved (p. 73).

To this graphic portrait we can add a trenchant psychoanalytic comment:

> . . . it is understandable that on the road back to primary narcissistic fusion the subject experiences his body as a worthless garment to be cast off in order to go beyond the bounds imposed by embodiment. . . . We are here faced with a gnostic way of thinking . . . the avatars of this are timeless. . . . For the gnostic, man

---

[10] See discussion of the Schreber case in chapter 1.

must free himself from matter, from his earthly trappings. His body must become a body of air, then an ethereal body and finally a pure luminous and spiritual essence. . . . For it is at that point that he will attain the Spirit and the Radiance of God. There is consubstantiality between his spirit and the divinity. Ridding himself of his body therefore allows him to accede to union with the divine, to perfect knowledge.

This fusion with the divine clearly represents a return to the union of ego and ideal, to the primary undifferentiated state. It seems to me to constitute at the same time a transgression of the incest barrier. "Knowledge" in the Bible is synonymous with coitus. To know a woman is to penetrate her, so would not perfect knowledge be that of the mother? Man must not eat of the fruit of the tree of knowledge. He must forever be separated, cut off from the supreme knowledge (Chasseguet-Smirgel 1985, pp. 58–59).

SECTION V

Psychoanalytic Perspectives
on the Cultic Process

13

Cult Characteristics and Dynamics

Introduction

Both cults and sects are deviant religious bodies existing in a state of relatively high tension with the sociocultural environment.[1] We have been concentrating on the cultic vicissitudes accompanying the origins and early development of Christianity. Our interest is in unearthing aspects of the intrapsychic dynamics sustaining and motivating the cultic processes we have been able to identify in the historical residues of these ancient cultures. We have learned a great deal about the cultic process and its psychological roots from the study of cultic variants in our own time and culture. I will argue that this understanding can shed light on the cultic process wherever and whenever it finds expression—whether in the turmoil of religious and cultural diversity of pre-Christian Palestine or in the anxiety-riddled maelstrom of religious uncertainty and doubt of our own troubled age. I presume that within certain limits, and with proper respect to the historical, social, economic, and cultural diversity of times and places, similar dynamics and process are at work in every expression of the cultic process. The processes in question would have to be regarded as at best analogous, with full awareness and acknowledgment of the significant differences engendered by historical and cultural diversities. If that assumption is

---

[1] See chapter 2 above.

valid, it allows us the latitude in exploring this remote terrain to read certain aspects of our understanding of contemporary cult dynamics back into the data and circumstances of cult and sectarian vicissitudes at the root of the Christian experience and to draw certain limited, but valid, if still tentative and tenuous, conclusions.

Cult Characteristics

In structural terms, cult characteristics were long thought to include small size, a yearning for mystical experience, minimal organizational structure, and the influence of a charismatic leader. In this perspective, cults would represent a sharp break from the dominant religious tradition and would tend to be short-lived, local in extent, and frequently centered on the teaching and charismatic influence of a dominant leader. The emphasis in cult structures in this reconstruction falls almost exclusively on individual needs with a tendency to minimize or disregard questions of social order and integration. The cult in this perspective is a religious mutant or a form of more extreme variation in the spectrum of processes by which man seeks to solve problems of existence by religious means.

Some cults have a positive influence, as legitimate forms of religious expression with the potential for constructive contributions to social and psychological development (Robbins and Anthony 1972; Richardson and Kilbourne 1984). Others seem to be less benign and more psychologically manipulative and even unethical (Kirsch and Glass 1977; Ofshe 1980; Temerlin and Temerlin 1982; Clark 1983). If history has anything to teach us from the study of sectarian movements, it is that even with the most constructive and best of intentions for the improvement of the human condition, cultic movements carry within them the seeds of deviant and destructive potentialities. As Spitz (1973) has noted all too tellingly:

> Utopia has always appealed to men conscious of the injustices of an existing order and attracted to an ideal commonwealth where disharmony and inequity no longer prevail. But this is not the lot of men. Utopias of whatever kind are always rooted in a rigid authoritarian model. This is because the new system, being perfect (or nearly perfect), cannot admit of change lest it lose its perfection. Utopias are thus static societies, and men within them, frozen into higher and lower orders, are soon frustrated and bored. The impulse to change cannot be eliminated, for while men have limited needs, they have unlimited wants; but if suppressed, that impulse will assume unorthodox and revolutionary forms. Hence the in-

evitable dilemma of utopia: to assure the maintenance of its perfect arrangements, it must preclude orderly processes of change; by precluding those processes, it only facilitates the emergence of other, disorderly and (probably) violent social movements. The reality of utopia becomes the death of utopia (p. 268).

One of the points at issue in this study is that every cultic movement has its share of the utopian vision, and consequently is open to this vulnerability in various forms and degrees. But this formula must be considered a stereotype or caricature. Not only is the model difficult to apply concretely, since so few marginal religious movements fit the description, but even when some reasonable approximation can be identified there is no apriori reason to think that the outcome will partake of the utopian or antinomian trends predicted for it by the model. In terms of the cultic process, the options are considerably more generous and variable. It is this pattern of development and progression, whatever the constructive or destructive components it involves or expresses, that I have described here in terms of the cultic process.

Origins

One important manner in which religious movements arise is in the form of crisis cults resolving inherent cultural problems not otherwise solved by the contemporary culture (LaBarre 1970). Accenting the psychological element, a social culture can be viewed as a system of defense mechanisms serving to buffer stress and anxiety and to preserve homeostasis in the social network. The emergence of revivalistic cults in the wake of cultural catastrophe or socio-economic deprivation reflects the loosening of social ties and structure as well as the dissolution of cultural norms and values—as was the case in pre-Christian Palestine. As Douglas (1970) observed, in the face of deteriorating social structure, "This is how the fringes of society express their marginality. . . . In relation to established authority, this area of the social structure is the wilderness from which prophets and new cults are observed to arise" (p. 83). Thus those who stand in the periphery of central authority and power tend to become possessed by spirits who are themselves in turn peripheral to the central pantheon and of dubious morality. Those on the periphery tend to occupy positions of servitude or subjection. Douglas rejected mere deprivation as the crucial factor in vulnerability to cult influences, since many so deprived do not react by embracing cultic movements. Even when the type and severity of deprivation are well known, as in the case of pre-Christian Palestine, prediction of the rise of a social movement and its specific ideology is impossible (Aberle 1966). Relative deprivation theory can propose no more than a necessary but not sufficient condition for the rise of any significant marginal religious movement.

In situations of cultural impoverishment, where people live deprived of meaningful categories, suffer from treatment as an undifferentiated and faceless mass, and express themselves with inarticulate and poorly differentiated symbols, their pattern of reaction becomes passive, accepting their subjection with hopeless resignation, without remedy or any sense of choice, their lives governed by impersonal and uncontrollable forces. Others may see that not only impersonal forces but real people are agents of change; may choose a course of direct action to alter deplorable conditions and establish clear distinctions and categories oppressors would have to recognize—such was the Zealot revolt against Roman oppression. Others choose the path of symbolic expression—as was the case for the Jesus movement, the Johannine community, and the majority of Gnostic communities. In these latter instances, actual persecution may have accompanied the process of segregation, but it seemingly remained secondary to ideological formations.

The effects of cultural collapse can be traced in the consequences of the destruction of Jerusalem and the Temple in A.D. 70. Christianity took root in a soil prepared by the failures of the Roman Empire to find solutions for its social, economic, and moral crises. The sacred culture of the Western world is "the ghost hovering over dead Graeco-Judeo-Roman cultures, the ghost dance of our forgotten psychological past" (LaBarre 1970, p. 45). Such religious movements were forms of crisis cult originating from the crisis of cultural disorganization, disintegration, or distress. Behind the emergence of a crisis cult, there is a cultural clash, a conflict between competing systems, a form of "cognitive dissonance" (Festinger 1957) resolved by the emergent crisis cult. Under conditions of stressful social crisis, perspective is focalized, adaptive resources are centered on the problem, contributing to the tendency for paranoid deviants to view the crisis in a sort of tunnel vision dictated by their own projective needs (Lofland 1966). This may also explain the resort to cognitively simplified schemata and an intensification of authoritarian responses among lower classes (Bord 1975; Kohn 1969; Lipset 1960).

Psychological Components

As LaBarre (1970) noted, cultures do not compete or confront each other: "Concretely, only a person can be in conflict within himself over alternative cultural beliefs and behaviors, only people in society in conflict with one another, and only societies of people in conflict with one another" (p. 277). Nor does cognitive dissonance always bring about or modify innovation. Even the failure of prophesy may not modify belief, especially when the cognitive system serves to do little more than rationalize pre-existing beliefs—I would regard this as a prime instance of persistent function of the paranoid construction (Meissner 1978b). Minority religious movements often thrive on their cognitive dissonance from the majority culture. Thus LaBarre (1970) argued:

> Whether ethnic or class, mere cognitive dissonance makes no difference to the presence or absence of crisis cults. And as far as acculturation is concerned, the notion that rational beings operate with rationally accessible alternative cultures is simply not the case. Cognition without affect toward what is "known" engenders no crisis cult. . . . Instead, the innovator's ambivalence toward his culture, his tribe's ambivalence toward either native or alien culture or both, the crisis of cultural faith, and the psychological relationship of innovator and group are all essential. In both prophet and group, mere cognition of cultural difference must in some way also involve emotional stress. Cognition and culture are bloodless; cults are always of people, by people and for people (pp. 278–79).

Disturbance of psychic equilibrium leads to efforts at adaptive restitution, whether psychologically or culturally. There is a limited value in the analogy between patterns of adjustment in individual psychic and socio-cultural terms. When cultural homeostasis is threatened by emerging cultural vicissitudes, there is a loss of confidence in our ability to satisfy basic needs and maintain our defenses against pain, disease and death. In the face of general privation, the strength to survive lies in ties to our fellow men. Their strength is our strength; their weakness our weakness. In the origin of crisis cults, people require the support of others to sustain their beliefs. Societies and cultures rest on common fears just as much as common ideals or values. "In subgroups, too, men of like belief join to preserve preferred emotional states and tend to consort only with those who will not disclose or criticize their peculiar mechanisms of defense, the 'authority' of their culture hero, the solace echoing the needed wish" (LaBarre 1970, p. 379). Ambivalences and loyalties are tested to the core. Doubts arise from the spectre of alternate belief systems and sow the seeds of fanaticism. Insofar as all sacred cultures are rooted in the attempt to master indominable anxieties (especially death), the rediscovery of the intolerable fact reactivates the radical trauma, calling for the erection of ever newer defenses of faith, to defend belief from recurrent doubt, to constantly devise new rituals and symbol systems to protect the unhealed wound and preserve psychic balance.[2]

In these terms the prophet or visionary must discover or reaffirm a source of power that can move the world by magic and provide the external authority to sanction his revelation and ritual. His voice becomes the voice of God, and his rules God's rules. But his ambivalence remains unresolved and his destructive hostility takes expression in apocalyptic visions and world cataclysms; his guilt takes the form of new and severe moral restrictions; and his regression to passive dependency comes to represent a utopia—a "no-place" that never was nor will be, a world vision without the demand for effort and without the encumbrance of evil.

The revelation thus becomes a reified dream,

> . . . an unconscious wish projected into reality. As a projective structure, the revelation has the identical homeostatic function as the dream; and it states the tensions of the inner known, the unconscious self, not the nature of the outer unknown, the world. . . . In the revelation, the visionary withdraws his trust and love from the Reality Principle, and offers them passionately to the Pleasure Principle. That a stubbornly unreasoning "will to believe" is at work is shown in the prophet's desperate hatred of the unbeliever and promise of dire punishments upon him. Such a critical unbeliever represents the ego functioning of the society. He is the vatic's worst enemy. The Apocalypse must overwhelm him for the sin of disbelief. The spectacle of unbelief (disobedience to the prophet's overwhelming wishes) is unbearable, an affront to his categorical and godlike id. The skeptic is to be as much hated as the reality, and for the same reason: wish frustration.
>
> Unbelief is no neutral matter, approachable by dispassionate secular means of proof. A ghost-dance theology is the more compulsive when doubt-riddled and or unsupported by manifest reality. The eternal church in each divinely right fanatic would burn the unbeliever at the stake. His own inner compulsions make the visionary compel belief in his communicants (LaBarre 1970, p. 382).

This portrait, while it seems overdrawn in the interest of displaying the raw dynamics of one form of pathological expression, does focus on

---

[2] This is not necessarily a statement of a pathological model. If the needs in question can be viewed as vulnerabilities (Singer and Lalich 1995), the dynamic of the cultic process set in motion to resolve the anxieties through cult formation and involvement can equally well be regarded as sources of strength and adaptive capacity. See Tabor and Gallagher (1995) on the distinction between a model of a "passive self" as opposed to a model of an "active self" as applied to cult members.

the central dynamics of the paranoid process as it finds its way into deviant and polarizing institution. The selectivity and deviance thus manifested cannot be taken as normative for all forms of crisis cult or the emergence of new, even marginal, religious movements. The scope of the paranoid process, as developed in this study, has a much further reach and scope.

Group Adherence

Once the originating forces have been set in motion and the cult emerges as an independent entity, the bonds unifying the members and reinforcing their adherence and loyalty to the group become powerful sources of motivation. This tenacity of adherence is very like that described in the analysis of nationalism—based on a fundamental need to belong to and to define one's sense of social and personal value in terms of such group belonging, even to make such group participation one of the major contributing factors in the maintenance of a sense of personal identity (Berlin 1979). The sense of belonging to a meaningful social group has its roots in early familial experiences and takes on connotations of a molding factor in the experience of self. Identity itself carries with it implications of social belonging and acceptance, of membership and participation in a larger social grouping (Erikson 1963). Such affiliative needs are optimally at work in the adherence to religious groups, particularly in the case of cult movements in which questions of belonging and separation from other religious movements are particularly pressing.[3] Nor does it seem necessary to appeal to a model of pathology to understand the dynamic of group affiliation and adherence (Beckford 1990). The importance of affiliative needs and the accompanying benefits of group membership, the sense of belonging, of participating in a shared meaningful enterprize, and the confirming and stabilizing of a sense of personal identity and the meaning and purposefulness of life (encompassed within the paranoid construction

[3] An alternate way of expressing such motivational concerns is in terms of power. Analyzing modern religious movements, Beckford (1990) observes: "In a nutshell, my interpretation of the movements with which I am familiar is that they are seen by prospective and actual members alike as *sources of various kinds of power*. The expectation and the experience of many recruits is that membership empowers them to cultivate and to achieve a number of things more easily than through other means. The chance to cultivate various spiritual qualities, personal goals, or social relationships is the attraction" (p. 55). With due allowance for historical and contextual differences, something similar could also be said about religious group conversion and adherence in the formation of early Christian groupings.

of a system of belief) can be powerful motivational factors. In this sense, I would not totally disagree with Beckford's disclaimer:

> In focusing on the capacity or function of religion to supply meaning, integration, and identity, the theoretical cart has been put before the empirical horse. Sociological interpretations of religious phenomena have been mistaken for their subjects' motives and intentions. In short, I agree that meaning and identity are important aspects of religion: but at the same time I dispute whether actors act out of consideration for them directly. Rather, I believe that *actors respond to perceived sources of power, and their responses may or may not supply the meaning and identity of which we have heard so much*. This is an empirical question: not something to be resolved by definition (p. 58).

Quite possibly so, and the criticism applies equally to psychological interpretations as to sociological. I would prefer to maintain the distinction, however, between external motivating factors and those that are internal and more psychologically relevant. Keeping in mind the historical context of this discussion, gaining power, particularly in the oppression-ridden contexts we have discussed, is undoubtedly relevant, but its focus is socio-political or even economic. The basic motivations, in my view, drawing early Judaic Christians into the Jesus movement would not satisfactorily be governed by the seeking for power. I would argue that something more subjective and personal was brought into play.

This sense of belonging and group adherence was expressed by Kohut (1976) in terms of the relation between the individual's sense of self and self-representation and the "group self." He commented:

> The sense of a person's identity, whether he views himself as an individual or as belonging to a particular group, pertains to his conscious or preconscious awareness of the manifestations of a psychological surface configuration—it concerns a self-representation which relates to the conscious and preconscious goals and purposes of his ego and to the conscious and preconscious idealized values of his superego. The psychoanalytic concept of a self, however—whether it refers to the self of an individual or to the self of a person as a member of a group or, as a "group self," to the self of a stable association of people—concerns a structure which dips into the deepest reaches of the psyche (p. 420).

The link between the group self and the individual self comes to rest on certain underlying narcissistic configurations expressed in Kohut's usage in the central ambitions and ideals and values of the nuclear group self. These core elements account for the continuity and cohesion of the group and determine the patterning of its actions, but also come to resonate with dynamic patterns within the individual nuclear self, particularly with unconscious ambitions of the grandiose self and the core unconscious ideals and values of the idealized parental image. By the same token, as Kohut (1973) has pointed out, the wounded self-esteem and narcissism of the group can be the source of endless hatred and lust for revenge, even at the cost of survival itself. The intense fanaticism of Islamic fundamentalism and the politico-religious Armageddon impelled by Saddam Hussein are cases in point.

Developmental experiences play a central role in shaping these patterns of affiliation to certain social groupings and differentiation from others.[4] The formation of early affiliative-affectionate bonds, as well as other differentiative-aggressive bonds serving to distance and separate the individual from other nonaffiliative and alien groups, has its roots in early childhood experiences reinforcing both attachment to affiliative groups and rejection of differentiated groups (Pinderhughes 1979, 1982, 1986; Volkan 1988). The very cohesion of the group often depends on this form of commitment to a leader or to an ideology.

At the same time, affiliative bonds decrease the degree of aggression within the group and allow it to be displaced externally—at times toward common tasks or the achievement of common goals, but frequently toward an external enemy who poses a threat to the group's survival. Submission to the leader involves some degree of identification with the aggressor (A. Freud 1937), allowing the deflection of aggression and enhancing the sense of cohesive bonding. Intrapsychically the leader becomes a substitute parental figure who guides, protects and dispenses favors. Submission to the leader in these contexts has group survival value. As Zaleznik (1974) pointed out:

> This classic model of group cohesion may also describe a condition of object surrender, where the followers hand over their egos to the leader and remain susceptible to his commands and directives. They submit in order to preserve their love of the leader, and whatever esteem they experience comes from the sense of devotion to the ideals and causes established in the leader's image (p. 228).

In the newly emerging religious movement, the tension between such in-group adherence and the missionary drive to expand and gain new members is central. In the development of early Pauline Christianity, for example, the ideological claim to possess the unique means of

---

[4] See the discussion of developmental aspects of the paranoid process in chapter 1.

salvation reinforced the group's cohesion, but also created separation and antagonism from out-groups. An outstanding characteristic of the movement guided by Paul was its missionary fervor which sought meaningful communication with the outside world—the outsider was, after all, a potential convert. This contrasted with the more introverted and inner-directed attitude of the Johannine communities. Thus, as Meeks (1983) notes, "There is a tension in the literature of the Pauline groups between measures needed to promote a strong internal cohesion, including rather clear boundaries separating it from the larger society, and the intention to continue normal and generally acceptable interactions with outsiders" (p. 107).

Ideology

New religious movements usually embrace or develop a doctrinal content, an ideology and an accompanying mythology, serving multiple purposes—offering hope in the face of deprivation and despair, responding in varying degrees to a variety of psychological needs of group members, enhancing the value of group belonging, providing a context that contributes meaning and purpose to the lives of believers, countering doubts regarding personal insignificance and vulnerability, alleviating the pain from group suffering and persecution, and so on. As Horowitz (1990) notes in reference to modern cults, "The new chiliastic religions and cults provide a wide variety of answers in a world of doubt, certainty in a world of uncertainty, and belief in a world of competing facts" (p. 74). In the Palestinian world of the first century, the proclamation of the kingdom of God must have sounded resonances of hope, the dawning of new vision of the world and the place of God in it, that opened new possibilities for life and the salvific future.

The belief system more often than not serves to reinforce the validity and value of group belonging by drawing a contrast between the group ideology and that of outside groups. The in-group ideology is enhanced and valued, the ideologies of other groups are in contrast impoverished, weak, foolish, meaningless, misguided, false, and deceptive. Mythic accounts and ideological formulations are cast in terms of aggrandizement of the group, its meaning and history, and the corresponding devaluation and derogation of other beliefs and value-orientations. As Mack (1983) observes with respect to nationalistic dynamics:

> The myths of being chosen by God are common among the national fantasies of peoples whose ethnic origins are associated with connection to a supreme being or deity. The collective notion of

being chosen, of being uniquely cherished, favored and protected by a supreme being from whom the highest value emanates is not only valuable for sustaining a positive sense of self-worth. It is also powerfully protective against the inevitable hurts to group pride or self-esteem, and the sense of helplessness which is experienced as a result of military defeat, floods, prejudice, scapegoating and other man-made and natural catastrophes that become part of a people's collective experience over time (p. 56).

The art of the charismatic leader often rests on his capacity to make propagandizing use of these ideological components to heighten the tension and division between the cult culture and the hostile and alien environment. Even more visionary and less exclusive belief systems can be promulgated and preached in such a way as to give them a narrow cult-bound focus fostering the interests and purposes of the group in opposition to the goals and purposes of other groups. Such ideologies can become the vehicles for powerful individual and group motivations binding personal identities to collective goals and purposes. As such they are prime targets for the manipulation and exploitation of narcissistic and self-aggrandizing charismatic leaders (GAP 1987).

When they are used in such exclusive and restrictive fashion, group ideologies exercise a powerful influence to persuade individual members to adhere to group rules and expectations. In the early stages of group recruitment and indoctrination the group ideology provides an initial rationale for submitting to the group norms, and a framework for reinterpreting personal issues in terms congruent with group ideals and values, and facilitates the continued engagement in the indoctrination process (Cushman 1986). Such self-sealing doctrines are usually presented as universally true and applicable. Contradictory facts are simply dismissed, subject to *ad hominem* and disparaging attack, or reinterpreted in support of group doctrine. This often generates a degree of rigid self-confidence and assurance in the maintenance of the group belief system. Cushman's (1986) observations are as valid for the indoctrination process as for the adherence of the believer to the belief system:

> The belief that there is one true faith that is universally applicable and completely effective keeps individuals enslaved to the idea of perfection. If the doctrine is perfect and yet the recruit continues to remain imperfect, it must be the recruit who is at fault (i.e., the *ad hominem* response to contradictory data). The recruit can be thought to be at fault for several reasons, depending upon the content of the ideology. The recruit may be lacking in faith, impure, holding back, refusing to "surrender," using intellect instead of

feelings, incorrectly applying the doctrine, burdened by the problems for a past life, and so forth. In whatever form, the result is a
membership of true believers who cannot refuse the leader's demands, question the doctrine, or in some cases even criticize the
leader's everyday decisions (p. 14).

The group ideology, in this distorted form, can become a form of alternative construction of reality that may be more or less vulnerable to
disconfirmation. Such groups reject the culturally transmitted sense of
reality and organize the data of reality into their own specific and distinctive interpretation. As Barkun (1974) commented:

> Adherents are shielded from competing views, and this social and
> often physical separation significantly alters the validation basis.
> Validation comes from fellow-believers, from the leader, and from
> distinctive truth-gathering techniques, be they scientific, revela-
> tory, or oracular. The leader in turn receives his own confirmation
> from the rank and file. The movement resembles a closed informa-
> tion system, in which each component confirms the value of others
> (p. 142).

It was this form of group ideology that Rokeach (1960) described as a
closed belief system.

If and when disconfirmation occurs, the result may not be dissolution of the group even though the crisis may be of major proportions.
Rather than destroying the movement, the doctrine is modified and
reinterpreted, specificity is reduced, and a relatively more passive
stance is induced. The inconsistencies must be rationalized away in
order that the profound psychic investment of the believer be maintained and preserved (Barkun 1974).

The Charismatic Leader

In the origin of any new religious movement, the leader or prophet
plays a critical role. The questions this raises have to do with the qualities of the prophet that establish his claim to a position of influence and
authority, and what aspects of the context and/or of the psychological
needs and dispositions of the followers contribute to this dynamic and
process. The question of psychopathology in the leader arises inevitably. In writing of the proponents of utopian visions, the Manuels
(1979) commented:

> An ideal visionary type, the perfect utopian, would probably both
> hate his father and come from a disinherited class. A bit of schizo-

phrenia, a dose of megalomania, obsessiveness, and compulsiveness fit neatly into the stereotype. But the utopian personality that is more than an item in a catalogue must also be gifted and stirred by a creative passion. . . . In the first instance the utopian is overwhelmed by the evil complexities of existence. The great utopians have all borne witness to their anger at the world, their disgust with society, their acute suffering as their sensibilities are assaulted from all sides. They withdraw from this world into a far simpler form of existence which they fantasy. . . . And their way back from utopia, their return to the real world they had abandoned, is often characterized by devotion to a fixed idea with which they become obsessed. They clutch frantically to this overvalued idea that at once explains all evil and offers the universal remedy, and they build an impregnable fortification around it. The one idea becomes a fetish that they worship and defend with marvelous ingenuity. To outsiders they are monomaniacs (p. 27).

Phenomenologically the leader comes close to the picture of the delusional paranoid. The gap between the Schrebers of this world and the charismatic cult leaders must have to do with charisma—cult leaders have it, Schrebers don't. The omnipotence and grandiosity of such leaders reaches back to the omnipotence of infancy or to the identification with the fantasied omnipotence of the father. As Kets de Vries (1977) noted, "in addition to developing delusions of grandeur, these leaders possess the ever-present potential for developing delusions of persecution. Suspiciousness may become a way of life" (p. 354). But this stereotypical assessment may not enjoy universal validity. Although he was not cast in the role of cult leader, Thomas More was one of the leading utopian dreamers of his time, but he holds his place in history as one of the great saints of the Catholic Church. If there is pathology in the mix producing the cult leader, there is also the potential for religious significance. History presents us with the profound question whether the one outlaws the other, or whether they are in any sense or degree synergistic.[5]

When the child cannot relinquish omnipotence and cannot adopt a more realistic position of limited and contingent potency, he runs the risk of becoming as an adult fixed in a chronically paranoid position. Ego boundaries become permeable and precarious, so that discrimination between the prophet and his God become doubtful—at times leading

---

[5] As I have argued elsewhere (Meissner 1992, 1996), in contradistinction to Freud (1927), the truth value of religious belief systems may be orthogonal to the pathology of their derivation or content. Freud's argument, *e contra*, was that the pathology of religious beliefs was an index of their falsity.

to adoption of an oracular function, at other times claiming the prerogatives of divinity. Omnipotence is purchased at the price of real and
symbolic potency. In the context of religious charismatic leadership,
"the paranoid is the *vatic personality*, the priest of his father's godhood,
condemned to a child's poverty, chastity and obedience—or he is himself spuriously a paranoid omnipotent god" (LaBarre 1970, p. 106). His
role is to become the prophet or seer, who utters the oracles of the God
as the instrument of divine power. He is the mouthpiece of divine
omniscience, driven by an inner impulse and need to speak with the
voice of God. Thus, in subjectively psychological terms, "the prophet is
psychologically parasitic upon a supposed external omnipotence that
is really an equally fictive internal one. Every paranoiac is a god in person, every god a paranoiac projected into space" (LaBarre 1970, p.
107).[6]

Rise of the Leader

The leader assumes his position by fashioning or enunciating the
new doctrine or revelation that seeds the origin of the cult. The circumstances of his appearance and of the acceptance of his doctrine demand
explanation. His appearance in contexts of social unrest may be fortui-
tous or providential, but the appearance of such a prophet in stable and
untroubled times might be ignored or regarded as deviant and pathological. Then again, the conjunction of the appearance of the prophet at
a point of elevated need and crisis may be neither accidental nor unre-
lated to the social conditions. Disaster creates situations in which the
capacity of traditional authority to adapt and absorb is strained or the
authority itself is even destroyed. The failure of traditional authority
leaves a vacuum for new leaders and ideas to emerge. To meet their
inner needs and anxieties, people turn to new sources of assurance and
hope (Barkun 1974).

The first objective of the prophet-leader is to bring some meaningful response to the emotional needs of uncertain and threatened listeners. He conveys his message in words as well as in the personal image
he casts before them. He takes the position of a role model who has

---

[6] The reader will undoubtedly have noted that the language regarding prophetic
leadership is cast in masculine terms. The intent of such terminology is in fact masculine (an implication reaching beyond the usage of generic pronouns), but probably should be interpreted with more generic import. While the history of religious
movements is overburdened with masculine prototypes, the dynamics are by no
means exclusively so and there is nothing to prevent any of the leadership roles discussed here from falling to feminine aspirants.

mastered the anxieties, achieved a state of assured conviction and belief, and experienced the transformation offered by the new dispensation and realized in some degree its hoped for effects. Without question, this is the portrait of Jesus painted by the evangelists. In order for this process to take place, the leader cannot become excessively deviant nor can he be regarded as essentially pathological or disturbed by potential followers. In certain cultural settings, aberrant characteristics may provide the basis for religious leadership roles—e.g., the shaman (Eliade 1964). In such cases society finds a way to provide an acceptable niche allowing eccentricities and peculiarities of behavior to be enlisted in the service of the spiritual and even physical needs of the group. The prophet's message may be received as originating in the "other world" or coming from the supernatural, often a translation for nothing more than the prophet's own unconscious (LaBarre 1970). On the contrary, there is no evidence to suggest that the followers who are drawn to and participate in the mission of pathologically deviant leaders are in any sense socially or psychologically any different than the ordinary members of the larger community (Barkun 1974; Meissner 1978b).[7]

The rise of such visionary leaders, especially in times of social crisis, when the cultic reform movement follows the pattern of revitalization movements (Wallace 1956), tends to take place when the index of individual stress in the population rises as a result of the failure of social stress-reduction processes to operate effectively—clearly the case in pre-Christian Palestine. Individual effects may be seen as regressive or increasingly pathological behaviors (alcoholism, drugs, socially deviant behaviors including sexually deviant, and so on), or as patterns of disengagement, withdrawal, and indifference. Cultural restructuring awaits emergence of the leader, a prophet, who often enough achieves leadership status by the use of techniques familiar in the cult of the shaman—divinely inspired visions, inspirations and messages of the spirit declaring the path to corrective action. The solution to individual anxieties and uncertainties is offered through mystical and supernatural devices (Johnson 1981).

---

[7] We need to remind ourselves that at times even evident pathology in the leader can be overlooked or recast in positive terms as evidence of his religious mission. The phenomenon of the shaman bears testimony to this aspect of the selection of religious leaders (Eliade 1964). We should also recall that Sabbatai Sevi, the mystical messiah (Scholem 1973) who became one of the last great messianic figures in medieval Judaism, was regarded as mentally disturbed and seems to have qualified as manic-depressive (Scholem 1973; Falk 1982; Meissner 1995).

Psychopathological Model

Perhaps the strongest argument for the origin of cults in some form of psychopathology was advanced by Bainbridge and Stark (1979). Their model of cult formation was set forth in eight points:

(1) Cults are novel cultural responses to personal and societal crisis. Most cults arise in periods of radical social change in which confidence in established institutions and cultural realities is weakened and undermined. Weakened confidence in established religious traditions and rituals is particularly characteristic.

(2) New cults are invented by individuals suffering from certain forms of mental illness. To the extent that the transforming religious vision arises as a form of religious delusion, the pathology in question would tend to take a paranoid form. This does not mean that such visionary prophets are clinically paranoid, but that their ideas take the form of a deviant ideology reflecting the dynamics of the paranoid process, particularly in the form of a paranoid construction providing the stability and cognitive integration required to satisfy underlying motivations and needs (Meissner 1984, 1987). In the early stages of cult formation, sharing of the delusional ideas may have the qualities of a *folie-à-deux* (Balch 1982).

(3) These individuals typically achieve their novel visions during psychotic episodes. Bainbridge and Stark (1979) associate the characteristics of such episodes with reactive schizophrenia; these features include a sudden disorganization of previous life style, predominantly auditory hallucinations, blunted affect, identity confusion, social withdrawal and isolation, periods of prolonged and intense self-absorption, and emphasis on the major themes of death, rebirth, cosmic catastrophe, and a sense of personal responsibility for the world's salvation. Again Schreber comes to mind. But the connection with a psychotic origin leaves many questions unanswered. How does the prophet develop from an apparently normal, if eccentric, individual to a religious visionary? How is it that the delusional message is interpreted by hearers of the message as religiously meaningful rather than as a psychotic production? (Balch 1982; Meissner 1976, 1986b).

(4) During such an episode, the individual invents a new package of compensators to meet his own needs, that is "sets of beliefs and prescriptions for action that substitute for the immediate achievement of the desired reward" (Bainbridge and Stark, p. 284).

(5) The individual's illness commits him to his new vision, either because his hallucinations appear to demonstrate its truth, or because his compelling needs demand immediate satisfaction. The similarity to the paranoid process here is striking. The process works to achieve a sense of consolidation and stability in the individual's inner world that contributes to his sense of self and identity. The paranoid construction contains and consolidates the other aspects of the process. When the process takes a pathological form, the delusional system represents the paranoid construction and has the effect of stabilizing and clarifying the patient's world view that until the crystallization of the delusional system has been uncertain, fraught with anxiety, doubt, insecurity and even terror. The unknown becomes known, the enemy is identified, and the drawbridges can be raised.

(6) After the episode, the prophet will most likely succeed in forming a cult around his vision if the society contains many others suffering from similar problems. The new religious vision must fall on fertile soil, else it cannot take root. The conditions for such soil may vary considerably, but it becomes essential that the new message strike a responsive chord in the hearers; it must resonate with some deeply felt psychological need in order to elicit the response of abandoning old beliefs and embracing the new. Why and how a message that is essentially irrational, unreasonable, unrealistic, and often fantastic comes to exercise such a powerful appeal at certain times and under certain conditions, becomes a central issue in the understanding of the origin and evolution of cults.

(7) Therefore, such new religious movements most often succeed during times of societal crisis, when large numbers of persons suffer from similar unresolved problems. This point falls back on the deprivation-disaster theory of the rise of cult movements. The approach has its inherent validity, as well as its limitations. The discriminating indices pertain to the nature and degree of stress and traumatic deprivation or disaster that bring about conditions of vulnerability in large numbers of people so that they will be moved to embrace and commit themselves to the vision and message of the prophet (Volkan 1988). In other words, the stimulus conditions must activate the victim introjective configuration in enough subjects to make them receptive to the salvific message.

(8) If the cult does succeed in attracting many followers, the individual founder may achieve at least a partial cure of his illness,

because his self-generated compensators are legitimated by other persons, and because he now receives true rewards from his followers. Yet it is not always clear that the leader's pathology remits after he gathers a group of followers around him. In some cases, the pathology clearly persists; in other cases, the union of the leader and the led may amount to little more than an expansion of the perimeter of the folie, a sort of folie-à-plus. These considerations lead us to the edge of the problem of charismatic leadership. As Balch (1982) comments:

> Because religious visionaries are unencumbered by the weight of institutionalization, they have a relatively free hand to invent whatever social forms they desire. We should not be surprised, then, if their hopes, fears, needs, and past experiences are reflected in the realities they create. A new religion, at least in its early stages, may be largely a projection of its leader's personality (p. 68).

The perspective offered by this pathological model has its appropriate range of application and validity, but is not an all-inclusive model, and may have to be supplemented by other models or even replaced by a nonpathological model in order to cover the range of variation found in the new religious movements. If the Stark and Bainbridge model places the emphasis on a pathological caricature, it is not thereby invalidated, but its range of valid application is thereby limited. While my comments on this model are intended to highlight the connections with the paranoid process, that process also finds its scope of application beyond the limits of this model. One of the basic issues raised by this discussion pertains to the question of the extent to which the rise of Christianity itself may or may not have developed on the basis of pathological dynamics, and what that may have to do with the religious meaning or significance of the religious movement itself. We can well ask the question at this juncture—was there any sense or any aspect of the charismatic leadership of Jesus of Nazareth that would have approximated the terms of the pathological model? And further, what would it mean if it did or didn't?

Narcissism

Narcissism is a predominant component of the personality organization of charismatic leaders. Freud (1921) characterized such leaders as having a masterful nature, narcissistic, self-confident, independent and needing to love no one but themselves. They tend to be self-centered, independent, difficult to intimidate, often fearlessly ready for action, counterphobic—strong personalities that step readily and willingly into the leadership position (Freud 1931). To this Kernberg (1979) adds, ". . . because narcissistic personalities are often driven by intense needs for power and prestige to assume positions of authority and leadership, individuals with such characteristics are found rather frequently in top leadership positions" (p. 33). Thus the leader's drive for leadership is rooted in his narcissism, a drive compelling him to take risks and undertake arduous tasks for the sake of winning a narcissistic prize and gaining a position of power and grandiose satisfaction.

The narcissism of the group becomes invested in the group ideology, viewing it as good and truthful, and opposed to the ideologies of outside groups which are declared to be false, deceptive, and destructive. The idealizing tendencies of group members make the person of the leader representative of the ideology with its conscious and unconscious fantasy components. The leader can thus become in terms of unconscious imagery both the father-protector of the group and its beliefs and the nurturing mother who sustains and succors the group and its needs, especially in the face of doubt and rejection (Volkan 1988).

Reactive narcissism in the leader involves a sense of lingering inadequacy that must be countered by an image of the self as special, an illusion of being unique and different, requiring denial of any discrepancy between wishes and reality and avoidance of any sense of limitation, loss or disappointment. Such leaders may have the capacity to ignore or minimize large segments of reality in the interest of preserving their narcissistic defenses and self-image. The vulnerability of the sense of self and the dependence on narcissistic defenses lends a strong paranoid bent to such a leader's personality (Volkan 1988). When such paranoid mechanisms come into play, the leader may become impervious to influence from outside or realistic sources of information. The potential for directing the group down a path of self-destructive or self-defeating behavior can become unbridled and reversible only by drastic means (Kets de Vries 1977; Meissner 1978b).

Such reactive leaders are often severe and demanding of their followers, preferring subservience and unquestioning obedience from their subordinates. Ideas contrary to the leader's own tend to be ignored or rejected. Subordinates who do not fit the mold are eliminated or expelled from the group. The leader can be ruthless in exploiting and manipulating others to meet his needs and wishes. His failings often are the result of his disregard of reality and his grandiose conviction that he can control and manipulate reality to suit his needs.

Self-deceptive narcissism in the leader has a somewhat different cast. Even though this type of leader may have many of the same qualities, they do not operate as dramatically in the leadership role. Their self-delusory and unrealistic self-image and ambition run afoul of more realistic limitations, imperfections, failures and disappointments. Both these forms of narcissism reveal pathological flaws and tend to employ relatively primitive defenses (Kernberg 1975), resulting in difficulties recognizing the complexities and ambiguities of human relationships and a tendency to polarize hatred, fear and aggression on one hand, and omnipotence and overidealization on the other. The latter qualities are attributed to the self and one's group, and the former to external groups and forces. It is common and vital to such religious leaders to see themselves as on the side of God, and to identify the enemy as Satan (Post 1986).

Self-deceptive leaders are more approachable, but at the same time they are hypersensitive, insecure, and have a need for approval and acceptance. Their insecurity demands constant scanning of the environment for possible sources of threat, often at the expense of a capacity for appropriate action. Failure looms at every turn, and with it the threat of loss of prestige and power. The adaptive strategy often becomes avoidant or conservative, making decisions at minimal risk.

Narcissism can also take a more constructive bent. *Constructive narcissism* does not generate the same need to distort reality or avoid life's frustrations. Primitive defenses are less frequent, so that they are less estranged from their feelings, wishes, or thoughts. Such leaders generally get on well with subordinates and can function well in task- and goal-oriented contexts. They wish to be admired, but have a better sense of their limitations and capacities. They can recognize, appreciate, and utilize competence in others. They can listen to subordinates, but take the ultimate responsibility for their own decisions. Their narcissistic needs put them at risk of appearing to be arrogant or insensitive. Religious leaders may fit into any one of these descriptive categories, but the charismatic leader, especially when he propounds a revelation that strains credibility or rationality, tends to follow the format of the more narcissistically pathological types (Kets de Vries and Miller 1977).

Charisma

The central figure in the origin of many cults and other marginal religious movements is the cult leader, especially when the cult arises as a crisis cult. In the crisis cult model, such leaders are invariably charismatic and come to the fore as cultural heroes bearing some inspiration or revelation responding to the crisis needs of the culture under stress. The effective religious leader is one who expresses and is responsive to the inner needs that play themselves out in the paranoid process. The most effective leader, then, is one who best embodies, gives form and shape to, and is responsive to those beliefs, values, attitudes and ideologies, which best express the interest and intents of the community of believers. The leader or prophet, therefore, serves as an appropriate figure to receive idealized projections from members of the group. To the extent that he succeeds in this, he serves as a channel of articulation of the values and beliefs the group must sustain and continue to promote and elaborate. The effective leader, then, serves as a unifying and consolidating force vis-à-vis the group allowing it to sustain a sense of cohesion and purposeful implementation. The effective political leader is able to mobilize these resources of the group and direct them in a way that provides members of the group with a sense of utility and purposeful action. It is specifically in these terms that the notion of "charism" takes on psychological meaning.

When the mix of contributing elements is right, a leader or prophet arises who acts as a catalyst bringing the cultic fantasies to an actualizing focus—be they millennarian, messianic, Gnostic, salvific or whatever (Meissner 1995). To the marginal and desperate masses, he announces his inspiration or revelation, for which he claims divine origin and authentication, and proclaims to his needy hearers a mission of lofty ideals and worldwide ambition. The conviction of divine mission, of being divinely appointed as the instrument of God to carry out this important role, conveys to the vulnerable and credulous masses the sense of significance, hope, the fulfillment of deepseated wishes and desires, the sense of narcissistic enhancement from association with God's messenger and God's purposes. For the needy and impoverished, there was no better mission in the messianic visions of Jewish and Christian apocalyptic than the total transformation of the world from a place of sickness, pain and suffering to one of wealth, luxurious ease, and the surcease of all pain and suffering. Where they had been poor, they would become rich. Where they had suffered deprivation, they would find the satisfaction of all desires. Where they had been persecuted and oppressed, their enemies would be put to flight and crushed, and they themselves would become the inheritors of the earth and exercise dominion and power in the name of Christ.

In Weber's (1922) original use of the term, charism referred to a type of personal authority based on "devotion to the specific sanctity, heroism or exemplary character of an individual person and of the normative patterns or order revealed or ordained by him." Despite the often contradictory usages, charismatic leadership seems to possess the following characteristics: (1) The leader is perceived by his followers to possess superhuman capacities; (2) The followers blindly accept and believe the leader's statements; (3) They unconditionally comply with and obey the leader's directives for action or behavior; (4) They give the leader unqualified emotional support and allegiance (Wilner 1984).

In more specifically Freudian terms, the charismatic relation can be described in libidinal terms as a special form of love relation based on a model of unconscious hysterical object love (Zaleznik 1974). The leader becomes a love object of sorts, giving rise to the peculiar devotion, intensity, and narcissistic enhancement of the leader (Volkan 1988). The love relation inherent in the charismatic relationship is analogous to analytic transference, and in fact may be compounded of the same elements (Hayley 1990). This emotional investment can become so powerful that it can result in the transformation of values and the overthrow of traditional and rational norms.

Interactional Model

Charism may also reflect a form of social relationship in which certain attributions and projections are involved on the part of the led. The prophet cannot be charismatic unless he is recognized as such. To say that the leader creates the movement is as valid as saying that the movement creates the leader. The leader is believed and followed because he embodies the values that are embraced or sought by the led. As LaBarre (1970) noted:

> The culture hero's charisma, that uncanny authority and supernatural ascendance he seems to have over his fellows, is in purely naturalistic terms merely the phatic attractiveness of his teaching to others under the same stress, an attractiveness aiding its diffusion from individual to individual. Charisma is only shared unconscious wishes and symbiotic thought paradigms in leader and communicants (p. 48).

Individuals strongly influenced by the charismatic attraction of the leader seem to have a certain need to submit themselves to some powerful personality, to be taken care of and guided by the knowledge and conviction of a powerful and idealized figure. The need to attach and subject themselves to the leader is based on basically narcissistic and erotic needs often deriving from quite infantile levels of development. They see others as more powerful and superior (the aggressive and superior narcissistic components) and themselves as weak, vulnerable and inferior (the victim and inferior narcissistic configurations).

While this psychological profile of the cult follower may entertain a degree of validity, the risks of overextending the model or using it to overinterpret cult dynamics looms large. While there may be cases in which the pathological model applies unequivocally, there is good question as to how far it can be extended before it verges into caricature and prejudicial stereotyping that might violate the realities of cult involvement and present a distorted picture of cult life. The image of cult organization and dynamics presented by Singer and Lalich (1995), for example, seems to veer toward the stereotypical, largely because of the concentration of their model of cult formation, almost exclusively centered on the role of the leader and the corresponding portrayal of cult members as passive, compliant, and mindlessly brainwashed. If the image obtains in those cults arising at a radical and extreme fringe, translation of the impressions they generate to the broad range of cult experiences would be prejudicial to say the least.

However, the divergence of viewpoints and interpretations does raise important questions when it comes to the effort in this study to look back through the dim obscurities of history and try to discern the manner in which some of these same dynamic factors played themselves out in the origins of the early Christian sect—or should I say sects. To what extent, in other words, can the charismatic leadership of Jesus, and after him the apostles, including Paul, be adequately encompassed in terms of a given model, pathological or otherwise? To what extent can the dynamic factors contributing to the emergence of the Christian movement and the scale of conversion that marked its early progress be connected with pathological determinants? Or are we closer to the truth by broadening our perspective to include more positive and constructive forces that may find their reflection in all culturally constructive religious movements?

Prophetic leaders seem to share in common an ability to stir primitive emotions in their followers and are masterful manipulators of symbols. Under the spell of charismatic leaders followers feel either powerfully grandiose or helplessly dependent. Leaders often induce regressive behavior in the group and are able to attune themselves to and exploit unconscious feelings and fantasies of their followers. The followers in turn seek to embrace an idealized, omnipotent image of the leader answering to their dependency needs and helplessness. Narcissistic gratifications for both leader and led can take precedence over more realistic task-related activity. The communication and sharing of regressive wishful fantasies is a central aspect of charismatic leader-led relations. The unconscious fantasy system operating behind such group ideologies is often paranoid, imagining some far-flung conspiracy, mysterious and frightening. LaBarre (1970) even concluded that "The distinction between a *cult* and a *folie à deux* is nonexistent" (p. 343). To which, we would have to add the cautious refrain—sometimes, but not always. There is a radical distinction between "often" and "always."

More than any other type of leader, however, the charismatic religious leader depends uniquely on the acceptance and support of his followers. He must be seen as a great man, narcissistically enhanced and idealized, or his program will not fall upon receptive ears (Bord 1975). The sources of his legitimate authority depend on the faith of his followers; but not on faith without proofs that provide some support for his claims. Realization to some degree of the consequences of charismatic belief in organizational or behavioral terms is essential to the maintenance of the belief. Thus the model for charismatic authority can be viewed as interactional—the followers accept the leader to the extent that he embodies and articulates their aspirations. He transposes these aspirations into concrete goals and collective beliefs that can be translated into action. The prophet's message thus attains central significance in the organization of the movement. The followers in their turn may accept the prophetic vision all too readily. They are quick to become the chosen people, the holy people of God, the saints, called to unqualified submission to the will of the prophet and devotion to his cause. They were to share in his power and in the fruits of his crusade—they could not fail or be disappointed because the cause was backed by the infinite and miraculous power of God. We can read the accounts of the early history of Christianity, as for example in the Acts of the Apostles, in this light. In a word, charismatic movements do not arise at the whim, inspiration or bidding of any prophetic figure; they depend on a context, on a mix of determining influences, and on the psychological dispositions in the mass of potential followers who are receptive to the stimulation of the prophetic message and the charism of the prophet, or interact in such a way as to elicit the conditions for prophet expectation and actualization (GAP 1987).

Paranoid Potential

The function of the leader is connected to the dynamics of the paranoid process. The effective religious leader is able to resonate with the inner needs of his followers embedded in the paranoid process. To this extent, the prophet serves as an appropriate figure to receive idealized projections from members of the group. To the extent that he succeeds in doing this, he serves as a focus for expression of the values and beliefs, which the group must sustain and for which it must exercise itself to promote and elaborate. The effective leader, then, serves as a unifying and consolidating force allowing the group to sustain a sense of cohesion and purposeful implementation. These circumstances make the prophetic role fragile and precarious, especially insofar as it depends on the unquestioning submission of the followers. The charismatic identity of the prophet often requires protection against subversion or challenge—by limiting general contact with the prophet, by excluding all who do not express complete submission and acceptance, and by insisting that any changes in doctrine be taken as tests of faith and commitment (Wallis 1982; Smith 1982).

The leader's sense of complete certainty and unwavering conviction may counteract any doubt and insecurity in the group, even as this stance can serve to ward off the leader's own inner doubts. Kohut (1971) emphasized the narcissistically fixated and even paranoid propensities found at times in such charismatic figures. They may be convinced that they are in the right and any who oppose them are in the wrong. They do not hesitate to hold themselves up as guides and leaders and as targets for the admiration and even reverence of others. They are capable of extremes of moral righteousness: they will typically disown and project to the outside world any unacceptable failing, imperfection or weakness they cannot acknowledge within themselves. The shell of conviction and certainty must be maintained in order to prevent inner doubts and vulnerabilities from showing through. In his paranoid rhetoric aggression is projected to external objects and groups who then become identified as the enemy. By expelling and destroying the weakness within, the leader and thus the group can become the strong and chosen people of God. Leader and led are caught up in an intoxicating whirl of mutual narcissistic reinforcement—the followers feed on the narcissistic enhancement and omnipotence of the leader, and the leader is sustained and reinforced by the idealizing elevation of his followers' admiration and praise (Post 1986).

When the leader realizes the power to shape fantasies into realities, he is at risk of yielding to his wishes for omnipotence and megalomaniacal ambition. Reality and its limitations fade into the background to be replaced by paranoid fantasies and delusions. To the extent that his omnipotence elicits corresponding savior images in his followers, the result may take the form of a kind of manic enthusiasm and delusion embracing the entire group. Attachment in the led and omnipotence in the leader can become mutually reinforcing, so that the leader's narcissistic grandiosity becomes a self-fulfilling prophecy in which everything becomes possible and all limits are denied (Kets de Vries 1977). When the group process moves in the direction of maximizing its pathological potential, this is an almost inevitable pattern. This does not answer the remaining difficult question as to why some emergent religious groups follow a path toward increasing pathogenicity while others lead to meaningful religious expression and coherence. But the psychoanalytic perspective would place the emphasis in focusing the determining factors on the inner psychic needs and dispositions of the participants, both leaders and followers.

14

The Cultic Process
and the Paranoid Process

In previous chapters we traced the role of the cultic process and its complex interweaving with social, political, economic, cultural and religious influences, in the emergence of Christianity and Gnostic cultic variants from their shared Palestinian background. But the interweaving of these social and ecclesial threads leads to further questions touching more immediately on psychoanalytic concerns. These forces could not have had their powerful consequences, had they not been drawing on deep psychological sources of motivation and conviction.

Relation to Belief Systems

The cultic process builds on and reflects several aspects of the psychological processes embraced by the paranoid process. One aspect is the formation of and commitment to a specific belief system; a second is the tendency to sectarian divisiveness and exclusivity. These two aspects do not exhaust the range of implication, but they will suffice to focus our discussion.

The belief system or ideology (Erikson 1959; Barratt 1986) of any of the religious groupings we have been considering is equivalent to a form of paranoid construction (Meissner 1978b; also chapter 1). The paranoid construction involves a cognitive system or elaboration providing a context of meaning supporting and making sense of particular projections or systems of projections and lending credibility, justification, and purposefulness to individual commitments. Insofar as projective elements themselves derive from introjective configurations in the individual subjective inner world, consolidation and coherence of these elements through the paranoid construction serves the further function of sustaining a coherent sense of self and identity built around the introjective organization that constitutes the core of the self structure. It serves this cohesive function in both individuals and the group.

In the religious context, then, commitment to the belief system brings with it a sense of meaning and purpose to one's human existence and suffering, it conveys a sense of significance and purpose in death, it confirms the believer in sharing in the life of a community of believers forming the in-group, and it indicates an ethic of salvation, a code of morality and ritualized praxis pointing the way toward right living and the ultimate fulfillment of human destiny. From a psychological perspective, the belief system serves the same function as the paranoid construction, namely providing a meaningful context with which the believer's sense of identity and self-integrity can find consolidation and confirmation. This connection with the paranoid process makes it understandable why belief systems come to play a discriminative role and why such ideological constructions tend at times to become divisive and exclusive.

The development of Christianity, centered around the mission of Paul, evolved from a Jewish apocalyptic sect into the form of Gentile Christianity found in the Pauline communities. The transformation had to involve a separation between the community of believers and the outside world. To his Gentile converts Paul preached avoidance of idolatry—a stance that marked them off from their fellow citizens. Paul also sought to drive a hard line of separation between his converts and Jewish Christians who adhered to the Law. The brand of apocalypticism Paul espoused also set his church apart from the traditional Judaic beliefs. As Segal (1990) puts it:

> Although many Jewish purity rules did not translate into the new Christian setting, apocalyptic dissatisfaction with the world found a ready audience among the disaffected gentiles, women, some Hellenistic Jews, and some half-proselytized God-fearers of the Roman Empire. The difference between Paul's apocalypticism and the traditional Jewish variety is that Paul brought with him the Pharisaic hopes for a gentile world won over to worship of the one God. He completely ignored the usual apocalyptic notion of condemning the gentiles for their sinning and mistreatment of Israel (p. 269).

Paul's unique blend of apocalypticism and mysticism defined a new way of living adapted to the needs of an apocalyptic Christian

Gentile community. The apocalyptic belief system dictated a separation between the in-group of the community and the outside world of non-believers, between the saved and the lost. Expulsion from the apostolic community was the most severe of punishments. In Qumran, so strict was such expulsion that the ostracized members often starved to death. Separation of the group of believers from others mirrors the apocalyptic belief in a heavenly dualism—for the Qumran devotees the dualism took the form of a cosmic battle between the forces of good and the forces of evil. Demonization of those outside the community was also found among Christian groups as well. Paul's apocalyptic view not only took a realized form but also did away with the special laws of Judaism defining the ceremonial borders between Judaism and the world. His view of the church as the body of those who had been saved through faith was based on an apocalyptic conviction—those within the community are to be saved and those outside it damned (Segal 1990). These same dynamics of in-group separation, exclusivism, and oppositional condemnation of outsiders—the Jews, the world—as hated and feared enemies of the cult were cast in even more dramatic terms in the Johannine community.[1]

Ambivalence

The resolution of ambivalence in oedipal development serves as a paradigm for the use of paranoid mechanisms both in the resolution of individual ambivalence more generally and on the level of group processes and cultural dynamics.[2] In the organization of groups and the working out of group behavior patterns, protection from the sense of loss and separation is accomplished by idealizing and libidinizing the values, attitudes, and beliefs of one's own group while simultaneously devaluing, rejecting, and opposing the values and attitudes of what does not belong to one's own group. Many aspects of these forms of group-related paranoid processes act to insure that group members will direct positive feelings towards one another and towards their own group and displace negative feelings towards outsiders. The process serves to resolve the inherent ambivalence in any such group relationship and provides for greater constancy and stability of psychic relationships. It is a form of normal delusion formation aggrandizing one object or set of objects and denigrating or devaluing all other objects.

---

[1] See the discussion of these dynamics in the Johannine community in chapter 9.

[2] See the discussion of the role of oedipal factors in relation to the paranoid process in chapter 1.

Thus the operation of paranoid mechanisms can serve highly adaptive functions in the elaboration of social groupings and in the working out of social processes. One of the primary adaptive functions in the mobilization of paranoid mechanisms is the avoidance of loss and the resolution of ambivalence. Where the levels of ambivalence are not excessively intense, where the susceptibility to loss is not catastrophic or overwhelming, and where sufficient ego resources have been allowed to emerge by way of significantly constructive introjections and internalizations, there will be a sufficient capacity for trust to enable individuals to form social bonds with other individuals and to align their paranoid responses with those of others to permit development of such nonpathological and group-related paranoid systems. Thus they can become members of an in-group and share a certain set of values, attitudes, positions, belief systems, or ideologies, etc., with other like-minded and comparably motivated individuals.

In these terms, such individuals are able to respond to and satisfy the needs underlying the paranoid process and thus achieve a sense of belonging and acceptance which mitigates the basic ambivalence threatening both their internal sense of self-consistency and their sense of participation and belonging extrinsically. However, where individuals are unable to muster a sufficient degree of trust to allow such participation and group commitment and are unable to form such social bonds, they become vulnerable to increasingly idiosyncratic belief systems, and the workings of the paranoid process must then begin to verge toward the pathological. The same dynamics are observable in religious movements that become so isolated and embattled that the paranoid mechanisms begin to take a pathological turn—examples abound, as we have seen—the Zealots of ancient Palestine, the messianic revolt of Bar Kochba, and certain Gnostic sects to name but a few.

Group Formation

The forming of social groupings involves shaping of an in-group, to which are aggregated aspects of value and belonging which provide the matrix of support for individual identities. A basic aspect of identity formation has to do with affiliation with such specific in-groups, within which the individual can define himself as a participating member with a sense of belonging and purposive participation. Along with these motivating dynamics, there may go a sense of empowerment and self-validation. However, the defining of the in-group is in part accomplished by setting it in opposition to the variety of out-groupings, representing divergent or oppositional sets of values and beliefs.

Thus Pinderhughes' (1971) hypothesis articulating the psychic aspects of processes connecting the emerging personality with social groupings is quite congruent with the point of view of the present study. He wrote:

> One relates by introjection to representatives of groups of which one feels a part, and one relates by projection to representatives of groups which one perceives as different from one's own. Thus, a group or its constituents are perceived and related to as if they were a single object. One is inclined to join or leave, to swallow or spit out, to accept or reject, and to associate pleasure or discomfort with social groups insofar as they are perceived as similar to one's own or different from one's own (p. 685).

Consequently, in so-called nonpathological group-related paranoias, psychic mechanisms operate to idealize by projection[3] the groups with which an individual affiliates himself and with which he identifies, and correspondingly to denigrate by projection the groups from which the individual dissociates himself. Thus the forming of such groups can provide a buffer against the loss of significant relationships and belonging within one's own group, but at the same time it provides a potent source for inter-group conflict.

Reciprocally, of course, the group process can also provide a context within which individual paranoid tendencies can assert and sustain themselves. Given the mutual support and reinforcement for the false belief system shared by the group, the belief system then becomes a matter of principle, an ideology, or a dogma, for which group members are willing to contend, fight, and even in certain extreme situations surrender their lives. In reflecting on the paranoid process, consequently, it is important to remember that the system of delusional belief characterizing paranoid distortion is driven by strong internal defensive and adaptive needs. It is motivated by the need to resolve intolerable ambivalence and/or to avoid the pain of loss—most poignantly and pressingly the pain of narcissistic loss and deprivation.

Thus the individual psyche resorts to any devices offering the promise of sustaining narcissistic impairment and integrating a sense of self

---

[3] For the sake of clarity, the in-group affiliation is thought here to involve projection of inherently positive introjective components to the in-group, that is aspects of the individual's self-organization that contribute to and sustain the integrity of the self and the sense of identity are attached to the image of the group and are thus regarded as sustaining attributes of the group. Projective mechanisms follow the opposite tack in respect to out-groups which tend to be invested with negative or destructive aspects of the self.

and identity, which is both internally consistent and coherent and articulated within a context of acceptance and belonging. It is precisely this aspect of the pressure toward identity which the group formation responds to most acutely. The absorptive and adaptive potential of these processes is a matter of great moment and social consequence. The degree to which such social and group processes have the effect of channeling and in a sense legitimizing latent pathologically paranoid potentials in the social organism can vary from group to group, but overall may serve the beneficial function of defusing and containing otherwise highly destructive forms of individual pathology and personal catastrophe.

Need for the Enemy

Another aspect of group formation, often playing a telling part in the dynamics of religious group formation and the cultic process, is the role of the enemy. The dynamics of group organization and interaction, particularly sustaining the integrity and strength of the group, may require setting itself over against an enemy. The group needs an enemy to bolster its own inner resources and maintain its own inner sense of value and purposiveness. The group sustains itself by idealizing its own values and setting them in conflict with the denigrated values of other groups. Furthermore, the dynamics of the situation will not tolerate a mere appraisal in terms of greater-or-lesser or more-or-less—the narcissistic basis on which the process operates demands a logic of extremes, in which there is a tendency for all value to be inherent in the in-group and no value or negative value to be inherent elsewhere. The natural extension of this logic is to set the respective value systems in opposition and to regard them as mutually exclusive and destructive. Thus what is in question here is not merely differences in degree but the narcissistically derived need for enemies.

The paranoid construction rationalizes the pattern of projections so that adherents to the belief system are viewed as bearers of truth and goodness, while those who reject or oppose the belief system or belong to deviant out-groups are regarded as agents of falsehood, error, even evil. This projective necessity requires the existence of an enemy[4] who becomes the bearer of projections. In the early vicissitudes of the evolution of the Christian cult, conflicts between Hellenizing and Judaizing factions, between Pauline and the Jerusalem factions, between Paul on

[4] The motif of the need for enemies has been proposed by a number of authors (Boyer 1986; Meissner 1978b; Pinderhughes 1970, 1979, 1982, 1986; Volkan 1985, 1988) and unquestionably plays a central role in the paranoid process.

one side and Peter and James on the other, between Gentile and Judaizing forms of nascent Christianity, between the Pauline and other churches, between the Johannine group and not only other groups of Christians but especially the "Jews," between orthodox and Gnostic ideologies, all involved such forms of ideological construction and adherence. Opposing factions were viewed as false, destructive, and misguided.[5]

The need for an enemy arises out of the developmental context[6] requiring projection of bad elements in the child's developing personalization to outside objects. These bad elements, primarily aggressive and destructive, are externalized and thus allow a more cohesive integration of the child's self with less conflicted and ambivalent internalizations (Meissner 1978b). But as the aggressivized projections develop, the enemy is painted in increasingly dehumanized and demonic colors, so that he easily becomes a monstrous, destructive, and evil entity seen as posing a dire threat to the integrity, purpose, and beliefs of the in-group. In religious movements, the enemy becomes the unbeliever, the infidel, who is colored with the dark shadows of deceit, evil intent, and demonic characteristics that earn him the label of Satan, the Devil, the Evil Archon, the Antichrist.

Finding or creating an enemy is integral to the consolidation and reinforcement of in-group dynamics. This inference derives from the basic hypothesis regarding the role of paranoid mechanisms in the constitution and sustaining of social groups—articulated here in terms of the paranoid process. The process, however, requires that suitable targets for such externalization be selected as safe and durable containers for bad self- and object-images—Volkan's (1988) "shared targets for projection." The designation of such suitable targets grows out of the child's internalization and identification with group norms and values —introjection as formulated here—and a separation and distancing from other less desirable and alien groups. Where suitable targets for externalization (projection) are not established as part of the child's development within the group and assimilation of the group culture, an important component of his emerging identity and sense of self may be lacking and have dire developmental consequences (Volkan 1986, 1988).

The existence of the enemy and the threat he poses has an indirect but beneficial effect within the in-group. The threat posed by the enemy forces members of the in-group to value all the more intently and fanatically what the in-group stands for and to commit themselves all the more convincingly to the purposes, beliefs, and values to which

[5] See sections III and IV.
[6] See the discussion of developmental aspects in chapter 1 above.

it directs itself. The more strongly the enemy confronts and attempts to undermine the group, the more powerful is the inner impulse to defend and cherish and adhere to what the group represents. The early Christian church was nourished by persecution and strengthened by the blood of martyrs.

As paranoid mechanisms find expression in group dynamics, they assume particular forms of expression. The group may invest in a "chosen trauma," that is, an event or episode causing the group to feel helpless, humiliated, or victimized by an outside group standing in the position of the "enemy" (Volkan 1992). The injury in such episodes is essentially narcissistic, and the injured group feels humiliated and violated. The injury becomes embedded in the history and seared into the memories of the members, together with its burden of hurt and shame and the defenses against them are passed on from generation to generation (Rogers 1979). They become markers of ethic identity so that the event and its consequences are incorporated into the identity and belief system of the group. Volkan (1992) argues that in order for an event to become a chosen trauma it must escape the capacity of the group to mourn. The group may be too angry, humiliated, too helpless and outraged to mourn—they are then unable and unwilling to reach any effective compromise with the perpetrator of the trauma and the resentment and wish for revenge is perpetuated from age to age.

From time to time succeeding generations may reach a point of wishing to repair the damage done to their ancestors and to free themselves from the humiliating burden that has become part of their history and identity. Volkan (1992) points to certain ritualistic outlets that operate unconsciously to reinforce prejudice and the need for separation and distinction from the enemy. The inability to mourn the chosen trauma and the evolution of social defenses plays a role in the formation of the group ideology. The first response is entitlement—the sense that the group has suffered an injury and is thereby entitled to restitution, special treatment and privilege above others and especially above those who have committed the injury. This may play a role in the political ideology of contemporary Israel (Moses 1990).

A second effect is the development of purification rituals—to the extent that the issues remain unresolved and unmourned, the group may view the enemy as so malignant and contaminated that distance and difference must be achieved through purification of oneself and one's group, shedding any vestiges of the influence of the out-group in order to consolidate its own group identity and sense of coherence. And lastly the group dynamic may take a masochistic turn turning its aggression inward leading to further victimization and potential humiliation.

When such rituals reach the point of malignant expression, they lead to dehumanization of the enemy, the formation of pseudospecies (Erikson 1966), increasing fear of and hostility toward the enemy, and absolving the group of any guilt from hostility or destructiveness unleashed against the enemy. These dynamics would have been at work in the persecutions of the early Christian era—on the part of the persecution of Christians by the Jews and Romans, in the Christian persecution of Jewish, Gnostic and pagan unbelievers, and in the persecution of Christians of each other. Dehumanization in its turn leads to further victimization and perpetuation of the state of hostility and the reciprocal enactment of paranoid mechanisms.

One can suggest that participation in communal paranoid undertakings, as may be involved in membership in religious groups, has an important function in terms of the adjustment capacity for such individuals. The commitment to the religious group and its ideology seems to absorb significant amounts of paranoid potentiality, so that instead of resorting to deviant forms of antisocial behavior, the group members are able to share in a communal effort to defend shared values and convictions. These individuals are accepted into a transient grouping, providing them with a context of usefulness and meaningful belonging and participation which helps to sustain and consolidate their fragile or fragmented sense of identity. The parameters of the paranoid process play a central and significant role in such manifestations. They can act to undercut the element of self-devaluation and self-rejection that plays such a central role in psychosocial deviance. At the same time, they provide the context of group participation and belonging that contributes powerfully to the maintenance of self-esteem. More than the need to have enemies, there is the need to have enemies to hate and a need to be able to hate our enemies (Stein 1986) as an important contributing and stabilizing force for the maintenance of both group and individual identity (Meissner 1978b). The mechanisms are no different in the context of religious cultic movements, and in large measure tend to bring about similar effects on individual psychic functioning.

Thus, the definition of one's self and particularly of one's self as a participant in the group with which he identifies is in part defined by contrasts with the other groups to which the individual does not belong and against which he defines his own sense of self. For these purposes, some enemies are better than others; the best enemy is the one who can optimally mirror and embody the negative identity of the group, the one that can best come to represent the disowned and projected aspects of the self (Stein 1986). The paradox is that the more we strive to differentiate our selves and our group from the enemy, the greater the resemblance seems to become on an unconscious level. As Volkan (1988) comments:

> Of the two principles that seem to dominate preoccupation with an enemy, the first deals in a paradoxical way with a sameness between ourselves and the enemy. Because the enemy, whatever realistic considerations may be involved, is a reservoir of our unwanted self- and object representations with which elements of our projections are condensed, there should be some unconscious perception of a likeness, a reverse correspondence that binds us together while alienating us. However, the externalizations and projections we have given our enemy are repugnant to us, so we disavow them and do not want to acknowledge this connection consciously. We feel ourselves obliged to see huge and important differences between us that support our sense of self and of membership in our own group (p. 99).

The process leads in the direction of the development of increasingly aggressive and threatening stereotypes that bypass any positive characteristics or qualities of the enemy, but increase a sense of psychological distance and differentiation between ourselves and them.

The relationship to the enemy is a complex psychological phenomenon. From one perspective it is necessary to maintain a sense of separation, difference, and distance—Volkan's (1988) second principle. From another perspective, aggression directed to the enemy binds us to him. It becomes necessary to control the psychological gap, maintaining simultaneously a sense of difference and connection (Volkan 1986). The gap serves to maintain a sense of unconscious connection through the unconsciously shared derivatives of aggression (Volkan 1986, 1987).

Sense of Self

The added step in the process concerns the motivation behind the projections. The paranoid process perspective suggests that projections become necessary to preserve the integrity of the self-system of individual believers, which embraces a configuration of introjects as core constituents. Whatever aspects of this core configuration cannot be integrated in the functional self must either be repressed or projected. These elements may be hostile or destructive; they may involve weakness or vulnerability; they may involve elements of shame and inferiority; or they may have the cast of omnipotence or grandiosity. The projection serves the stability of the self by internal denial and repression and by attribution of such conflictual qualities to the external objects.

The overall function of the paranoid system, then, is to achieve and preserve the integrity and meaningful existence of the self. This likewise is the basis of its motivation (Meissner 1978b).

It is my contention that these powerful motives were at work in the drama of contending religious forces in the early history of Christianity. The Palestinian origins took place in the context of the struggle of an oppressed people against Roman domination and of the destruction of Jerusalem. For the Jews this meant profound humiliation and desperation. Jewish Christians sought refuge in an adherence to the Mosaic law and a reaffirmation of messianic hopes. Hellenistic Christians, for a variety of reasons (Meissner 1988),[7] sought to dissociate themselves from judaizing influences and associations. Their common lot was persecution.

What impact must these influences have had on their individual inner lives? My hypothesis is that desperate external circumstances and the crisis in religious belief served to activate profound psychological conflicts and needs, and that these were salvaged by mobilization of restitutive aspects of the paranoid process. The divergent groups found different ideologies, each under different sets of complex historical and cultural influences, to resolve the inner crisis. The Judaizers made their commitment to the leadership of Peter and James, and to the conviction that adherence to the traditional Law was the vehicle of salvation. For them, Hellenizing influences were a cultural and religious threat that meant abandonment of the religious connection with the traditional belief system. The conviction that theirs was the true belief, together with messianic anticipations of ultimate vindication and victory over their enemies, were vehicles for narcissistic restitutive processes overburdened with elements of idealization and the triumph of narcissistic superiority.

The Hellenizers responded to a different set of cultural and religious determinants. For them, connection with Palestinian roots and particularly the Jewish rebellion against Rome, was a stigma that would doom the new religion of Christ to failure and oblivion. Jewish beliefs and practices would have found little acceptance or credibility in the Hellenizing world of the Roman Empire. Thus the struggle was joined, fueled by inner needs and conflicts that found their partial resolution in variant ideological commitments. The conflicts we have been able to identify, for example, between the churches of Antioch and Jerusalem, as well as within the Antioch, Corinthian, and Johannine communities, reflect the oppositional and divisive influences of the paranoid process, feeding on divergent contextual differences and emphases, but driving the conflicts in the direction of elimination of oppo-

[7] See also chapters 7, 8, and 9.

sition and vindication and supremacy of the in-group ideology. The result was in part a joining of ranks of more moderate and orthodox factions against their common enemies—at one level against more radical groups at either extreme, and at the same time in reaction to the constant threat of external persecution.

Where the sense of self is more profoundly threatened by unresolved ambivalences, the need for an enemy becomes a predominant influence in the shaping and sustaining of a sense of self (Kets de Vries 1977; Meissner 1978b). We can recognize in this aspect of the process the effects of unresolved narcissistic needs. Primitive unresolved narcissism, with its tendency to unremitting and exclusive demands, leaves little room for sharing or alliance, and sees external objects as generally threatening to its need for omnipotence and omnivorous possessiveness. Such pathogenic narcissism carries within itself the potentiality and the need for enemies.

Paranoid Mechanisms

The burden of these conclusions is obvious, since it points in the direction of delineating broad areas of social and religious conflict in terms of underlying paranoid mechanisms. As Pinderhughes (1970), in a lucid discussion of these issues, has observed:

> Nonpathological paranoia well might be viewed as a pervasive, even universal, process stimulated by and dealing with conflicting psychic impulses. Such a concept is consistent with the vast scale on which we find conflict, exploitation, discrimination, and destruction taking place between human beings.
>
> One of the reasons why we have made so little progress in curbing and eliminating discrimination, exploitation, violence and war lies in our refusal to recognize and acknowledge that all human beings depend heavily upon paranoid processes throughout their lives. Most persons are too narcissistic to conceptualize themselves as primitive or irrational in thinking and behavior. They prefer instead to view themselves as intelligent and rational, while failing to observe that their intelligence and reason are impaired in the service of paranoid processes which aggrandize those with whom they identify and denigrate those they project upon. Intellect and reason are employed unconsciously to maintain and advance the position, benefits, and comforts of some persons at the expense of others (p. 608).

Groups tend to exaggerate their distinguishing differences from other groups in ways which denigrate the others and enhance their own status as "special." As the GAP report (1987) comments:

> Tragically, as groups "discover" themselves to be special and supe-
> rior to others, they behave as though they are unaware that all
> groups engage in this kind of assessment—and for the same rea-
> son. All draw attention to their culture and direct it away from the
> vulnerable identity core they use culture to defend. What a para-
> dox—the insistence on uniqueness is universal; only the cultural
> trimmings differ, and the core—the core purpose—of identity re-
> mains the same (pp. 22–23).

Erikson (1966) pointed to the role of ritualization in this process, particularly in its function of deflecting feelings of unworthiness onto outside objects. In adolescence certain rituals of confirmation serve to integrate earlier childhood identifications and introjections into ideological beliefs to which one gives allegiance and to the crystallization of foreign belief systems, wishes, fantasies, and images that have become alien and undesirable. The assignment of these alien ideological elements to the outside group serve to consolidate the boundaries between the in-group and the out-group. Ritualization has as its purpose the overcoming or at least tolerance of ambivalence within the group by projection of negative characteristics to outside objects in a process of pseudospeciation. The assimilation of these cultural norms are the mark of the individual's participation in the culture of the group, an aspect of his group belonging, and of his integration of his own sense of self and identity in social and cultural terms.

In the perspective proposed in the present study, however, I wish to emphasize the adaptive aspects of the paranoid process. It is my conviction that only when we can envision and appreciate the positive, constructive and adaptive role of paranoid mechanisms, both in the organization and sustaining of individual personalities and in the formation and function of broader social groupings and processes, will we be able to come to terms effectively either with the pathological distortions which affect individual personalities or the patterns of social distortion and conflict which afflict the broader ranges of social, cultural, and religious experience.

From Psychodynamics to Social Reality

An interesting aspect of this whole problem is that—according to the crucial insight of W. I. Thomas that if situations are perceived or defined as real, they are real in their consequences—there is a decisive pressure in such events for such paranoid distortions to become realities. There is not only a general tendency for human beings to behave in ways that they are expected to behave, but the paranoid process operates in such a way as to elicit its own validation. Thus acts of barbarity and inhumanity are perpetrated, and intensify and reinforce paranoid distortions. This was undoubtedly the case throughout the history of the development of religious movements in ancient times, nor was it any less in evidence in the many cases of religious prejudice and persecution that have repeatedly stained the pages of religious history.

Such examples can be endlessly multiplied, and the paranoid quality pervading them is in little need of documentation. It may be worth, however, noting the quality of the thinking which attends such processes. There is clearly a logic of all-or-nothing, either-or, black-and-white; one side is right and the other is wrong—completely and more or less absolutely. All virtue and truth and goodness is aggregated to one side of the controversy, while evil, wrongdoing, destructiveness, error, and falsehood are attributed to the other side. The capacity for discrimination becomes obfuscated and impoverished, so that thinking becomes stereotypical. Passions run high, and the individuals involved seem to be impervious to reason or to evidence.

These are all familiar expressions of the paranoid process gone haywire. We can recognize that the attitudes, feelings, and points of view characteristic of these situations are driven by inner needs rather than by external realities or evidences. On both sides of these situations of confrontation and conflict, there is at work a pervasive fear and an impending sense of vulnerability and threatened loss. We can also recognize the characteristic paranoid mechanisms—the paranoid construction organizing and rationalizing perceptions of reality into a framework that supports and justifies the underlying projections; the sense of vulnerability and narcissistic fragility we have identified in all situations of paranoid defense. We can also detect the intolerance of ambivalence which seeks to resolve itself by resorting to paranoid mechanisms.

While the paranoid aspects of these situations are relatively transparent and easily identifiable, we should not lose sight of the adaptive aspects which also serve in important ways to sustain these processes. One of the salient rewards accruing to the individual by reason of his affiliation to the group is a sense of acceptance and belonging, and identification with a set of values esteemed and accorded regard within the community. By assimilating, adopting, and internalizing these values, therefore, the individual aggregates himself to the community and assimilates to himself some of the esteem and sense of value that is derived from and inherent in the community.

In conclusion, the various aspects of the cultic process under examination in these pages can be seen to have an intrinsic and inherent connection with the underlying dynamic forces of the paranoid process. The emotional power and intensity of religious beliefs and commitments derives in significant degree from unconscious forces of libidinal, narcissistic, and even aggressive motivation embedded in and shaped by the mechanisms of the paranoid process. It is through these mechanisms that these derivatives find their way into communal expression in a variety of social, cultural, and religious settings. The interpenetration of these dynamic components with other factors, operating at more conscious and group-oriented levels of action and interaction, provides a deeper and more comprehensive understanding of the impact of religious beliefs and movements, adding another dimension to the understanding of human religious experience and its psychic meaning.

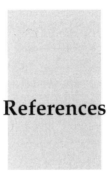

References

Aberle, D. F. (1966) *The Peyote Religion Among the Navaho.* New York: Wenner-Gren Foundation for Anthropological Research [Viking Fund Publs. in Anthroplogy, 42].

Ahlstrom, S. E. (1972) *A Religious History of the American People.* New Haven, Ct.: Yale University Press.

Albright, W. F. (1957) *From the Stone Age to Christianity: Monotheism and the Historical Process.* Garden City, N.Y.: Doubleday Anchor Books.

Bainbridge, W. S., and Stark, R. (1979) Cult formation: three compatible models. *Sociological Analysis,* 40:283–95.

Balch, R. W. (1982) Bo and Peep: a case study of the origins of messianic leadership. In Wallis, R. (ed.) *Millennialism and Charisma.* Belfast, N. Ireland: Queen's University Press, 13–72.

Barkun, M. (1974) *Disaster and the Millennium.* New Haven, Ct.: Yale University Press.

Barratt, B. B. (1986) Psychoanalysis as critique of ideology. *Psychoanalytic Inquiry,* 5:437–70.

Beckford, J. A. (1990) Religion and power. In Robbins, T., and Anthony, D. (eds.) *In Gods We Trust: New Patterns of Religious Pluralism in America.* 2nd ed. New Brunswick, N.J.: Transaction Publishers, 43–60.

Berlin, I. (1979) Nationalism: past neglect and present power. *Partisan Review* 46:337–58.

Bord, R. J. (1975) Toward a social-psychological theory of charismatic social influence processes. *Social Forces,* 53:485–97.

Borg, M. J. (1987) *Jesus—A New Vision: Spirit, Culture, and the Life of Discipleship.* San Francisco: Harper and Row.

Boyer, L. B. (1986) On man's need to have enemies: a psychoanalytic perspective. *Journal of Psychoanalytic Anthropology* 9:101–20.

Brandon, S.G.F. (1967) *Jesus and the Zealots.* Manchester: Manchester University Press.

Brown, P. (1968) Approaches to the religious crisis of the third century A.D. In Brown, P. *Religion and Society in the Age of St. Augustine.* New York: Harper and Row, 1972, 74–93.

Brown, P. (1972) *Religion and Society in the Age of St. Augustine.* New York: Harper and Row.

Brown, S.S., R. E. (1979) *The Community of the Beloved Disciple.* New York: Paulist Press.

Brown, R. E., Fitzmyer, J. A., and Murphy, R. E. (eds.) (1968) *The Jerome Biblical Commentary.* Englewood Cliffs, N.J.: Prentice-Hall.

Brown, R. E., Fitzmyer, J. A., and Murphy, R. E. (eds.) (1990) *The New Jerome Biblical Commentary.* Englewood Cliffs, N.J.: Prentice-Hall.

Brown, S.S., R. E., and Meier, J. P. (1983) *Antioch and Rome.* New York: Paulist Press.

Buie, D. H., Meissner, S.J., W. W., Rizzuto, A.-M., and Sashin, J. (1983) Aggression in the psychoanalytic situation. *International Review of Psychoanalysis* 10:159–70.

Buie, D. H., Meissner, S.J., W. W., Rizzuto, A.-M. (1996) The role of aggression in sadomasochism. *Canadian Journal of Psychoanalysis* 4:1–27.

Bultmann, R. (1941) *Das Evangelium des Johannes,* 17th ed. Göttingen: 1962.

Camara, H. (1971) *Spiral of Violence.* London: Sheed and Ward.

Cerfaux, L. (1959) *The Church in the Theology of St. Paul.* New York: Herder and Herder.

Charlesworth, J. H. (1968–69) A critical comparison of the dualism in 1QS 3.13–4.26 and the 'dualism' contained in the gospel of John. *New Testament Studies,* 15:389–418.

Charlesworth, J. H. (1987) From Jewish messianology to Christian christology: some caveats and perspectives. In Neusner, J., Green,

W.S., and Frerichs, E.S. (eds.) *Judaisms and Their Messiahs at the Turn of the Christian Era.* Cambridge: Cambridge University Press, 225–64.

Chasseguet-Smirgel, J. (1985) *The Ego Ideal.* New York: Norton.

Clark, J. (1983) On the further study of destructive cultism. In Halperin, D. (ed.) *Psychodynamic Perspectives on Religion, Sect and Cult.* Boston: John Wright PSG Ltd.

Cohn, N. (1970a) Medieval millenarism: its bearing on the comparative study of millenarian movements. In Thrupp, S.L. (ed.) *Millennial Dreams in Action: Studies in Revolutionary Religious Movements.* New York: Schocken Books, 31–43.

Committee on Internal Relations (GAP). (1987) *Us and Them: The Psychology of Ethnonationalism.* New York: Brunner/Mazel.

Cullmann, O. (1956) *The State in the New Testament.* New York: Scribner.

Cullmann, O. (1962) *Peter: Disciple, Apostle, Martyr.* London: SCM Press.

Cullmann, O. (1970) *Jesus und die Revolutionären seiner Zeit.* Tübingen: J.C.B. Mohr.

Cushman, P. (1986) The self besieged: recruitment-indoctrination processes in restrictive groups. *Journal for the Theory of Social Behaviour* 16:1–32.

Daniélou, J. (1973) *A History of Early Christian Doctrine. Vol. II: Gospel Message and Hellenistic Culture.* Philadelphia: Westminster Press.

Davies, W. D. (1966) *The Sermon on the Mount.* Cambridge: Cambridge University Press.

de Jonge, M. (1991) *Jesus, the Servant-Messiah.* New Haven, Ct.: Yale University Press.

Denzer, G. A. (1968) The pastoral letters. In Brown, R. E., Fitzmyer, J. A., and Murphy, R. E. (eds.) *The Jerome Biblical Commentary.* Englewood Cliffs, N.J.: Prentice-Hall, vol. II, 350–61.

Dodd, C. H. (1968) *The Interpretation of the Fourth Gospel.* Cambridge: Cambridge University Press.

Dodds, E. R. (1965) *Pagan and Christian in an Age of Anxiety.* London: Cambridge University Press.

Douglas, M. (1970) *Natural Symbols: Explorations in Cosmology.* London: Cresset Press.

Dowling, S., and Rothstein, A. (eds.) (1989) *The Significance of Observational Research for Clinical Work with Children, Adolescents, and Adults.* Madison, Ct.: International Universities Press.

Dupont, J. (1949) *Gnosis: La Connaissance Religieuse dans les Epître de Saint Paul.* Louvain: Louvain Dissertations 2/40.

Edwards, G. R. (1972) *Jesus and the Politics of Violence.* New York: Harper.

Eliade, M. (1964) *Shamanism: Archaic Techniques of Exstasy.* Princeton, N.J.: Princeton University Press.

Eliade, M. (1982) *A History of Religious Ideas. Vol. 2: From Gautama Buddha to the Triumph of Christianity.* Chicago: University of Chicago Press.

Erikson, E. H. (1959) The problem of ego identity. In: *Identity and the Life Cycle.* New York: International Universities Press, 101–64. [Psychological Issues. Monograph 1].

Erikson, E. H. (1963) *Childhood and Society.* New York: Norton.

Erikson, E. H. (1966) Ontogeny of ritualization. In Loewenstein, R. M., Newman, L. M., Schur, M., and Solnit, A. J. (eds.) *Psychoanalysis —A General Psychology: Essays in Honor of Heinz Hartmann.* New York: International Universities Press, 601–21.

Erikson, E. H. (1978) *Life History and the Historical Moment.* New York: Norton.

Falk, A. (1982) The Messiah and the qelippoth: on the mental illness of Sabbatai Sevi. *Journal of Psychology and Judaism.* 7:5–29.

Festinger, L. (1957) *A Theory of Cognitive Dissonance.* Evanston, Ill.: Row, Peterson.

Festugière, O.P., R. P. (1949–1953) *La Révélation d'Hermès Trismégiste.* 4 vols. Paris: J. Gabalda et Cie.

Festugière, O.P., R. P. (1967) *Hermétisme et Mystique Paienne.* Paris: Aubier-Montaigne.

Fitzmyer, S.J., J. A. (1981) The Dead Sea Scrolls and the New Testament after Thirty years. *Theology Digest,* 29 (4) 351–67.

Freud, A. (1937) *Ego Psychology and the Mechanisms of Defense.* New York: International Universities Press.

Freud, S. (1911) Psycho-analytic notes on an autobiographical account of a case of paranoia (dementia paranoides). *Standard Edition* 12:1–82.

Freud, S. (1917) Mourning and melancholia. *Standard Edition* 14:237–60.

Freud, S. (1921) Group psychology and the analysis of the ego. *Standard Edition* 18:65–143.

Freud, S. (1923) The ego and the id. *Standard Edition* 19:1–66.

Friedländer, M. (1898) *Der vorchristliche jüdische Gnosticismus.* Göttingen: Vandenhoeck und Ruprecht.

Gerth, H. H., and Mills, C. W. (eds.) (1946) *From Max Weber: Essays in Sociology.* New York: Oxford University Press.

Gilhus, I. S. (1984) Gnosticism—a study in liminal symbolism. *Numen* 31:106–28.

Girard, R. (1979) *Violence and the Sacred.* Baltimore: Johns Hopkins University Press.

Girard, R. (1986) *The Scapegoat.* Baltimore: Johns Hopkins University Press.

Grant, R. M. (ed.) (1961) *Gnosticism: A Source Book of Heretical Writings from the Early Christian Period.* New York: Harper and Bros.

Grant, R. M. (1966) *Gnosticism and Early Christianity.* 2nd ed. New York: Columbia University Press.

Grant, R. M. (1970) *Augustus to Constantine: The Thrust of the Christian Movement into the Roman World.* New York: Harper and Row.

Grassi, M.M., J. A. (1968) The letter to the Colossians. In Brown, R. E., Fitzmyer, J. A., and Murphy, R. E. (eds.) *The Jerome Biblical Commentary.* Englewood Cliffs, N.J.: Prentice-Hall, 334–40.

Hall, J. R. (1995) Public narratives and the apocalyptic sect. In Wright, S.A. (ed.) *Armageddon in Waco: Critical Perspectives on the Branch Davidian Conflict.* Chicago: University of Chicago Press, 1995, 205–35.

Harrington, S.J., D. J. (1980) Sociological concepts and the early church: a decade of research. *Theological Studies* 41:181–90.

Harrington, S.J., D. J. (1982) *The Light of All Nations: Essays on the Church in New Testament Research.* Wilmington, Del.: Glazier.

Hayley, T. (1990) Charisma, suggestion, psychoanalysts, medicine-men and metaphor. *International Review of Psychoanalysis* 17:1–10.

Hobsbawm, E. J. (1981) *Bandits.* New York: Pantheon.

Hofstadter, R. (1967) *The Paranoid Style in American Politics and Other Essays.* New York: Vintage Books.

Horowitz, I. L. (1990) The limits of modernity. In Robbins, T., and Anthony, D. (eds.) *In Gods We Trust: New Patterns of Religious Pluralism in America.* 2nd ed. New Brunswick, N.J.: Transaction Publishers, 63–76.

Horsley, R. A. (1987) *Jesus and the Spiral of Violence: Popular Jewish Resistance in Roman Palestine*. San Francisco: Harper and Row.

Horsley, R. A. (1989) *Sociology and the Jesus Movement*. New York: Crossroad.

Horsley, R. A., and Hanson, J. S. (1985) *Bandits, Prophets, and Messiahs: Popular Movements in the Time of Jesus*. Minneapolis: Winston Press.

Isenberg, S. (1975) Mary Douglas and hellenistic religions: the case of Qumran. *SBL 1975 Seminar Papers*, 179–85.

Johnson, B. (1963) On church and sect. *American Sociological Review* 28:539–49.

Johnson, C. L. (1981) Psychoanalysis, shamanism and cultural phenomena. *Journal of the American Academy of Psychoanalysis* 9:311–18.

Jonas, H. (1963) *The Gnostic Religion*. 2nd edit. Boston: Beacon Press.

Kaesemann, E. (1964) *Essays on New Testament Themes*. London: SCM.

Kaesemann, E. (1969) *New Testament Questions of Today*. Philadelphia: Fortress.

Kee, H. C. (1987) Christology in Mark's gospel. In Neusner, J., Green, W. S., and Frerichs, E. S. (eds.) *Judaisms and Their Messiahs at the Turn of the Christian Era*. Cambridge: Cambridge University Press, 187–208.

Kernberg, O. (1975) *Borderline Conditions and Pathological Narcissism*. New York: Aronson.

Kernberg, O. (1979) Regression in organizational leadership. *Psychiatry* 42:29–39.

Kets de Vries, M.F.R. (1977) Crisis leadership and the paranoid potential: an organizational perspective. *Bulletin of the Menninger Clinic* 41:349– 65.

Kets de Vries, M.F.R., and Miller, D. (1985) Narcissism and leadership: an object relations perspective. *Human Relations* 38:583–601.

Kirsch, M., and Glass, L. (1977) Psychiatric disturbances associated with erhard seminar training, II: Additional cases and theoretical considerations. *American Journal of Psychiatry* 134:1254–58.

Kohn, M. (1969) *Class and Conformity*. Homewood, Ill.: Dorsey.

Kohut, H. (1971) *The Analysis of the Self*. New York: International Universities Press.

Kohut, H. (1976) Creativeness, charisma, group psychology: reflections on the self-analysis of Freud. In Gedo, J.E., and Pollock, G.H.

(eds.) *Freud: The Fusion of Science and Humanism.* New York: International Universities Press, 379–425 [Psychological Issues, Monograph 34/35].

Koschorke, K. (1978) *Die Polemik der Gnostiker Gegen das Kirchliche Christentum.* Leiden: E.J. Brill.

Kselman, S.S., J. S. (1968) Modern New Testament criticism. In Brown, R. E., Fitzmyer, J. A., and Murphy, R. E. (eds.) *The Jerome Biblical Commentary.* Englewood Cliffs, N.J.: Prentice-Hall, vol. II, 7–20.

Kugelman, C.P., R. (1968) The first letter to the Corinthians. In Brown, R. E., Fitzmyer, J. A., and Murphy, R. E. (eds.) *The Jerome Biblical Commentary.* Englewood Cliffs, N.J.: Prentice-Hall, vol. II, 254–75.

LaBarre, W. (1970) *The Ghost Dance: Origins of Religion.* Garden City, N.Y.: Doubleday.

Lacarriere, J. (1977) *The Gnostics.* London: Peter Owen.

LaVerdiere, S.S.S., E. A., and Thompson, S.J., W. G. (1976) New testament communities in transition: a study of Matthew and Luke. *Theological Studies* 37:567–97.

Lebreton, S.J., J., and Zeiller, J. (1962) *Heresy and Orthodoxy.* New York: Collier Books.

Leahy, S.J., T. W. (1968) The epistle of Jude. In Brown, R. E., Fitzmyer, J. A., and Murphy, R. E. (eds.) *The Jerome Biblical Commentary.* Englewood Cliffs, N.J.: Prentice-Hall, vol. II, 378–80.

Lipset, S. M. (1960) Working-class authoritarianism. In *Political Man: The Social Bases of Politics.* Garden City, N.Y.: Anchor Books, 1963.

Lofland, J. (1966) *Doomsday Cult.* Englewood Cliffs, N.J.: Prentice-Hall.

Lohfink, G. (1984) *The Last Day of Jesus.* Notre Dame, Ind.: Ave Maria Press.

Mack, J. (1983) Nationalism and the self. *Psychohistory Review* 2:47–69.

Manuel, F. E., and Manuel, F. P. (1979) *Utopian Thought in the Western World.* Cambridge, Mass.: Harvard University Press.

MacRae, S.J., G. (1966) Biblical news: gnosis in Messina. *Catholic Biblical Quarterly* 28:322–33.

MacRae, S.J., G. (1970) The Jewish background of the gnostic Sophia myth. *Novum Testamentum* 12:86–101.

MacRae, S.J., G. (1978) Nag Hammadi and the New Testament. *Gnosis: Festschrift H. Jonas,* ed. B. Aland. Göttingen: Vandenhoeck and Ruprecht, 144–57.

Mahler, M. S., Pine, F., and Bergman, A. (1975) *The Psychological Birth of the Human Infant: Symbiosis and Individuation.* New York: Basic Books.

McDevitt, J. B. (1975) Separation-individuation and object constancy. *Journal of the American Psychoanalytic Association* 23:713–42.

McGuire, A. (1986) Conversion and gnosis in the *Gospel of Truth. Novum Testamentum* 28:338–55.

Meeks, W. A. (1983) *The First Urban Christians: The Social World of the Apostle Paul.* New Haven, Ct.: Yale University Press.

Meier, J. P. (1990) The historical Jesus: rethinking some concepts. *Theological Studies* 51:3–24.

Meissner, S.J., W. W. (1970) Notes on identification. I. Origins in Freud. *Psychoanalytic Quarterly* 39:563–89.

Meissner, S.J., W. W. (1971) Notes on identification. II. Clarification of related concepts. *Psychoanalytic Quarterly* 40:277–302.

Meissner, S. J., W. W. (1972) Notes on identification. III. The concept of identification. *Psychoanalytic Quarterly* 41:224–60.

Meissner, S.J., W. W. (1974) Differentiation and integration of learning and identification in the developmental process. *Annual of Psychoanalysis* 2:181–96.

Meissner, S.J., W. W. (1976) Schreber and the paranoid process. *Annual of Psychoanalysis* 4:3–40.

Meissner, S.J., W. W. (1978a) The conceptualization of marriage and family dynamics from a psychoanalytic perspective. In Paolino, T.J., and McCrady, B.S. (eds.) *Marriage and Marital Therapy: Psychoanalytic, Behavioral, and Systems Theory Perspectives.* New York: Brunner/Mazel, 25–88.

Meissner, S.J., W. W. (1978b) *The Paranoid Process.* New York: Aronson.

Meissner, S.J., W. W. (1981) *Internalization in Psychoanalysis.* New York: International Universities Press. [Psychological Issues, Monograph 50].

Meissner, S.J., W. W. (1984) The cult phenomenon: psychoanalytic perspective. *Psychoanalytic Study of Society* 10:91–111.

Meissner, S.J., W. W. (1986a) Can psychoanalysis find itself? *Journal of the American Psychoanalytic Association* 34:379–400.

Meissner, S.J., W. W. (1986b) The oedipus complex and the paranoid process. *Annual of Psychoanalysis* 14:221–43.

Meissner, S.J., W. W. (1986c) *Psychotherapy and the Paranoid Process.* Northvale, N.J.: Aronson.

Meissner, S.J., W. W. (1987) The cult phenomenon and the paranoid process. *Psychoanalytic Study of Society* 12:69–95.

Meissner, S.J., W. W. (1988) The origins of Christianity. *Psychoanalytic Study of Society* 13:29–62.

Meissner, S.J., W. W. (1989) Cultic elements in early Christianity: Antioch and Jerusalem. *Psychoanalytic Study of Society* 14:89–117.

Meissner, S. J., W. W. (1991a) Aggression in phobic states. *Psychoanalytic Inquiry* 11:261–83.

Meissner, S.J., W. W. (1991b) Cultic elements in early Christianity: Rome, Corinth, and the Johannine community. *Psychoanalytic Study of Society* 16:265–85.

Meissner, S.J., W. W. (1992) The pathology of belief systems. *Psychoanalysis and Contemporary Thought* 15:99–128.

Meissner, S.J., W. W. (1994a) Prejudice. *Psychoanalytic Study of Society,* to be published.

Meissner, S.J., W. W. (1994b) *Psychotherapy and the Paranoid Process.* (Softcover edition) Northvale, N.J.: Aronson.

Meissner, S.J., W. W. (1995) *Thy Kingdom Come: Psychoanalytic Perspectives on the Messiah and the Millennium.* Kansas City, Mo.: Sheed and Ward.

Meissner, S.J., W. W., Rizzuto, A.-M., Sashin, J., and Buie, D. H. (1987) A view of aggression in phobic states. *Psychoanalytic Quarterly* 56:452– 76.

Melton, J. G. (1991) Introduction: when prophets die: the succession crisis in new religions. In Miller, T. (ed.) *When Prophets Die: The Postcharismatic Fate of New Religious Movements.* Albany, N.Y.: State University of New York Press, 1–12.

Miller, T. (Ed.) *When Prophets Die: The Postcharismatic Fate of New Religious Movements.* Albany, N.Y.: State University of New York Press, 1991.

Modell, A. H. (1968) *Object Love and Reality.* New York: International Universities Press.

Monti, M. R. (1981) Scienza, paranoia, pseudoscienza. *Rivista di Storia delle Idee* 1:395–424.

Moses, R. (1990) Shame and entitlement. In Volkan, V. D., Julius, D. A., and Montville, J. V. (eds.) *The Psychodynamics of International*

Relationships: Concept and Theories, vol. I. Lexington, Mass.: Lexington Books, 131–41.

Neusner, J. (1984) *Judaism in the Beginning of Christianity.* Philadelphia: Fortress Press.

Neyrey, S.J., J. H. (1988) *John's Christology in Social-Science Perspective.* Philadelphia: Fortress Press.

Niebuhr, H. R. (1929) *The Social Sources of Denominationalism.* New York: Holt.

Niederland, W. G. (1974) *The Schreber Case: Psychoanalytic Profile of a Paranoid Personality.* New York: Quadrangle/New York Times Book Co.

Nock, A. D. (1972) *Essays on Religion and the Ancient World.* 2 vols. ed. by Z. Stewart. Oxford: Clarendon Press.

Ofshe, R. (1980) The social development of the Synanon cult: the managerial strategy of organizational transformation. *Sociological Analysis* 41:109–27.

Oldham, J. M., and Bone, S. (eds.) *Paranoia: New Psychoanalytic Perspectives.* Madison, Ct.: International Universities Press.

Pagels, E. (1976) The demiurge and his archons—a gnostic view of the bishop and presbyters? *Harvard Theological Review* 69:301–24.

Pearson, B. A. (1990a) Biblical exegesis in gnostic literature. In *Gnosticism, Judaism, and Egyptian Christianity.* Minneapolis: Fortress Press, 29–38.

Pearson, B. A. (1990b) Friedländer revisited: Alexandrian Judaism and gnostic origins. In *Gnosticism, Judaism, and Egyptian Christianity.* Minneapolis: Fortress Press, 10–28.

Peel, M. L. (1970) Gnostic eschatology and the New Testament. *Novum Testamentum* 12:141–65.

Perkins, P. (1980) *The Gnostic Dialogue: The Early Church and the Crisis of Gnosticism.* New York: Paulist Press.

Perkins, P. (1990a) Gnosticism. In Brown, R. E., Fitzmyer, J. A., and Murphy, R. E. (eds.) *New Jerome Biblical Commentary.* Englewood Cliffs, N.J.: Prentice-Hall, 1350–53.

Perkins, P. (1990b) The gospel according to John. In Brown, R. E., Fitzmyer, J. A., and Murphy, R. E. (eds.) *New Jerome Biblical Commentary.* Englewood Cliffs, N.J.: Prentice-Hall, 942–85.

Perkins, P. (1991) Gnosis as salvation: a phenomenological inquiry. In Haase, W. (ed.) *Aufstieg und Niedergang der Römische Welt.* Berlin: Walter de Gruyter. [Mimeograph version; to be published].

Pinderhughes, C. A. (1970) The universal resolution of ambivalence by paranoia with an example of black and white. *American Journal of Psychotherapy* 24:597–610.

Pinderhughes, C. A. (1971) Somatic, psychic, and social sequelae of loss. *Journal of the American Psychoanalytic Association* 19:670–96.

Pinderhughes, C. A. (1979) Differential bonding: toward a psycho-physiological theory of stereotyping. *American Journal of Psychiatry* 136:33–37.

Pinderhughes, C. A. (1982) Paired differential bonding in biological, psychological and social systems. *American Journal of Social Psychiatry* 2:5–14.

Pinderhughes, C. A. (1986) Differential bonding from infancy to international conflict. *Psychoanalytic Inquiry* 6:155–73.

Post, J. M. (1986) Narcissism and the charismatic leader-follower relationship. *Political Psychology* 7:675–88.

Puech, H.-C. (1951) Gnosis and time. In Campbell, J. (ed.) *Man and Time: Papers from the Eranos Yearbooks.* Princeton, N.J.: Princeton University Press, 1973, 38–84.

Rahner, S.J., H. (1963) *Greek Myths and Christian Mystery.* New York: Harper and Row.

Richardson, J. T., and Kilbourne, B. (1984) Psychotherapy and new religions in a pluralistic society. *American Psychologist* 39:237–51.

Rizzuto, A.-M., Sashin, J., Buie, D. H., and Meissner, S.J., W. W. (1993) A revised theory of aggression. *Psychoanalytic Review* 80:29–54.

Robbins, T., and Anthony, D. (1972) Getting straight with Meher Baba: a study of drug rehabilitation, mysticism and post-adolescent role conflict. *Journal for the Scientific Study of Religion* 11:122–40.

Robinson, J. M. (ed.) (1977) *The Nag Hammadi Library in English.* San Francisco: Harper and Row.

Rochlin, G. (1965) *Griefs and Discontents: The Forces of Change.* Boston: Little, Brown.

Rogers, R. R. (1979) Intergenerational exchange: transference of attitudes down the generations. In Howells, J. (ed.) *Modern Perspectives in the Psychiatry of Infancy.* New York: Brunner/Mazel, 339–49.

Rokeach, M. (1960) *The Open and Closed Mind.* New York: Basic Books.

Saldarini, A. J. (1988) *Pharisees, Scribes and Sadducees in Palestinian Society: A Sociological Approach.* Wilmington, Del.: Michael Glazier.

Schatzman, M. (1974) *Soul Murder: Persecution in the Family.* New York: New American Library.

Scholem, G. (1973) *Sabbatai Sevi: The Mystical Messiah.* Princeton, N.J.: Princeton University Press.

Schreber, D. P. (1903) *Memoirs of My Nervous Illness.* Ed. by Macalpine, I., and Hunter, R. A. Cambridge, Mass.: Robert Bentley, 1955.

Scroggs, R. (1975) The earliest Christian communities as sectarian movement. In: *Christianity, Judaism and Other Greco-Roman Cults —Studies for Morton Smith at Sixty,* ed. J. Neusner, vol. II: 1–23. Leiden: Brill.

Segal, A. F. (1987) *The Other Judaisms of Late Antiquity.* Atlanta, Ga.: Scholars Press.

Segal, A. F. (1990) *Paul the Convert: The Apostolate and Apostasy of Saul the Pharisee.* New Haven, Ct.: Yale University Press.

Shengold, L. (1989) *Soul Murder: The Effects of Childhood Abuse and Deprivation.* New Haven, Ct.: Yale University Press.

Singer, M. T., and Lalich, J. (1995) *Cults in Our Midst.* San Francisco: Jossey-Bass.

Sloyan, G. S. (1973) *Jesus on Trial: The Development of the Passion Narratives and Their Historical and Ecumenical Implications.* Philadelphia: Fortress Press.

Smith, P. (1982) Millenarianism in the Babi and Baha'i religions. In Wallis, R. (ed.) *Millennialism and Charisma.* Belfast, Ireland: Queen's University Press, 231–83.

Spitz, D. (1973) The higher reaches of the lower orders. *Dissent* 20:243–69.

Stark, R., and Bainbridge, W. S. (1979) Of churches, sects, and cults: Preliminary concepts for a theory of religious movements. *Journal for the Scientific Study of Religion* 18:117–33.

Stein, H. F. (1986) The influence of psychogeography upon the conduct of international relations: clinical and metapsychological considerations. *Psychoanalytic Inquiry* 6:193–222.

Stendahl, K. (1968) *The School of St. Matthew and Its Use of the Old Testament.* 2nd ed. Lund: Gleerup.

Stern, D. N. (1985) *The Interpersonal World of the Infant: A View from Psychoanalysis and Developmental Psychology.* New York: Basic Books.

Tabor, J. D., and Gallagher, E. V. (1995) *Why Waco? Cults and the Battle for Religious Freedom in America.* Berkeley: University of California Press.

Temerlin, M., and Temerlin, J. (1982) Psychotherapy cults: an iatrogenic perversion. *Psychotherapy: Therapy, Research, and Practice* 19:131–41.

Theissen, G. (1978) *Sociology of Early Palestinian Christianity.* Philadelphia: Fortress Press.

Theissen, G. (1982) *The Social Setting of Pauline Christianity: Essays on Corinth.* Philadelphia: Fortress.

Tracy, D. (1987) *Plurality and Ambiguity: Hermeneutics, Religion, Hope.* Chicago: University of Chicago Press.

Trevor-Roper, H. R. (1969) *The European Witch-craze of the Sixteenth and Seventeenth Centuries and Other Essays.* New York: Harper Torchbooks.

Vawter, C.M., B. (1968) The gospel according to John. In Brown, R. E., Fitzmyer, J. A., and Murphy, R. E. (eds.) *The Jerome Biblical Commentary.* Englewood Cliffs, N.J.: Prentice-Hall, vol. II, 414–66.

Vermes, G. (1977) *The Dead Sea Scrolls.* Philadelphia: Fortress.

Volkan, V. D. (1985) The need to have enemies and allies: a developmental approach. *Political Psychology* 6:219–47.

Volkan, V. D. (1986) The narcissism of minor differences in the psychological gap between opposing nations. *Psychoanalytic Inquiry* 6:175–91.

Volkan, V. D. (1987) Psychological concepts useful in building of political foundations between nations: track II diplomacy. *Journal of the American Psychoanalytic Association* 35:903–35.

Volkan, V. D. (1988) *The Need to Have Enemies and Allies: From Clinical Practice to International Relationships.* Northvale, N.J.: Jason Aronson.

Volkan, V. D. (1992) Ethnonationalistic rituals: an introduction. *Mind and Human Interaction* 4:3–19.

Wach, J. (1944) *Sociology of Religion.* Chicago: University of Chicago Press.

Wallace, A.F.C. (1956) Revitalization movements. *American Anthropologist* 58:264–81.

Wallis, R. (1982) Introduction: millennialism and charisma. In Wallis, R. (ed.) *Millennialism and Charisma.* Belfast, N. Ireland: Queen's University Press, 1–11.

Wallis, R. (ed.) (1982) *Millennialism and Charisma.* Belfast, N. Ireland: Queen's University Press.

Weber, M. (1922) *The Sociology of Religion.* Boston: Beacon Press, 1963.

Weber, M. (1947) *The Theory of Social and Economic Organization.* T. Parsons, ed. New York: Oxford University Press.

Weber, M. (1968) *Max Weber on Charisma and Institution Building.* S.N. Eisenstadt, ed. Chicago: University of Chicago Press.

Westphal, M. (1990) Paranoia and piety: reflections on the Schreber case. In: *Psychoanalysis and Religion,* ed. J. H. Smith and S. A. Handelman. Baltimore, Md.: Johns Hopkins University Press, 117–35.

Wilner, A. R. (1984) *The Spellbinders.* New Haven, Ct.: Yale University Press.

Wilson, B. R. (1959) An analysis of sect development. *American Sociological Review* 24:3–15.

Wilson, R. M. (1958) *The Gnostic Problem: A Study of the Relations between Hellenistic Judaism and the Gnostic Heresy.* London: Mowbray.

Winnicott, D. W. (1965) *The Maturational Processes and the Facilitating Environment.* New York: International Universities Press.

Wisse, F. (1978) Gnosticism and early monasticism in Egypt. In Aland, B. (ed.) *Gnosis: Festschrift H. Jonas.* Gottingen: Vandenhoeck and Ruprecht, 431–40.

Worsley, P. (1968) *The Trumpet Shall Sound.* New York: Schocken Books.

Wright, S. A. (1995) Introduction. In Wright, S.A. (ed.) *Armageddon in Waco: Critical Perspectives on the Branch Davidian Conflict.* Chicago: University of Chicago Press, 1995, xiii–xxvi.

Yinger, J. M. (1957) *Religion, Society and the Individual.* New York: Macmillan.

Yoder, J. H. (1972) *The Politics of Jesus.* Grand Rapids, Mich.: Eerdmans.

Zaleznik, A. (1974) Charismatic and consensus leaders: a psychological comparison. *Bulletin of the Menninger Clinic* 38:222–38.

Index